A TRAINER'S GUIDE TO

THE CREATIVE CURRICULUM® FOR PRESCHOOL

Candy Jones

Diane Trister Dodge

Teaching Strategies® Inc.
Washington, DC

Editor: Toni S. Bickart
Cover: Based on an original design by Kathi Dunn
Book design and computer illustrations: Carla Uriona
Illustrations: Jennifer Barrett O'Connell and Anthony Woods

Teaching Strategies, Inc.
P.O. Box 42243
Washington, DC 20015
www.TeachingStrategies.com
ISBN 1-879537-44-3

Publisher's Cataloging-in-Publication
(Provided by Quality Books, Inc.)

Jones, Candy, 1956-
    A trainer's guide to The creative curriculum for preschool. Volume 1, Getting started / Candy Jones, Diane Trister Dodge.
        p. cm.
        LCCN: 2003097824
        ISBN 1-879537-44-3

    1. Education, Preschool--Curricula--Handbooks, manuals, etc. 2. Curriculum planning--Handbooks, manuals, etc. 3. Child development--Handbooks, manuals, etc. I. Dodge, Diane Trister. II. Dodge, Diane Trister. Creative curriculum for preschool. III. Title.

LB1140.4.J66 2003   372.19
                          QBI03-200790

Printed and bound in the United States of America
First Printing

Acknowledgments

Many people helped in the preparation of this *Trainer's Guide*. First, we would like to thank the highly talented trainers in the Teaching Strategies' Staff Development Network who have been using many of these workshops and have given us feedback and ideas. Toni Bickart, Cate Heroman, and Sherrie Rudick read and reread versions of each workshop, used the material in training, and helped us with revisions. We thank Monica Vacca and Whit Hayslip for their contributions toward extending the workshops to help teachers think about children with disabilities.

We appreciate the substantial work of Toni Bickart, our editor, and her assistants, Rachel Friedlander Tickner and Laurie Goold. Thanks to Carla Uriona, for her design and production management, and to her assistant, Terri Rue-Woods, for both their skill and their patience. Anthony Woods provided many of the illustrations for the Cooking chapter handouts that we know will be used by teachers everywhere. We thank all the staff of Teaching Strategies for helping us to stay focused (despite a hurricane and a move) on seeing this book through to production, especially Larry Bram and Fran Simon, who reminded us often of the many requests they were getting for a trainer's guide to *The Creative Curriculum for Preschool*.

We thank all the early childhood educators who support teachers in making classrooms great places where young children can learn and thrive.

Table of Contents

# Introduction

This book is the first of two volumes of *A Trainer's Guide to The Creative Curriculum® for Preschool*. Volume I, "Getting Started," offers detailed workshops and handouts on the foundation of the Curriculum and on introducing four components of the Curriculum framework—"How Children Develop and Learn," "The Learning Environment," "The Teacher's Role," and "The Family's Role"— and applying the framework to the 11 interest areas. Volume II, "Content in *The Creative Curriculum*," focuses on a fifth component of the framework, "What Children Learn." It contains workshops on how literacy, math, science, social studies, the arts, and technology are addressed in *The Creative Curriculum*, and how teachers can use in-depth studies to teach content and address developmental goals.[1]

The Creative Curriculum for Preschool is a comprehensive resource for establishing and sustaining a quality preschool program. It describes the theory and research that form the foundation, and it applies this knowledge to everyday practices, giving teachers a roadmap for teaching. Some teachers will pick up the Curriculum, read it, and use it independently. Other teachers will not have time to read the entire Curriculum. They will need someone to guide them through the content and help them to apply the approach in their own classrooms.

The purpose of this *Trainer's Guide* is to support the critically important role of program administrators, education coordinators, and staff development specialists who are responsible for helping teachers to learn about and implement the Curriculum. It is equally useful to educators who wish to incorporate the workshop activities into courses and seminars. You are the people who bring the Curriculum to life.

How This *Trainer's Guide* Is Organized

The first section of *A Trainer's Guide* helps you to develop a plan for implementing *The Creative Curriculum* in your program. The remainder of *A Trainer's Guide* presents the workshops. Part I contains workshops that explore the foundation of the Curriculum as well as four of the five components of the Curriculum framework. Each workshop series begins with a description of the purpose of the workshops and the important ideas to be learned. Part II includes workshops on each interest area. Each workshop series addresses how children's development and learning are fostered through play in the interest area; how to set up and equip the area; and how the teacher supports, promotes, and extends children's learning. A chart identifies points to be covered in each workshop, the materials and supplies (including handouts or transparencies, books, and videos) that are needed, the pages from the Curriculum that are referenced, and the approximate amount of time required. Since the purpose of *A Trainer's Guide* is to help staff developers work with teachers to learn the Curriculum, the content of the workshops mirrors the content presented in each chapter of *The Creative Curriculum for Preschool*.

The workshop instructions have four parts. The **Preparation** section explains how to prepare for the workshop. The **Introduction** gives suggestions for introducing the workshop. The **Activity** section guides the trainer in conducting the activity. Each workshop ends with **Summary** points to be made. Handouts and transparencies are at the end of each workshop series.

---

[1] Volume II will be published in mid-2004.

Planning for Training

Most workshops are designed for 30- to 90-minute periods. Times will vary depending on group size and participants' needs, interests, and level of engagement. This design allows programs that have only short periods for training to offer engaging activities that can be built upon over time. For programs wanting lengthier, more intensive training, the design allows workshops to be combined.

The activities suggested in *A Trainer's Guide* engage people in many ways and at many different levels. Unless indicated otherwise, the activities in each workshop assume that participants are able to work at tables in groups of 6–8 persons. They will work alone, with a partner, and with the whole group. Many activities call for sharing or brainstorming ideas or practicing new strategies to use with children.

The most important guidance to users of this *Trainer's Guide* is to make the workshops your own. No one should consider using every workshop as presented. Here are suggestions to consider:

- Read *The Creative Curriculum for Preschool* thoroughly. As the workshop presenter, you will have more credibility if you have a thorough knowledge of the book.

- Carefully select the workshop activities you want to present based on two criteria: 1) what you know about your group and 2) what you feel comfortable presenting.

- Prepare ahead of time. In some activities we have listed "possible responses" in italics. Where we have not done that, write down the responses you expect to hear and prepare your own stories to share. Sharing personal stories is a powerful way to make people comfortable and more willing to share their experiences.

- Adapt the activities and instructions to fit your situation. For example, if time is limited, you might decide to have each group respond to one question on a handout rather than have all groups do all the tasks. If you do this, allow time for the groups to share their ideas.

- Wherever you see text presented in bullet format, these are suggested words, points, and questions. Use them as talking points, putting them into your own words.

- If some of the participants in your group are not fast readers, consider reading aloud the scenarios in some of the workshops.

- Since the underlying goal of the workshops is to familiarize participants with the content of *The Creative Curriculum* and apply it to their own settings, it is best if participants have their own books. Provide small Post-its and encourage participants to mark pages and write notes.

- Call participants' attention to the "Frequently Asked Questions" at the end of the interest area chapters. Members of your group may have similar questions.

The following resources are needed for the workshops in this *Trainer's Guide*: *The Creative Curriculum for Preschool*; *The Creative Curriculum* video; *Room Arrangement as a Teaching Strategy* video; *The Creative Curriculum for Preschool Implementation Checklist*; and a set of continuum cards made from the Appendix.

Implementing *The Creative Curriculum* in Your Program

A curriculum is like an architectural blueprint; it will remain on paper unless it is interpreted and used accurately. A well-designed blueprint gives everyone involved in the process a picture of what they are creating together. Once the building is constructed, the process does not end. People move into the structure and make it their own. Their individual interests and work styles influence how the building is actually used and changed. As new resources and information become available, they may modify and enhance the building to keep it up-to-date and responsive to new needs.

In a similar way, all those responsible for implementing *The Creative Curriculum* need to have a shared vision of what they want to achieve and what the program should look like. The curriculum should reflect this vision and provide a blueprint for achieving it. Like contractors, administrators take time to read and understand the approach. They use a variety of approaches to provide ongoing direction and support to teachers, who then use the Curriculum as a guide for decision making each day. While the philosophy and approach that guide decision making remain the same, the Curriculum, as implemented by each program, takes on the special characteristics and individuality of those involved—the director, teachers, children and their families, and the community.

As you begin to develop your plan for helping teachers learn about and implement *The Creative Curriculum for Preschool*, it will be helpful to think about the different phases in curriculum implementation. Each of these phases is described below.

Create a Shared Vision

A first step in preparing to implement *The Creative Curriculum* is to build a shared vision. Questions you might pose for the staff and families to consider include:

- What are our hopes and dreams for the children and families we serve?

- What skills and abilities will the children need to lead satisfying and successful lives as adults?

- What requirements must our program meet (e.g., performance standards, state requirements, mandated outcomes)?

- What do we know about how children learn best?

- What are the expectations of kindergarten teachers and how can we collaborate with them?

Once the vision is defined, you can present current research and reports that describe the practices that lead to these outcomes. You can then show how *The Creative Curriculum for Preschool* is based on this body of research and is consistent with the vision.

Determine Training Needs

The next step is to determine the training needs of the staff who will implement the Curriculum. Many variables have an impact on where you decide to start, including

- the backgrounds and experiences of the staff

- the staff's familiarity with the curriculum and the approach

- the degree to which each classroom is set up as a *Creative Curriculum* environment and teachers are already carrying out the approach

- the opportunities and time that can be allocated for staff development

To ensure that teachers receive the training and support they need, every program should develop a training plan for the year. It should outline the variety of professional development opportunities that will be offered and when. To assist you in determining training needs, we have developed *The Creative Curriculum Implementation Checklist*. It is a tool for determining the degree to which the Curriculum is being implemented as intended, and it can be used to assess needs.

Using the *Implementation Checklist*

The *Implementation Checklist* highlights key aspects of the Curriculum in a checklist format. It is organized in five sections:

- physical environment
- structure
- teacher-child interactions
- assessment
- families

By using the *Implementation Checklist*, teachers can be involved in determining which aspects of the Curriculum are already in place and where they need more information and skills. The data can help you focus training and support.

Teachers can begin by reading through the *Implementation Checklist* and marking the items that are already in place. Those who are just beginning to use *The Creative Curriculum* will feel reassured by discovering that many of their current practices are already a part of the Curriculum. Teachers are not as overwhelmed when they can see, in writing, that they are now implementing various aspects of the Curriculum. They also see specific areas that they need to learn more about, practices they need to incorporate, or materials they need to acquire in order to implement the Curriculum well.

Trainers can look at a teacher's self-assessment to see how to focus the training. A trainer may have the opportunity to visit the classrooms and complete the *Implementation Checklist* before designing a training plan for a program. The trainer can meet with the program administrator to discuss the findings and focus training on the particular aspects of the Curriculum that need the most attention. The time spent on various topics can be adjusted according to the findings.

Administrators can use the *Implementation Checklist* as a tool to help keep the program on track and to assess the degree of implementation in each classroom. After teachers have learned about a new part of the Curriculum, administrators can use the *Implementation Checklist* to follow up in the classroom to see if what was learned is being applied. Administrators can also use the *Implementation Checklist* to see what materials, furnishings, and equipment should be purchased in order to help teachers implement the Curriculum effectively. On page 20 of the *Implementation Checklist Classroom Profile*, you will see an example of how to create a spreadsheet to see at a glance the results of all teachers in your program. These classroom visits and your follow-up analysis will help you to develop a training plan for your program.

Develop a Training Plan

In developing your training plan, keep in mind what is known about how adults learn best.

Adults bring a great deal of experience and knowledge to their work and to the learning process. Training is more meaningful if it builds on the life experiences of each person. Use approaches that encourage teachers to think about their own experiences and use the insights they gain in their work with children and families. Meaningful learning occurs when people can make connections between what they know and what they are learning.

Adults need time to assimilate new ideas and information. Workshops spaced over time are more effective than intensive training crammed into a few days. People need time to think about what they learned, try out new ideas, and come back to talk about their experiences and what they observed.

Adults are often uneasy about taking risks. Keep in mind that when you ask people to try something new, they may feel uncomfortable. It is safer and more comfortable to keep doing things the same old way. People are more willing to change, however, if they see a reason to try a new approach and if they know that experimentation is encouraged rather than punished. Make it safe for people to take risks by reassuring them that mistakes are part of the process of learning and we can all learn from them.

Think about how you will plan for orientation, classroom support, ongoing training and support, staff time, and workshops.

- **Orientation:** How many days can I allocate to introduce the Curriculum? Who should attend? Where will the training take place? How will I orient staff members hired mid-year?

- **Classroom support:** How often will I observe in the classrooms? When will I make these observations? How will I build in time for follow-up conversations and feedback?

- **Ongoing training and support:** What arrangements can I make for teachers to meet together to share ideas and experiences in implementing the Curriculum? What other programs might teachers visit? How can I continue to guide teachers in using the Curriculum?

- **Staff time:** How will I provide time for teachers to participate in training sessions? Do I have money in my budget to compensate them for this time if it is outside of the school day? How often will the staff need to meet together to plan?

- **Workshops:** What workshops will deepen teachers' understanding of the Curriculum? How can I space workshops to allow teachers time to implement the ideas we cover?

As you plan for staff development, try to have all training experiences count toward meeting the teachers' professional development requirements. In most states, this involves verifying that formal training sessions, such as courses, workshops, study groups, and seminars, are led by certified trainers; that the hours of attendance and completion of assignments are documented; and that these experiences fall into one of the core competencies outlined by the early childhood profession. Whenever possible, college credit should be offered. Training experiences and course credits should lead to increased responsibilities and compensation.

Introduce the Curriculum

It is very important that all those implementing the Curriculum have a common understanding of the philosophy and approach and know how to apply these concepts to everyday decision making. If you are just introducing the Curriculum, plan for at least three full days and arrange for all staff members to attend. If you have been using the Curriculum and the staff is familiar with its approach, you still might find it useful to provide an overview of the framework before focusing intensively on specific topics of interest to the staff. The "Setting the Stage" workshops in this *Trainer's Guide* offer guidance on how to do this.

To help teachers get started, allow time to work with them in the classrooms on setting up and equipping interest areas, labeling materials, and preparing for the first few days. Refer them to the sections in the Curriculum that address these topics.

One of the strengths of *The Creative Curriculum* is the link between the goals and objectives for children and the *Developmental Continuum* Assessment System. While assessment is an integral part of implementing the Curriculum, you will have to judge the best time to introduce this system to the staff. It's most important to focus first on getting started with the program, itself. Once teachers have established a good learning environment and the children have learned to function well in the classroom, you can plan to introduce the assessment system.

Provide Ongoing Training and Support

The most important phase in implementing any curriculum is the ongoing support and training teachers receive throughout the year. This is when you can individualize your training and support on the basis of your observations and the results of a teacher's self-assessment. Together, you can design a staff development plan that reflects each teacher's preferred way of learning and the topics of greatest importance to the teacher. Here are some options for offering ongoing training and support.

Classroom visits and support. There's no substitute for observing and supporting teachers in their classrooms. Only by visiting classrooms can you determine exactly how well teachers understand and to what extent they are implementing *The Creative Curriculum*. You will also learn about particular challenges each teacher has encountered and how you can offer support.

Seminars and courses. The orientation is just the beginning of training on the Curriculum. If possible, arrange for ongoing training through workshops, seminars, and courses that address different topics in depth. Select workshop activities that will work for your group of teachers and that correspond to their interests and aspects of curriculum implementation that need strengthening.

Weekly e-mails. Once a week, send a short e-mail to the staff highlighting a section of *The Creative Curriculum* that is relevant to what is occurring. These bite-size tidbits can include quotes of short passages and refer the staff to the pages that will help them address an issue, such as "Setting up Interest Areas" (pp. 62-67) and "Preparing for the First Few Days" (pp. 100-101).[1]

Staff meetings. Most programs have regular staff meetings, weekly or at least once or twice a month. Try to use some of the time for discussions that focus on one aspect of the Curriculum. You might have everyone read a section that is particularly relevant to the staff and come prepared to discuss their reactions and thoughts. Having an agenda item for each meeting that is related to the Curriculum reminds everyone that the book is a guide to consult regularly, not something kept on the shelf.

Visiting other classrooms. Teachers can learn a great deal by observing other classrooms where *The Creative Curriculum* is being implemented well. Such visits might reveal the effect of good room arrangement, positive adult-child interactions, a long-term study that is in progress, classroom management strategies, and how to handle transitions and routines. Participating in the visit enables you to focus the teachers' observations and discuss what you and the teachers observe.

Mentoring. The first year of working with children in a group setting can be overwhelming. An experienced staff member can help a new teacher with the daily nuts and bolts of working in the program, as well as offer practical tips on how to implement the Curriculum. A mentoring relationship can be a growth experience for both the mentor and the new staff member.

Connecting via the Internet. The Internet provides the staff with access to databases, discussion groups, and files on early childhood education. There is a special section on *The Creative Curriculum for Preschool* at www.TeachingStrategies.com. Not only can teachers learn from colleagues in their schools or centers, but technology also gives them the opportunity to network with teachers all over the world. The Creative Curriculum Listserv is an electronic discussion group that operates through e-mail. Participants can submit questions on their use of the Curriculum that will be answered by the authors and by other users from around the world. It's a wonderful forum for sharing experiences and ideas.

Use Learning Teams for Ongoing Professional Development[2]

A learning team is a small group of professionals who meet on a regular basis over the course of the year to learn more about a topic in a very disciplined way. These learning teams (sometimes referred to as study groups) strengthen teachers' knowledge and skills in order to improve child outcomes. Learning teams also provide opportunities for networking with colleagues, as well as a support system as teachers implement new ideas and strategies.

Learning teams are a cost-effective way to provide professional development over an extended period of time. Teams meet during the workday for short periods of time, such as rest or planning periods.

The director, education coordinator, or principal usually initiates the learning team concept. Teachers, however, must be brought in to the decision-making process in order for learning teams to be successful. They must understand the idea of learning teams as a powerful tool for improving classroom practices and as an interesting and productive vehicle for personal growth.

As the idea of creating learning teams is being discussed, teachers and other participants need to understand that each team will be very focused. Learning will take place in a systematic way. Learning teams are not committees that develop policies or take care of everyday business. The goal is to increase knowledge and understanding of teaching and learning. Implementation of *The Creative Curriculum* is the content of learning team meetings.

Initially, all teachers, assistants, and administrators must have a common understanding of the learning team concept. Everyone needs to be introduced to *The Creative Curriculum*. This may mean bringing in a specialist or conducting in-house training. As new staff members join, they, too, must have a good understanding of the Curriculum.

Once all teachers have received initial training on *The Creative Curriculum*, learning teams can be formed. We recommend no more than six persons to a team. Learning teams should meet once a week during the school day for an entire year. Administrative leadership is crucial in finding an hour's block of time for each meeting and protecting these meetings from disruptions.

To form the teams and to establish a focus for the year, start with the data. What are the strengths of the children in this program? What areas need more attention? By looking at the child progress reports and outcome data, teachers and administrators can easily identify priority areas that need to be addressed.

Data collected from classroom observations and self-assessments can also be analyzed. Teachers can complete a self-assessment using the *Implementation Checklist*, to reflect on their practices. This tool will help them to assess the degree to which the Curriculum is being implemented. Administrators can use this tool to conduct classroom observations. Teachers and administrators can compare their ratings and use them to begin discussion. The entire program can be analyzed by placing ratings on a chart or a spreadsheet. Such analysis might prompt conclusions such as these:

- Teachers A, B, and D need work in setting up their physical environments.

- Teacher E is strong in most areas and could serve as a facilitator, mentor, or coach. Teacher E also needs more challenging professional development, such as an exploration of appropriate studies for children.

- Teacher-child interactions, especially in content areas, were rated low for most teachers.

- All teachers rated highly in observation and documentation, but they rated much lower in other parts of assessment, such as analyzing and evaluating facts.

- All teachers in the program were rated highly in the items related to families.

The primary goal of the learning teams is to improve child outcomes by strengthening teachers' knowledge and skills. Both the child outcome data and the *Implementation Checklist* data are useful in forming learning teams to plan staff development. Learning teams then focus their year-long study. It is important that the team stay with a topic and not change topics from week-to-week. Teachers should have time to learn about a new strategy, concept, or technique; try it out in the classroom; and then evaluate its effectiveness. Change takes time.

Develop a Learning Team Plan

Once the learning team has been formed and the focus has been selected, it is time to develop a plan. The plan must be tailored to meet the needs of the program, so it should address the following questions:

- What knowledge and skills do children need to improve?

- What do teachers need to know and be able to do in order to help children progress in this focus area?

- How will teachers gain or strengthen the necessary knowledge and skills?

- What resources are needed in this focus area?

- How will the direct impact of the learning team's work be evaluated?

Developing a plan is a starting point. The plan should be considered dynamic. It will be revised and refined as the year progresses.

The individual members of each learning team can be tremendous resources. Take the time to discover the strengths of each person in the group. Consider the topic you will be working on and find out from each learning team member:

- What training have you had?

- Has this topic been covered in any courses you have taken?

- What has worked well for you? What didn't work well?

- What related resources do you have (or know about) to share with the group?

Each learning team should have a leader or facilitator, as well as a recorder. You may want to create other roles, such as a timekeeper or a materials manager. We suggest that you take turns in the different roles so that everyone has experience with the different tasks involved. In addition, leadership is shared to avoid having one member become more responsible than other members for the group's success. This joint responsibility results in a higher level of commitment. Create a rotation schedule of roles for the year or by the month.

The leader or facilitator confirms the logistics and reminds people about each meeting. This person leads discussions and makes sure that all team members have a chance to participate. The leader is also responsible for keeping the group focused. The recorder captures the important ideas of the group and completes a learning team log for the session.

Initially, much time is devoted to reviewing sections or chapters of *The Creative Curriculum*, viewing video clips, communicating with experts, and reading articles. This *Trainer's Guide* can be used for learning team activities. The learning team discusses the main ideas and classroom implications of each new piece of information.

Reading and discussion are not enough. Knowledge must be put into action. There may be visits to each other's classrooms to see a new dramatic play setting or to share different ways of managing assessment portfolios or observational notes. The group may try out new ideas or use them as homework to be completed before the next team meeting.

At the close of each team meeting, the recorder documents what was learned in the "Learning Team Log." To make the team's learning useful to others, the log is placed where others can read it, such as the work room or staff lounge. Administrators use this log to keep up to date with the work of the team.

Periodically, learning teams should reflect on their work:

- Is the team working effectively?

- Are learning team meetings productive?

- Are changes being made in the classroom based on the learning team's work?

- Are participants gaining a deeper understanding of *The Creative Curriculum*?

At the end of the year, it is time to go back to the data again to plan a focus for the teams' work next year.

Learning teams, as described here, help teachers accomplish what they are already expected to do. With learning teams, teachers share the work. The group sets common goals and works cooperatively to achieve them. When this happens, the results are positive for both adults and children.

---

[1] Van Avery, S. Education Coordinator, Northern Michigan Head Start Association (personal communication, September, 2003).
[2] Richardson, J. (August/September 2001). Learning teams: When teachers work together, knowledge and rapport grows. *Tools for Schools*. National Staff Development Council. Retrieved from http://www.nsdc.org/library/tools/tools8-01.pdf.

Setting the Stage

PURPOSE

In recent years, published research and reports have expanded our understanding of how children develop and learn. They also outline approaches most likely to ensure children's success and ways to address content with preschool children. *The Creative Curriculum for Preschool* incorporates these research findings as well as new requirements for addressing content. With its emphasis on the role of the teacher in connecting content, teaching, and learning, the Curriculum is a comprehensive approach to working with young children.

This workshop series begins by having participants explore the concept of curriculum and its value in helping teachers achieve their goals for young children. Participants are introduced to the components of the *Creative Curriculum* framework and begin exploring the book—their guide to creating quality preschool programs where children thrive.

BIG IDEAS:

- A quality curriculum provides a vision of what a program should look like and a framework for making decisions about how to achieve that vision.

- A curriculum can help teachers implement developmentally appropriate practice.

- Programs that emphasize social and emotional development help children acquire skills essential for success in school and in life.

- *The Creative Curriculum* provides teachers with a framework for creating quality preschool programs.

important

plan study areas

Setting the Stage

WORKSHOPS

⚷ Key Points	⚙ Workshop	🗒 Materials	🕐 Time (minutes)
The goal of early childhood education is to help children develop the skills and dispositions to be successful, life-long learners.	**Defining Successful Learners** (p. 4)	☐ Transparency **0A:** Characteristics of Successful Learners ☐ Chart paper, markers	20
Programs are more likely to achieve their vision and goals for children when staff share the same or similar beliefs and those beliefs align with the curriculum being implemented.	**What Do You Believe About Early Childhood Education?** (p. 8)	☐ Handout **0B:** What Do You Believe About Early Childhood Education? ☐ Handout **0C:** Fundamental Beliefs ☐ Chart paper, markers, adhesive dots	25
The Creative Curriculum offers teachers a framework for planning and implementing a developmentally appropriate program.	**Introduction to *The Creative Curriculum for Preschool*** (p. 10)	☐ Chart paper, markers, masking tape ☐ Transparency **0D:** Framework ☐ *Creative Curriculum*, p. xiv ☐ Variation-Handout **0E:** A Scavenger Hunt Through *The Creative Curriculum* ☐ *Creative Curriculum* video	20
Theory and research provide the foundation for understanding child development. A knowledge of child development helps teachers understand and determine the best approaches for designing a preschool program.	**Wall of Fame** (p. 16)	☐ Chart paper, various art supplies ☐ Handout **0F:** Theory and Research Behind *The Creative Curriculum* ☐ Handout **0F-Trainer:** Theory and Research Behind *The Creative Curriculum* ☐ *Creative Curriculum* video	45–60

Define "Curriculum"
Define "Creative Curriculum"

Defining Successful Learners

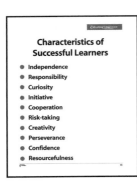

Characteristics of Successful Learners

- Independence
- Responsibility
- Curiosity
- Initiative
- Cooperation
- Risk-taking
- Creativity
- Perseverance
- Confidence
- Resourcefulness

☐ Transparency **0A**
☐ Chart paper, markers

⬤ PREPARATION

Prepare the transparency.

⬤ INTRODUCTION

Introduce the workshop:

- Research confirms that high quality preschool programs make a positive difference in the lives of young children and contribute to children's success in school.

- A quality curriculum provides a vision of what a program should look like and a framework for making decisions about how to achieve that vision.

- The purpose of this workshop is to have you examine your values and beliefs about early childhood education and determine the degree to which your practices align.

⬤ ACTIVITY

Introduce the activity:

- A good way to begin thinking about curriculum for young children is to consider the big goals of education.

- Think for a moment about your goals for the children enrolled in your program.

- Turn to your neighbor and share your thoughts.

Ask participants how many said that they want children to become successful, life-long learners, or something similar.

Explain that the purpose of this first activity is to examine what it means to be a successful learner and to discuss the role curriculum plays in the process.

Give each group a piece of chart paper and a marker and have them fold it in half, lengthwise to form two columns. Give the following instructions:

- Think of someone you know who is a successful learner. Think about two or three characteristics that make that person a successful learner.

- Take a few minutes to share your ideas with others at your table.

- Choose someone at your table to be a recorder and create a collective list of the characteristics you discussed. Record your ideas in one column.

Have the groups share one or two of their ideas.

Show the transparency and discuss any characteristics not mentioned by the groups. Make the following points:

- Teaching and learning should be about nurturing these characteristics.

- Successful learners are able to define problems, secure needed resources and information, work well with others, and apply what they have learned to new situations.

 - How we teach is as important as what we teach.

Next, have participants think about someone they know—an adult or a child—who has good social skills. Ask them to record their ideas in the other column.

When the groups are finished, have them open their chart papers to compare the two lists. Have the groups note similarities between their lists.

> **Possible responses:**
> *Strong communication skills (good listener, expresses self well), attentive, confident, friendly, able to develop good relationships with peers, independent, yet works well with others, positive attitude, strong self-concept, team player, leader*

Make the following points:

- The socialization process during the preschool years involves children learning the values and behaviors accepted by society.

- Children develop skills and participate in activities that help them become competent and feel confident.

- Research confirms that social and emotional readiness is critical to a successful kindergarten transition, early school success, and, later, accomplishments in the workplace.

- Preschool is a prime setting for helping children gain social and emotional competence and these skills should be an important focus for teachers.

Refer again to the transparency and pose the following questions:

- How do you nurture these characteristics?

- What strategies do you use in the classroom?

  Possible responses:

  Independence—Organize the environment so children can manage themselves and their play.

  Responsibility—Assign jobs.

  Curiosity—Provide interesting materials and experiences that encourage children to ask questions, explore, and experiment.

  Initiative—Offer materials that encourage children to try new things and create on their own.

  Cooperation—Provide opportunities for working in small groups or on group projects.

  Risk-taking—Provide a safe environment where children feel free to try new things and make mistakes.

  Creativity—Provide many open-ended materials to explore and create.

  Perseverance—Provide extended time for children who are deeply engaged in play or a project.

  Confidence—Offer challenging yet doable experiences; celebrate accomplishments.

  Resourcefulness—Provide tools for exploration, interesting materials for building.

SUMMARY

Summarize the workshop with the following points:

- The goal of early childhood education is to help children develop the skills and dispositions that enable them to become successful, life-long learners.

- Social and emotional competence are essential to children's well-being and success in school and in life.

- By focusing on social competence, we also promote the characteristics of a successful learner.

- Anything we do to discourage the development of these skills and attitudes works against our central goals.

NOTES

What Do You Believe About Early Childhood Education?

☐ Handout **0B**
☐ Handout **0C**
☐ Chart paper, markers,
   adhesive dots

◖ PREPARATION

Prior to the training, write the numbers 1–20 along the left-hand side of a piece of chart paper. Put three adhesive dots on each table. Prepare the transparency and duplicate the handout.

◖ INTRODUCTION

Lead a discussion about how beliefs affect both classroom practice and a program's ability to achieve its vision and goals for children.

Explain that during this activity, each person will be asked to examine his or her true beliefs about early childhood education.

◖ ACTIVITY

Distribute handout 0B and give the following instructions:

* Individually, read each statement and put a checkmark next to the ones that you believe to be true.

* Choose a partner at your table. Of the statements you have both checked, agree on five that are most important to both of you.

* Share your top five statements with others at your table.

* As a group, come to consensus on your three most widely held beliefs.

* On the chart numbered 1–20, put a colored dot next to the corresponding statement for each of your three choices.

Discuss the beliefs that received the most number of votes. Examine how they influence attitudes, actions, and classroom and program practice. Emphasize the importance of having shared beliefs among teaching colleagues, administrators, families. Most important, focus on beliefs aligned with *The Creative Curriculum*.

Distribute handout 0C and discuss the fundamental beliefs that underlie *The Creative Curriculum*:

- Constructive, purposeful play is a vehicle for meaningful learning.

- The development of social competence is a key focus of the preschool years.

- Curriculum and assessment must be linked.

- Families are partners in children's learning.

- The teacher's role is vital in connecting content, teaching, and learning.

- All children, including those with special needs, can thrive in an appropriate preschool classroom.

SUMMARY

Summarize with the following points:

- If programs are to achieve their vision or goals for children, it is important that staff share the same, or similar beliefs and that those beliefs align with the curriculum being implemented.

- *The Creative Curriculum* is a blueprint for planning and implementing a developmentally appropriate program.

- Positive results can only be achieved if the Curriculum is implemented as designed. This does not mean that every program will look exactly alike, but it does mean that your philosophy must be in line with that of the Curriculum.

WORKSHOP

Introduction to
The Creative Curriculum for Preschool

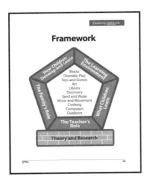

☐ Chart paper, markers, masking tape
☐ Transparency **0D**
☐ *Creative Curriculum,* p. xiv
☐ Variation-Handout **0E**
☐ *Creative Curriculum* video

PREPARATION

Prepare the transparency. Cue the video and duplicate the handout if you are using the Variation.

INTRODUCTION

Introduce the workshop:

• Often, people have different ideas about how to define curriculum for young children.

• The purposes of this activity are to clarify what is meant by curriculum and to introduce *The Creative Curriculum* so that you can feel comfortable using it to plan your program and as an ongoing reference.

ACTIVITY

Give each group a piece of chart paper and a marker. Have the groups talk among themselves to complete the sentence, "Curriculum is…" When they are finished, ask them to write their definitions of curriculum on chart paper and hang them on the wall.

Allow time for participants to walk about and read the various definitions.

Make the following points:

• The field of early childhood education has evolved over the years. There is consensus among leading professional organizations such as the National Association for the Education of Young Children (NAEYC) and the National Association of Early Childhood Specialist in State Departments of Education (NAECS/SDE) as well as Head Start about the importance of a comprehensive curriculum.

• Such a curriculum includes the goals for children's development and learning, what teachers do to achieve the goals, the content children are to learn as well as the processes and activities through which they learn, and the environment or context in which teaching and learning occur.

- Various research and reports (*Eager to Learn*, *From Neurons to Neighborhoods*, *Preventing Reading Difficulties in Young Children*, the *Report of the National Reading Panel: Teaching Children to Read*, and state and national content standards) have

  expanded our understanding of how children develop and learn

  outlined approaches most likely to ensure children's success

  identified ways to address academic content with preschool children

- There are insights about what it takes to provide high-quality programs. Teachers need to

  make the connection between curriculum and assessment

  use a variety of approaches and teaching strategies as they work with children

  know how to integrate content while helping children develop and learn important skills

- A high-quality comprehensive curriculum combines research with desired results, forming a logical plan.

- *The Creative Curriculum* is one such curriculum—offering a comprehensive picture of a high-quality program, and strategies for bringing the program to life in the classroom.

Introduce the Curriculum by asking what participants know about *The Creative Curriculum*.

Invite them to share their thoughts.

Note that the Curriculum has two distinguishing characteristics that set it apart from other approaches.

- It offers a framework for decision-making.

- There is a focus on interest areas.

Provide time for them to look through the book and identify features that immediately catch their attention. Have them share what they discover.

Put up transparency 0D showing the framework and refer participants to the illustration of the framework on page xiv. Use the points below to describe the framework.

Research and Theory

- The Curriculum has always rested on a foundation of research and theory, in particular, the work of Piaget, Maslow, Erikson, and Smilansky.

- This foundation has been strengthened through the work of Vygotsky and Gardner, as well as new information about learning, the brain, and resiliency.

- All of these influence the Curriculum, its view of children, and the recommendations the authors make to teachers.

How Children Develop and Learn

- Teaching begins with knowing children. This component describes what children ages 3–5 are like in four areas of development: social/emotional, physical, cognitive, and language.

- Children enrolled in preschool programs around the country are diverse and have unique needs. *The Creative Curriculum* addresses the differences teachers encounter in individual children, such as gender, temperament, interests, life experiences, learning styles, culture, special needs, and second language learners.

- Children with disabilities are guaranteed access to preschool programs through the Americans with Disabilities Act. The Individuals with Disabilities Act (IDEA) requires early childhood programs to support children's access to their typical peers and to the general curriculum. These requirements for preschoolers can be met using *The Creative Curriculum*.

- The needs of the second language learner can be met in a *Creative Curriculum* classroom as well. Teachers learn how to support a child's continued learning in his or her primary language and, at the same time, provide rich experiences that foster a child's ability to learn to speak English.

- The *Developmental Continuum*, based on the goals and objectives of the Curriculum, is a tool for observing children's development, supporting learning, and tracking their progress.

The Learning Environment

- The learning environment is the starting point for actually implementing *The Creative Curriculum*.

- This component addresses how teachers set up and maintain the physical environment, establish a structure for the day, and create a classroom community conducive to teaching and learning.

What Children Learn

- This component describes the content preschool children learn in six areas: literacy, math, science, social studies, the arts, and technology.

- It gives examples of how children use process skills to learn this content and how teachers integrate content throughout the day.

The Teacher's Role

- The fourth component of the framework shows how teachers engage in an ongoing cycle of observing, guiding learning, and assessing children's progress.

- Observation is the basis for building relationships with children and for planning experiences that will enable every child to grow and learn. Teachers guide children's learning by using a variety of instructional strategies, and integrate learning by engaging children in studies.

- The Curriculum describes how teachers track children's progress using a systematic approach, and how they use assessment to inform their decisions and ensure that every child is making progress.

The Family's Role

- Families are the first and lifelong influence on a child.

- This component focuses on how teachers can build partnerships with families to support children's learning and development.

Interest Areas

- Inside the framework are 11 interest areas.

- If you turn to any one of the 11 interest area chapters, you'll see that the framework is applied in each one.

- Each chapter describes the various materials that meet the developmental needs of young children and enhance learning and teaching in that area.

- You will see a connection between the Curriculum's 50 objectives and academic content and strategies for guiding and assessing children's learning.

- Each chapter ends with frequently asked questions and a letter to families that explains ways to support children's learning at school and at home.

SUMMARY

Summarize by emphasizing the following points:

- *The Creative Curriculum* is a blueprint for planning and implementing a developmentally appropriate program.

- Like a blueprint, the Curriculum must be reviewed, studied, and interpreted accurately in order to build a program that will achieve your desired results.

- Every program using the Curriculum will not look the same. Teachers' own interests and teaching styles should be incorporated, as well as the unique characteristics of the children and families in their programs and the community in which the program is located.

- Consistency results from staying true to the philosophy, using the framework as a guide for decision-making, and focusing on interest areas.

- Implementing a curriculum requires a commitment to learn it and use it as a guide to make decisions.

VARIATION

A Scavenger Hunt Through *The Creative Curriculum*

Ask participants if they have ever gone on a scavenger hunt. Explain that they will begin learning about *The Creative Curriculum* pretending that they are on a scavenger hunt searching through for the location of answers to questions.

Distribute handout 0E and give the following directions:

- Read each statement on the handout.

- Search through the Curriculum to find where the issue is discussed.

- Write the chapter, section, and page number in the space below each statement.

- Each group may divide up the questions if they wish.

Allow time for participants to complete the task and share what they learned.

Add additional comments if necessary.

Show "Part I: Setting the Stage" of the video to give participants an idea of what a *Creative Curriculum* classroom looks like.

Explain that "Part II" highlights most interest areas and will be shown in conjunction with training on "The Teacher's Role."

NOTES

Wall of Fame

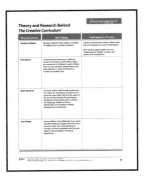

□ Chart paper,
   various art supplies
□ Handout **OF**
□ Handout **OF-Trainer**
□ *Creative Curriculum*
   video

PREPARATION

Duplicate the handout. Review the trainer's version of the handout.

INTRODUCTION

Introduce the workshop with the following points:

- *The Creative Curriculum* is based on accepted theories and research that explain how children develop and learn.

- Teachers who understand the theory and research will know what they are doing and why, and be able to make informed decisions about children and daily classroom practice.

- The purpose of this workshop is to introduce the theory and research that form the foundation of the Curriculum and to consider how each impacts program design, daily practice, and decision making. Additional research and reports that relate to specific topics (e.g., *Preventing Reading Difficulties*) are referenced at the end of each chapter.

ACTIVITY

Have participants form eight groups and explain that they are going to build a Wall of Fame to represent the findings of important theorists and researchers in the field of early childhood education. Assign each group one of the theorists or a research topic and then provide these instructions:

- Pages 2–14 in your book explain the theory and research that are the foundation of the Curriculum. Find and read the section describing the theorist or research you have been assigned. Then talk among yourselves to share what you have learned.

- Next, brainstorm a way to showcase the main ideas by making a poster using any of the art materials on the table. (Offer a demonstration or show a sample poster if necessary.)

- Turn to handout OF. Look at the findings on the handout and discuss the implications of this research for classroom practice. Consider how these ideas influence what you do every day. Record your thoughts in column 3 on the handout.

- When finished, you will present your posters highlighting the findings and then share the implications for practice.

Allow time for the groups to complete their posters and present them. During the presentations, have other participants record the implications for practice in the appropriate boxes on the handout. Add any comments you feel are needed using the completed handout for trainers.

After each presentation, hang the poster on the wall to create the "Wall of Fame." Display them at subsequent workshops and revisit them as the other parts of the *Creative Curriculum* framework are explored.

SUMMARY

Summarize the workshop:

- Understanding theory and research about how young children develop and learn helps teachers plan a program and work with children in ways that match the way children learn. In turn, children become more successful learners.

- These theories and research influenced the design of the Curriculum, the view of children, and the recommendations that the authors make to teachers.

VARIATION

Use handout 0F on its own as a separate activity. Explain the following:

- The purpose of reviewing the theory and research is to consider how each impacts program design, daily practice, and decision-making.

- The first two columns of the handout show the name of the theorist or body of research and the key findings from the research.

- In column 3, you will list some of the ways each finding affects daily classroom practice.

Review the key findings from Maslow and the implications for practice. Then, have participants read Erikson's theories and suggest some implications. Ask:

What do you do to promote children's sense of trust, autonomy, and initiative?

Have participants record their ideas in the appropriate box in column 3 of the handout.

Divide participants into six small groups. Assign one of the remaining theorists or research topics to each group then give these instructions:

- Look over the key findings on the handout and discuss the implications for practice—how would these ideas influence what you do every day?

- Record your ideas in column 3 of the handout. When you have a few ideas listed, turn to pages 2–14 in the Curriculum and find the section on your theorist or research topic. After reading, discuss whether you want to add any additional implications for practice.

Allow time for each group to present the implications for their theorist or research. Add any comments you feel are needed by using the completed handout for trainers.

Characteristics of Successful Learners

- **Independence**

- **Responsibility**

- **Curiosity**

- **Initiative**

- **Cooperation**

- **Risk-taking**

- **Creativity**

- **Perseverance**

- **Confidence**

- **Resourcefulness**

What Do You Believe About Early Childhood Education?

1. Play is an important vehicle for learning in all areas of development.

2. It's impossible to meet today's demands for academic achievement and remain developmentally appropriate.

3. A primary role of the early childhood teacher is to provide an appropriate learning environment and many first-hand experiences that invite children to investigate, represent, and share.

4. Academic skills are best presented to young children in separate subject areas, i.e., reading, math, science, social studies.

5. Teachers must use a wide range of teaching strategies, including both child-initiated learning and direct teaching.

6. Children's development and learning can and should be assessed in the context of classroom activities. This assessment is the key to planning for the individual needs of children.

7. All children, including those with special needs and second language learners, can benefit from a developmentally appropriate preschool program.

8. Children do better on tests when greater emphasis is placed on academics in the early years.

9. Grouping children by ability helps less-able and brighter children learn better.

10. When families are an integral part of a school program, children's self-esteem and achievement are enhanced.

11. Children are less likely to stay focused when family members and other volunteers are in the classroom.

What Do You Believe About Early Childhood Education? continued

12. Social/emotional readiness is critical to children's success in school and in life and should therefore, be the focus of preschool programs.

13. Standardized tests given in the early years reveal a great deal about a child's potential for learning.

14. Group administered achievement tests are necessary for accountability in early childhood programs.

15. Peer modeling, lively interaction, and conversation are essential parts of the early childhood curriculum.

16. Children who attend early childhood programs where they can make choices of activities and materials and engage in active learning are more likely to succeed in school and in life than children who attend more teacher-directed programs.

17. To improve child outcomes, more time must be spent on academic subjects and less time on outdoors and nap.

18. A print-rich environment that allows children to practice literacy skills in real-life experiences, combined with intentional teaching of key concepts, is the foundation of literacy learning in preschool.

19. Content such as science and social studies should be reserved for children in upper grades of school.

20. School board members, school administrators, and the public in general should be knowledgeable about developmentally appropriate practices for young children.

Fundamental Beliefs

1. Constructive purposeful play is a vehicle for meaningful learning.

2. The development of social competence is a key focus of the preschool years.

3. Curriculum and assessment must be linked.

4. Families are partners in children's learning.

5. The teacher's role is vital in connecting content, teaching, and learning.

6. All children, including those with special needs, can thrive in an appropriate preschool classroom.

0C

Framework

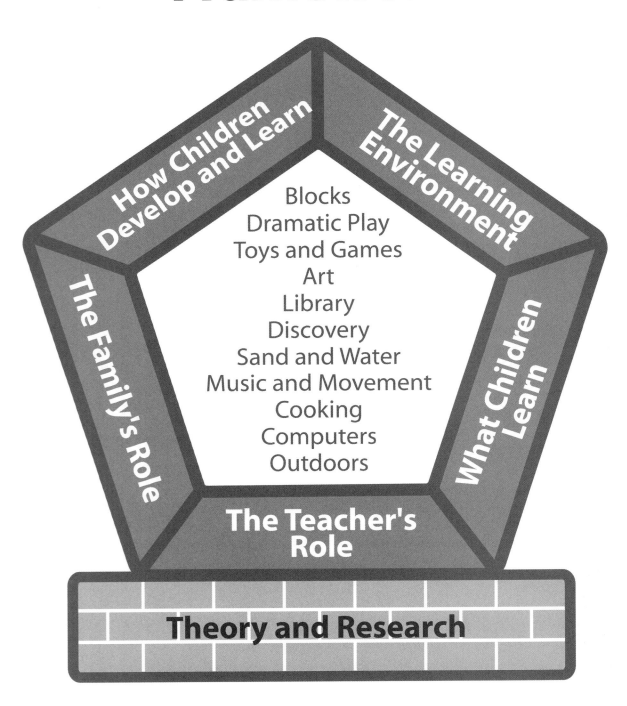

Blocks
Dramatic Play
Toys and Games
Art
Library
Discovery
Sand and Water
Music and Movement
Cooking
Computers
Outdoors

How Children Develop and Learn

The Learning Environment

The Family's Role

What Children Learn

The Teacher's Role

Theory and Research

A Scavenger Hunt Through
The Creative Curriculum® for Preschool

1. You are a new preschool teacher and quite nervous about the beginning of school. Where could you find suggestions for planning the first few days?

2. A parent is concerned that her child does not share or take turns with other children. What information from *The Creative Curriculum* could you share?

3. You have many children whose primary language is not English. You have no idea what to expect or how to work with these children. Where could you look for guidance?

4. A parent complains that she wants her child to stop playing and work on getting ready for kindergarten. What information would you share?

5. Parents regularly ask if their children are learning academics. What section(s) of *The Creative Curriculum* could help you explain the nature of academics in the preschool classroom?

6. Your outdoor area is just a big empty yard. Where do you look to find ways to make it more stimulating for children?

7. A parent tells you she wants to be involved in the program, but her job requires her to work irregular hours. Where would you find suggestions for involving all parents?

8. Children in the class often reject a child. Where can you find strategies to help this child learn to make friends?

9. You have a number of toys and games. You are unsure of where to put them and how to arrange them. Where could you look?

10. You need to know the best and most accurate way to document children's learning and development. How could *The Creative Curriculum* help you?

Theory and Research Behind
The Creative Curriculum®

Theory/Research	Key Findings	Implications for Practice
Abraham Maslow	Meeting children's basic needs is essential to helping them succeed as learners.	Create an environment where children feel safe and experience a sense of belonging. Plan learning opportunities that are challenging yet "doable" to foster self-esteem and competence.
Erik Erikson	Social/emotional learning is a lifelong process that begins at birth. When adults are responsive to children's needs, children learn to trust, develop independence, and take initiative to assert themselves in socially acceptable ways.	
Brain Research	The brain builds itself through experience. The richer the experiences a child has, the more the brain grows. The first five years of life are sensitive periods for developing emotional control, attachment to others, and language. Stable, nurturing relationships are essential to healthy development and learning.	
Jean Piaget	Young children think differently from adults and their thinking changes over time. They construct their own understanding of concepts as they manipulate real, concrete objects and participate in firsthand experiences.	

From *The Creative Curriculum*® *for Preschool*, 4ᵗʰ Edition.
©2004 Teaching Strategies, Inc., PO Box 42243, Washington, DC 20015, www.TeachingStrategies.com

0F

Theory and Research Behind The Creative Curriculum®, continued

Theory/Research	Key Findings	Implications for Practice
Lev Vygotsky	Children grow cognitively not only by acting on objects but also by interacting with knowledgeable peers and adults.	
Howard Gardner	People can be intelligent in many different ways: linguistic, logical, musical, spatial, bodily, interpersonal, intrapersonal, naturalistic.	
Sara Smilansky	Children learn through play: functional play, constructive play, games with rules, and dramatic or pretend play.	
Resilience Research	Children who have faced hardship are not doomed. They can develop the strength and skills necessary to deal with adversity when teachers use good early childhood practices.	

Theory and Research Behind
The Creative Curriculum®

Theory/Research	Key Findings	Implications for Practice
Abraham Maslow	Meeting children's basic needs is essential to helping them succeed as learners.	Create an environment where children feel safe and experience a sense of belonging. Plan learning opportunities that are challenging yet "doable" to foster self-esteem and competence.
Erik Erikson	Social/emotional learning is a lifelong process that begins at birth. When adults are responsive to children's needs, children learn to trust, develop independence, and take initiative to assert themselves in socially acceptable ways.	**Trust**—Follow a consistent schedule, develop a positive relationship with each child, follow through on promises. **Autonomy**—Provide appropriate materials (challenging but not too difficult), acknowledge children's efforts, provide responsibilities. **Initiative**—Value children's ideas, offer choices, promote problem solving and risk taking, encourage creativity.
Brain Research	The brain builds itself through experience. The richer the experiences a child has, the more the brain grows. The first five years of life are sensitive periods for developing emotional control, attachment to others, and language. Stable, nurturing relationships are essential to healthy development and learning.	Focus on social/emotional development as well as language and music skills. Ensure that each child has access to a well-balanced diet and daily exercise. Provide rich and varied learning experiences. Provide time and opportunities for children to practice new skills. Respond to children in ways that let them know that you respect and value their ideas and efforts.
Jean Piaget	Young children think differently from adults and their thinking changes over time. They construct their own understanding of concepts as they manipulate real, concrete objects and participate in firsthand experiences.	Offer many firsthand experiences that invite children to explore, experiment, and make discoveries. Provide experiences that are responsive to where children are in their development.

From *The Creative Curriculum*® *for Preschool*, 4ᵗʰ Edition.
©2004 Teaching Strategies, Inc., PO Box 42243, Washington, DC 20015, www.TeachingStrategies.com

Theory and Research Behind The Creative Curriculum®, continued

Theory/Research	Key Findings	Implications for Practice
Lev Vygotsky	Children grow cognitively not only by acting on objects but also by interacting with knowledgeable peers and adults.	Offer opportunities for children to work with and interact with children of all ability levels. Provide challenging experiences, that is, those that can be accomplished with sensitive guidance.
Howard Gardner	People can be intelligent in many different ways: linguistic, logical, musical, spatial, bodily, interpersonal, intrapersonal, naturalistic.	Provide activities and experiences that allow children to explore all intelligences. Focus on children's strengths as they learn new skills.
Sara Smilansky	Children learn through play: functional play, constructive play, games with rules, and dramatic or pretend play.	Set up an environment that helps children get the most out of their play experiences. Interact with children in ways that invite them to explore, talk about their work, and expand their thinking. Encourage sociodramatic play and provide materials that stimulate imagination.
Resilience Research	Children who have faced hardship are not doomed. They can develop the strength and skills necessary to deal with adversity when teachers use good early childhood practices.	Provide a safe, secure environment. Provide experiences that enable children to feel successful and competent. Be responsive to children, offering them encouragement and hope.

From *The Creative Curriculum® for Preschool*, 4ᵗʰ Edition.
©2004 Teaching Strategies, Inc., PO Box 42243, Washington, DC 20015, www.TeachingStrategies.com

How Children Develop and Learn

PURPOSE

In order to plan and implement an appropriate preschool program for children ages 3–5, teachers must know what young children are like developmentally as well as what makes each child unique. This means understanding the sequence of growth in social/emotional, physical, cognitive, and language development. It also means learning about each child's strengths, interests, needs, experiences, and learning styles. By knowing children, teachers can build relationships that help them to make decisions about how to support learning and development.

This workshop series presents participants with a basic knowledge of child development and individual differences, and introduces them to the *Developmental Continuum*. They learn how to apply this knowledge to everyday classroom practices.

BIG IDEAS:

- Child development is the accepted body of knowledge about how children grow and learn.

- There are four areas of development that, together, give us a picture of the whole child: social/emotional, physical, cognitive, and language.

- These developmental areas are interrelated—development in one area affects other areas.

- Understanding the stages of development of 3-, 4-, and 5-year-old children gives teachers a head start in knowing what children will be like, how they may react to and use the materials teachers select, and how they will relate to others.

- All children bring to school a set of unique characteristics and experiences that affect how they respond to school experiences, relate to others, and learn.

- Effective teachers get to know each child in order to individualize teaching and learning.

How Children Develop and Learn

WORKSHOPS

Key Points	Workshop	Materials	Time (minutes)
Preschool children demonstrate predictable behavior in terms of their social/emotional, physical, cognitive, and language development. Knowing about how children develop and learn is the basis for planning a program, selecting materials, and guiding children's learning.	**Applying What You Know About Child Development to Your Classroom** (p. 32)	☐ Handout **1A:** Applying What You Know About Child Development ☐ *Creative Curriculum* video ☐ Handout **1A-Trainer:** Applying What You Know About Child Development ☐ *Creative Curriculum*, pp. 18–26 ☐ Variation 1-Handout **1B:** Applying What You Know About Child Development to Your Classroom— Play Scenarios ☐ Variation 1-Handout **1C:** Applying What You Know About Child Development to Your Classroom—Worksheet	30–45
Every person is unique and has specific interests, experiences, and learning styles. Getting to know what makes each child unique enables teachers to build a relationship and help every child succeed.	**How Well Do You Know Your Children?** (p. 36)	☐ Transparency **1D:** Individual Differences ☐ Handout **1E:** How Well Do You Know Your Children? ☐ *Creative Curriculum*, pp. 27–41	45
The *Developmental Continuum* is the tool for determining where each child is developmentally, for tracking each child's progress, and for planning learning.	**Looking at Development on a Continuum** (p. 40)	☐ Transparency **1F:** *The Creative Curriculum* Goals and Objectives at a Glance ☐ Transparency **1G:** Developmental Continuum #40 ☐ Post-it notes ☐ Continuum cards, 2–3 sets per table (see Appendix) ☐ *Creative Curriculum*, pp. 19–22, 42–58	45–60

WORKSHOP

Applying What You Know About Child Development to Your Classroom

◖ PREPARATION

Review handout 1A-Trainer. Duplicate the handouts.

Set up TV/VCR.

◖ INTRODUCTION

Introduce the workshop with the following points:

- Curriculum begins with knowing what preschool children are like and how they grow and learn in four areas of development: social/emotional, physical, cognitive, and language.

- Most preschool children demonstrate predictable patterns of development in each area.

- Learning and development in these areas occur in an interrelated fashion.

- Understanding child development enables teachers to anticipate what young children are like so they can respond appropriately.

Ask participants to give examples of what preschool children are like in terms of their social/emotional, physical, cognitive, and language development.

> **Possible responses:** *active, curious about their world, love to talk, like to play, explore using senses, developing small muscles, ask a lot of "why" questions, like to do things on their own, like to try new things, like to please you, feel competent, tire easily, can't sit still for long periods of time.*

☐ Handout **1A**
☐ *Creative Curriculum* video
☐ Handout **1A-Trainer**
☐ *Creative Curriculum*, pp. 18–26
☐ Variation 1– Handout **1B**
☐ Variation 1– Handout **1C**

Take one or two of the characteristics named (e.g., preschool children are active) and ask how these characteristics would influence teachers when

- planning experiences (**Possible responses:** *hands-on, sensory*)

- arranging the physical environment (**Possible responses:** *make sure it is safe and secure, spacious yet well defined to prevent running and rough housing*)

- selecting materials (**Possible responses:** *materials children can manipulate, actively explore, and experiment with*)

- designing the daily schedule (**Possible responses:** *children are likely to tire easily, therefore build in periods of rest, must have reasonable/sufficient amount of time for children to engage in play oriented activities, limit time spent in activities where children are required to sit and listen*)

- creating the social atmosphere (**Possible responses:** *must have realistic rules to guide behavior, provide opportunities for children to work together and cooperate*)

- planning group times (**Possible responses:** *plan participatory activities, make large-group times short*)

ACTIVITY

Distribute handout 1A and give the following instructions:

- Read each statement in column 1 to review examples of what preschool children are like in each of the four areas of development: social/emotional, physical, cognitive, and language.

- Discuss each statement with others at your table and brainstorm practices that are responsive to each statement. Record your ideas in column 2.

Allow time for each group to share some of its ideas.

Ask participants to read pages 18–26 and then discuss the section, "What Preschool Children Are Like."

Show "Part I: Setting the Stage" of the *Creative Curriculum* video and highlight any points related to your previous discussion. Explain that Part II highlights most interest areas and will be shown in conjunction with those workshops.

SUMMARY

Summarize with the following points:

- Knowledge of child development and the typical behaviors of young children gives you a general basis for planning a preschool program.

- *The Creative Curriculum* is based upon research and knowledge of child development and shows teachers how to apply this information to everyday practices in the classroom.

- Each child develops on an individual timetable and may respond to a program in different ways. Therefore, it is important to get to know each child and to appreciate each child's special characteristics.

VARIATIONS

Variation 1:
Distribute handouts 1B and 1C. Give the following instructions:

- Read each scenario.

- Working as groups at your tables, identify the characteristics demonstrated by the children in each scenario. Ask yourselves, "What does this tell me about preschoolers' development?"

- Record each characteristic you identify in a box in column 1.

Have each group share one or two ideas. Expect that their responses will be similar in nature, rather than identical to one to another. Continue with the following instructions:

- Discuss ways in which teachers can respond to each of the characteristics you identified.

- Record your ideas in column 2.

Variation 2:
Ask each group to read about one area of development (social/emotional, physical, cognitive, or language) discussed on pages 18–22.

Have participants list examples of opportunities (indoor and outdoor) they provide for children to develop in this area. They should consider how the schedule, environment, materials and equipment, and activities contribute to development.

NOTES

How Well Do You Know Your Children?

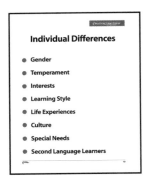

☐ Transparency **1D**
☐ Handout **1E**
☐ *Creative Curriculum,*
   pp. 27–41

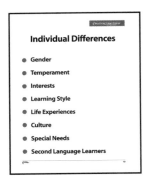

PREPARATION

Review pages 27–41. Prepare the transparency and duplicate the handout.

INTRODUCTION

Begin the workshop with the following instructions:

- Talk with the people at your table to find one thing you all have in common that might not be obvious.

- Next, identify a unique characteristic or ability that is not shared by anyone else at the table.

- Let's hear what you found out.

Make the following points:

- We share many similarities; some are quite obvious while others are not so apparent.

- While we are similar in many respects, we each possess unique characteristics, interests, and abilities.

Ask: "How do you think these two points might have influenced planning for this training?" Respond to the ideas presented.

> **Possible responses:**
>
> *We are all concerned about outcomes.*
>
> *We are all interested in learning more about* The Creative Curriculum.
>
> *One person is hard of hearing; another loves to sing.*
>
> *Some people like to speak in a large group; others prefer sharing their ideas with a partner.*

Make the following points:

- We have to adapt training to meet diverse needs.

- Regardless of the similarities in patterns of development, every child brings specific interests, experiences, skills and abilities, and learning styles to the preschool classroom.

- These unique characteristics influence what a child is like and how he or she reacts to a program.

- Learning what is unique and special about each child, enables a teacher to

    build positive relationships

    help every child feel comfortable in the classroom and ready to learn

    tailor practices to the individual

    build a classroom community

Ask participants to name ways they learn about the children in their programs.

> **Possible responses:** *records, family members, observation, or interaction.*

ACTIVITY

Distribute handout 1D to participants and explain that this activity will help them assess how well they know the unique qualities and characteristics of each of the children in their classes. Give the following instructions:

- Write the names of the children in your class in column 1, labeled "Child's Name."

- Reflect on the following questions and then discuss your response with others at your table.

    Were you able to remember all of the children in your class?

    Which children were easier or more difficult to remember?

    Why do you suppose that is?

Show transparency 1E. Ask participants to choose one of the differences discussed on pages 27–41 to read about. Then offer a few remarks about each. Ask participants to then complete the chart:

- In column 2, record something you know about each child that makes that child unique or special.

- Consider one of the differences highlighted on pages 27–41.

Allow time for participants to complete the task. Ask them to share any observations or insights about their ability or inability to complete this phase of the activity.

Stress that knowing the unique characteristics and abilities of children is key to individualizing instruction. When teachers regularly reflect on what they know about each child, they can make plans to adapt the daily program to support a child's strengths and address individual needs.

Ask participants to think about ways to use what they know about a child to build a relationship, strengthen it, or to support learning. They can record their ideas in column 3.

If necessary, offer an example such as this:

A visual learner is one who learns best by looking. He is drawn to color, shape, and motion. He literally thinks in the form of pictures. This child would benefit more from seeing how things are done rather than just being told.

A teacher might

- provide materials that invite the child to draw or represent learning in pictorial form, or

- show a child how to hold a pair of scissors or turn the paper to cut, in addition to giving oral directions.

Remind participants to consider how they might use the environment, daily routines and events, and studies to individualize, as well as how they might interact with a child.

Invite a few people to share some of their ideas. Encourage participants to continue using this process as a means to think about each child's strengths and abilities and to determine strategies that support learning and development.

SUMMARY

Summarize by highlighting the following points:

- Knowing what preschool children are like means knowing them individually as well as developmentally.

- Each child's unique interests, abilities, and learning styles affect how he or she reacts to your program.

- Knowing what is unique about each child helps you to build a relationship and guide learning.

NOTES

Looking at Development on a Continuum

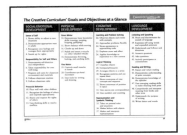

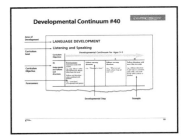

☐ Transparency **1F**
☐ Transparency **1G**
☐ Post-it notes
☐ Continuum cards, 2–3
   sets per table
   (see Appendix)
☐ *Creative Curriculum*,
   pp. 19–22, 42–58

PREPARATION

Prepare the transparencies. Use 8" x 11" cardstock to create continuum cards for the forerunner and each step of **one** of the hypothetical objectives below. Do not label the cards Forerunner, Step I, Step II, or Step III.

Objective: Uses the computer and Internet

   Watches others use the computer

   Turns the computer on and off

   Sends e-mail with attachments

   Develops own personal website and updates it regularly

Objective: Uses a VCR

   Turns on VCR

   Puts a video in the VCR and watches it

   Records a program while watching it

   Programs a week's worth of TV programs

Prepare the continuum cards from the master set in the Appendix. Copy the cards for each developmental area on a different color of paper (e.g., Social/Emotional—yellow; Physical—green). If you plan to use the cards more than once, copy them onto card stock paper for greater durability.

Put several sets of the continuum cards on each table. Shuffle the cards so the steps of each objective are out of order. You may wish to use only the Social/Emotional and Physical continuum cards and use those from the Cognitive and Language areas of development during other workshops.

INTRODUCTION

Show transparency 1F. Have participants locate the goals and objectives listed on pages 42 and 530 and elaborate on the following points:

- The goals and objectives of *The Creative Curriculum* are a guide for planning a program that fosters learning and development in four areas—social/emotional, physical, cognitive, and language.

- The goals are described in the discussion of each area of development in the section, "What Preschool Children Are Like," on pages 19–22. The objectives are first introduced on page 42.

- We know that children do not achieve objectives all at one time. Most go through a series of steps when learning a skill.

Introduce the idea of a continuum of development by having participants think about the steps one follows when working toward one of the hypothetical objectives—using a computer or a VCR.

Ask for three volunteers, and give each a card describing one of the steps of the objective. Have them read their cards aloud in random order, and then arrange themselves to depict the correct sequence of steps. Ask the rest of the group if they agree with the order.

Make the following points:

- The steps you outlined are typical levels of development that most people go through when learning to use a computer and the Internet or a VCR.

- Some people might proceed quickly through the steps; others may progress more slowly.

- The steps are not defined by age.

- The *Developmental Continuum* shows the sequence of steps children go through as they achieve the goals and objectives of the Curriculum. The three steps we just looked at are similar to steps I, II, and III on the *Developmental Continuum*.

Pass out the Forerunner card to another volunteer and make the following points:

- Everyone is not at the typical level of development for various reasons—perhaps someone has never seen a computer or VCR, has had little or no experience using a computer or VCR, or has a disability that prevents him from successfully accessing this equipment.

- Everyone exhibits some prerequisite behavior or skills related to achieving this objective. In the *Developmental Continuum*, these are called Forerunner skills.

Have the volunteer read the last step aloud and stand next to the person holding step I. Invite the group to offer other examples of Forerunner skills.

Point out that other people may go beyond step III.

Show the transparency 1G. Ask participants to turn to page 43 and follow along as you explain how the Continuum is formatted and how each objective is broken into developmental steps. Emphasize the following points:

- The boxes labeled I, II, or III represent the developmental steps, which are particular points in skill development. These steps do not represent specific age levels, i.e., step I is not necessary equivalent to a 3-year-old's behavior, step II a 4-year-old's, or step II a 5-year-old's.

- Behaviors listed for each step are only **examples**. There are numerous and varied ways children show what they know and can do.

- There may be some children who are not yet in the typical range of development but who will exhibit emergent, or Forerunner, skills and behaviors.

- Forerunner behaviors listed on the Continuum are **examples** of ways children **might** show their knowledge or skill.

- Children who are not in the typical range of development may have had limited experiences, lacked opportunity to develop a skill, or have a special need.

- Some children will go beyond the scope of the Continuum. Referring to step III will give you an idea of how to increase the complexity of a task.

- All children have strengths and abilities upon which to build.

ACTIVITY

Introduce the activity:

- The purpose of this next activity is to become familiar with the *Developmental Continuum*.

- The sets of colored cards on each table include the objectives in two areas of development: yellow—social/emotional; green—physical. Each card has the number of a specific objective and one developmental step or the forerunners printed on it.

- The first task is to sort the cards according to objective. There are four cards for each numbered objective.

- Once you have the cards sorted, divide up the sets so each person at the table has several objectives. You may work with a partner or on your own.

- Decide on the developmental sequence and sort the cards accordingly, beginning with the forerunner (which is a "freebie").

As each group completes the task, invite them to share among themselves to see if others at the table agree with what they are doing. Then invite participants to compare their work with the *Developmental Continuum* found on pages 46–58 and discuss any differences. Pose these questions:

- How did you do?

- Did you find any objectives or steps particularly challenging?

- What are some of the benefits of looking at objectives on a continuum?

SUMMARY

Review the following points:

- The goals and objectives of the Curriculum are a guide for planning learning opportunities in four areas of development.

- The *Developmental Continuum* takes the goals and objectives of the Curriculum and shows the progression of development for all 50 objectives.

- Each child is on an individual timetable. The *Developmental Continuum* enables teachers to determine where each child is in terms of development, track progress, and plan experiences that will enhance learning and encourage development.

Applying What You Know About Child Development

Child Development Characteristics	How Teachers Can Respond
Social/Emotional Development Learning to get along with others	
Take initiative	
Express feelings in actions and words	
Physical Development Enjoy moving the large muscles of the body, especially the arms and legs	
Like doing puzzles and putting things together	
Tire easily	

Applying What You Know About Child Development, continued

Child Development Characteristics	How Teachers Can Respond
Cognitive Development Use all of their senses to learn	
Use their imaginations and are creative in their thinking	
Learn to identify, compare, match, and classify by color, shape, and size	
Language Development Use language to think, learn, imagine, plan, make requests, direct others, and solve problems	
Can retell stories and recite favorite parts of books and songs	
Explore and use writing	

Applying What You Know
About Child Development

Child Development Characteristics	How Teachers Can Respond
Social/Emotional Development Learning to get along with others	• Comment positively on relationships: "You and Sonya help out each other. That's what friends do." • Teach children skills involved in making friends, such as asking another child to play. • Teach children the words and actions needed to enter a group of children at play.
Take initiative	• Provide interesting materials that invite children to explore, experiment, and create on their own. • Offer children opportunities to make choices. • Value children's ideas. • Promote problem solving and risk taking
Express feelings in actions and words	• Help children to label their emotions: "I can tell that you're angry by the way you threw the book on the floor." • Model appropriate ways of expressing emotions. • Help children to use words instead of actions: "Why don't you tell Zack that you're still looking at the book? When you throw the book on the floor, you crease and tear the pages."
Physical Development Enjoy moving the large muscles of the body, especially the arms and legs	• Include music and movement activities and outdoor times in the daily schedule. • Provide many types of movement props such as scarves, hoops, beanbags, balls, and a parachute. • Play games such as "hot potato" so children can practice catching skills.
Like doing puzzles and putting things together	• Provide toys and games that encourage children to coordinate their hand and eye movements, such as puzzles, patterning toys, beads and string, and Legos. • Offer children old watches, clocks, toys, and appliances that they can take apart and try to reassemble.
Tire easily	• Include quiet activities and rest periods in the daily schedule. • Offer children who require more rest alternatives to more active experiences.

Applying What You Know About Child Development, continued

Child Development Characteristics	How Teachers Can Respond
Cognitive Development Use all of their senses to learn	• Create an environment rich in sensory opportunities: fabrics of different textures that can be used in collage; fall leaves for graphing; cooking experiences to stimulate the senses, etc.
Use their imaginations and are creative in their thinking	• Provide open-ended toys and materials for children to explore, experiment, and create. • Create an environment in which children feel free to experiment and take risks. • Provide time and opportunity for children to engage in dramatic play.
Learn to identify, compare, match, and classify by color, shape, and size	• Provide collections of leaves, keys, buttons, and shells for children to sort and graph. • Use transitions that sort the children into groups: all of the girls, those wearing red, everyone whose shoes tie, etc.
Language Development Use language to think, learn, imagine, plan, make requests, direct others, and solve problems	• Speak with children about their work and ask open-ended questions to encourage them to express ideas. • Set up each interest area to encourage all kinds of language learning. Include magazines and note pads in dramatic play, books on buildings in blocks, a sign-in sheet for snack, alphabet letters at the writing table, etc. • Label objects and materials with pictures and words. • Encourage children to refer to books for answers questions. • Take dictation of children's stories or write descriptions of their art on drawings and paintings.
Can retell stories and recite favorite parts of books and songs	• Read or sing children's favorites often, letting them join in on refrains. • Encourage children to retell stories in their own words. • Encourage children to recite these stories and songs for families and other groups.
Explore and use writing	• Create a place specifically for writing in the Library Area. • Incorporate writing materials into other interest areas of the classroom. • Write with children to demonstrate the purposes and functions of writing. Talk about the features of words and letters and the processes used. • Offer words of encouragement as children express themselves creatively through writing.

Applying What You Know About Child Development to Your Classroom—Play Scenarios

Scenario 1:

As Tasheen enters the Sand and Water Area at choice time, she immediately heads to a water table that is filled with warm, soapy water. She touches the water and says, "Oooo, it feels warm and slippery." Tasheen swishes her hand gently through the water, watching small bubbles appear. She begins moving both hands through the water, and soft suds form on top of the water.

Leo, who is looking on from the sandbox, joins Tasheen at the water table. He says to Tasheen, "What would happen if we both put our hands in the water?" The children play quietly alongside one another, swishing their hands, scooping up suds with their hands, putting them on their arms, and making "suds mountains." Leo sees a whisk from a nearby tub of props. Taking it, he says, "I'm going to make pancakes like my Grandma does!" He begins moving the whisk vigorously back and forth through the water. Leo smiles, moving his hand faster and faster as the soft, frothy, bubbles begin to rise. Leo tells Tasheen, "I learned how to make lots of pancake mix." Leo pretends to cook pancakes, then puts his hand to his mouth and says, "These sure don't taste like my Grandma's pancakes!" Both children giggle with delight.

Scenario 2:

Carlos arrives at school on Monday morning, excited about his weekend with his Dad at the stock car races. At circle time, Carlos shares a poster of car #24, the winning car. Ben and Janelle have many questions for Carlos, who offers as much information as he can. He talks about the drivers' uniforms, helmets, the sounds of the engines, and even the food sold at the concession stands. Choice Time arrives, and Ben and Janelle choose to work with Carlos in the Block Area to build a race track where cars can go "really fast!" They begin by resting the ramps on the first level of the block shelf, but are disappointed when the cars gently roll down the ramp. Carlos suggests that they provide the cars with "more engine power" by pushing the cars down the ramp. Unfortunately, the cars jump the track. Returning to their original plans, the children try resting the ramps, first on a chair, then the wall, until finally each holds a ramp. Calling Mr. Alvarez over, Carlos announces, "We learned how to make cars go really fast! And, Janelle was the winner of the race." When asked how she became the winner, Carlos explains that, when holding the ramps, Janelle's was the highest, and that made her car go the fastest.

Scenario 3:

Kate, Dallas, and Susie are in the Dramatic Play Area that has been converted into a Pet Shop. Suddenly, Susie announces, "Boots is missing! She's not in her basket!" Boots is one of the stuffed kittens that is used in play. Dallas and Kate quickly join in the search for Boots. "She's not in another kitten's basket or in the bathtub," calls Kate. "Let's ask some other people if they have seen Boots," says Dallas. Susie, Kate, and Dallas begin asking other friends in the classroom if they have seen Boots. Having no luck, Susie says, "We need to make some signs." Susie gets paper and markers while Kate and Dallas clear space at the table to make signs. The children begin drawing pictures of Boots. "Now, how do you write 'Lost Kitten'?" asks Susie. Ms. Tory writes the words on a piece of paper, and the children quickly copy them onto their signs. Working together they hang their signs around the room and outside their classroom door. The children are sure that the signs will help them find Boots.

Scenario 4:

During outdoor time, Derek, Ben, and Zack frequently wear colorful pieces of fabric tied around their shoulders and say, "I'm Spiderman," "I'm Superman," or "I'm Batman" as they jump and swing on the outdoor climbers. They collect leaves, rocks, and acorns during outdoor play and sort them into neat piles. When asked about their collections, they are quick to explain that these are "energy foods" that help them stay strong so they can help people in trouble.

The boys often enlist other children to join their play, inviting them to help build a hideout or vehicle out of PVC pipe and other loose parts. The building consists of putting pieces together and taking them apart until they fit just right. Other favorite activities include throwing and kicking balls, because these are the "superhero's exercises."

Applying What You Know About
Child Development to Your Classroom—Worksheet

Child Development Characteristics	How Teachers Can Respond
Social/Emotional Development	
Physical Development	
Cognitive Development:	
Language Development	

Individual Differences

- **Gender**

- **Temperament**

- **Interests**

- **Learning Style**

- **Life Experiences**

- **Culture**

- **Special Needs**

- **Second Language Learners**

How Well Do You Know Your Children?

Child's Name	Something Special I Know About This Child	How I Can Use What I Know to Build a Relationship and Support Learning
1		
2		
3		
4		
5		
6		
7		
8		
9		
10		
11		
12		
13		
14		
15		
16		
17		
18		
19		
20		

1E

The *Creative Curriculum®* Goals and Objectives at a Glance

SOCIAL/EMOTIONAL DEVELOPMENT

Sense of Self

1. Shows ability to adjust to new situations
2. Demonstrates appropriate trust in adults
3. Recognizes own feelings and manages them appropriately
4. Stands up for rights

Responsibility for Self and Others

5. Demonstrates self-direction and independence
6. Takes responsibility for own well-being
7. Respects and cares for classroom environment and materials
8. Follows classroom routines
9. Follows classroom rules

Prosocial Behavior

10. Plays well with other children
11. Recognizes the feelings of others and responds appropriately
12. Shares and respects the rights of others
13. Uses thinking skills to resolve conflicts

PHYSICAL DEVELOPMENT

Gross Motor

14. Demonstrates basic locomotor skills (running, jumping, hopping, galloping)
15. Shows balance while moving
16. Climbs up and down
17. Pedals and steers a tricycle (or other wheeled vehicle)
18. Demonstrates throwing, kicking, and catching skills

Fine Motor

19. Controls small muscles in hands
20. Coordinates eye-hand movement
21. Uses tools for writing and drawing

COGNITIVE DEVELOPMENT

Learning and Problem Solving

22. Observes objects and events with curiosity
23. Approaches problems flexibly
24. Shows persistence in approaching tasks
25. Explores cause and effect
26. Applies knowledge or experience to a new context

Logical Thinking

27. Classifies objects
28. Compares/measures
29. Arranges objects in a series
30. Recognizes patterns and can repeat them
31. Shows awareness of time concepts and sequence
32. Shows awareness of position in space
33. Uses one-to-one correspondence
34. Uses numbers and counting

Representation and Symbolic Thinking

35. Takes on pretend roles and situations
36. Makes believe with objects
37. Makes and interprets representations

LANGUAGE DEVELOPMENT

Listening and Speaking

38. Hears and discriminates the sounds of language
39. Expresses self using words and expanded sentences
40. Understands and follows oral directions
41. Answers questions
42. Asks questions
43. Actively participates in conversations

Reading and Writing

44. Enjoys and values reading
45. Demonstrates understanding of print concepts
46. Demonstrates knowledge of the alphabet
47. Uses emerging reading skills to make meaning from print
48. Comprehends and interprets meaning from books and other texts
49. Understands the purpose of writing
50. Writes letters and words

Developmental Continuum #40

Area of Development → **LANGUAGE DEVELOPMENT**

Curriculum Goal → **Listening and Speaking**

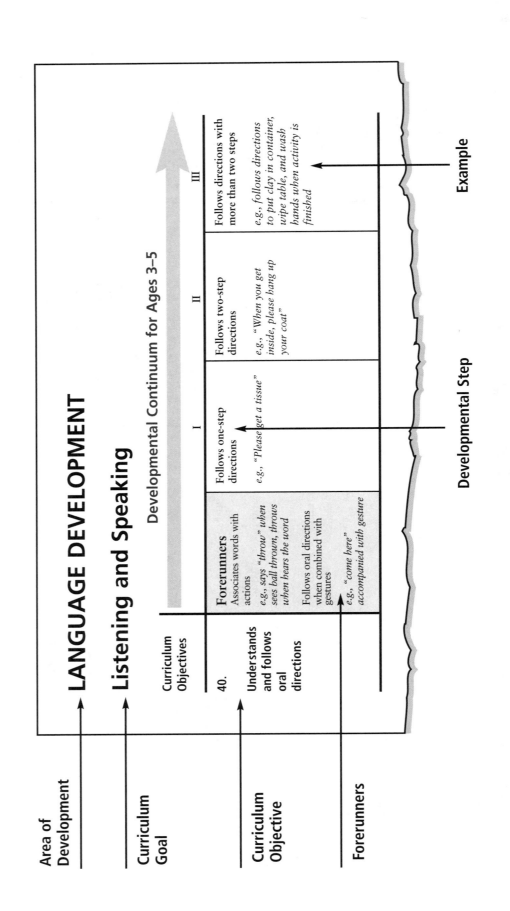

Developmental Continuum for Ages 3–5

Curriculum Objectives	Forerunners	I	II	III
40. **Understands and follows oral directions**	Associates words with actions *e.g., says "throw" when sees ball thrown, throws when hears the word* Follows oral directions when combined with gestures *e.g., "come here" accompanied with gesture*	Follows one-step directions *e.g., "Please get a tissue"*	Follows two-step directions *e.g., "When you get inside, please hang up your coat"*	Follows directions with more than two steps *e.g., follows directions to put clay in container, wipe table, and wash hands when activity is finished*

Curriculum Objective

Forerunners

Developmental Step

Example

NOTES

The Learning Environment

PURPOSE

1st

important

The learning environment has a profound impact on how people feel, how they behave, and how they learn. Teachers use their knowledge of how children develop and learn to create an environment in which children are safe and comfortable, and feel they belong. An effective learning environment also helps children develop independence and confidence as learners. The second component of the *Creative Curriculum* framework includes three aspects of the learning environment: how to set up and maintain the classroom, how to establish a structure for each day, and how to create a classroom community.

These workshops will help participants to appreciate how the environment affects behavior, to select and display materials, and to evaluate their own room arrangements. They explore how to design an appropriate daily schedule, facilitate routine times of the day, and use the Weekly Planning Form. Finally, participants learn about establishing a classroom community, including forming positive relationships, establishing rules, setting limits, and guiding children's behavior.

BIG IDEAS:

- The learning environment is the starting point for implementing *The Creative Curriculum*.

- The physical environment sets the stage for learning and affects children's behavior.

- The daily routines and schedule bring order to the day and help children function as a group.

- Classrooms that function as a community help children relate positively to others and resolve conflicts peacefully.

The Learning Environment

WORKSHOPS

Key Points	Workshop	Materials	Time (minutes)
In an effective learning environment, children become independent and confident learners.	**Elements of an Effective Learning Environment** (p. 60)	☐ Handout **2A:** Different Kinds of Classrooms—Skits	25
The physical environment affects how people feel and behave.	**Setting Up and Maintaining the Classroom** (p. 62)	☐ Handout **2B:** Setting Up the Classroom ☐ Blank transparency or chart paper ☐ *Creative Curriculum*, pp. 63, 81	30
The arrangement of furnishings and organization of materials convey messages and support goals for learning.	**Messages in the Environment** (p. 66)	☐ *Creative Curriculum*, pp. 76–78 ☐ *Room Arrangement* video ☐ TV/VCR ☐ Handout **2C:** Messages in the Environment	45
Teachers must consider the particular needs of individual children when adapting the environment.	**Adapting the Environment for Children With Disabilities** (p. 68)	☐ *Creative Curriculum*, pp. 72, 76–78	30
When the environment is comfortable and attractive, both teachers and children learn better.	**Making Your Space Comfortable and Attractive** (p. 70)	☐ *Creative Curriculum*, p. 71 ☐ Handout **2D:** Elements of a Comfortable and Attractive Setting ☐ Variation-Pictures of two classrooms ☐ Variation-*Creative Curriculum*, p. 71	30
Materials should be varied, challenging, interesting, and carefully arranged.	**Selecting Materials That Support *Creative Curriculum* Goals and Objectives** (p. 72)	☐ *Creative Curriculum*, p. 530 ☐ Toys and other learning materials ☐ Chart paper, markers, tape	30–45
Interest areas appeal to the range of children's interests.	**Why Interest Areas Are Important** (p. 74)	☐ Post-it notes	15–30
A checklist can help you evaluate the effectiveness of your classroom environment.	**Using the *Implementation Checklist* to Evaluate Your Classroom Environment** (p. 76)	☐ *Creative Curriculum*, pp. 62–81 ☐ *Implementation Checklist* ☐ Transparencies	20–30
Consistent routines promote a well-managed classroom.	**Daily Events: What Is Their Value?** (p. 78)	☐ Handout **2E:** The Value of Daily Events	20

The Learning Environment

WORKSHOPS

🔑 Key Points	⬡ Workshop	🗎 Materials	🕐 Time (minutes)
Orderly events scheduled to suit the developmental and individual needs of children help the day go more smoothly. A good schedule for preschool children offers a balance of various types of activities.	**Using What You Know About Children to Structure the Day** (p. 80)	☐ Chart paper, markers, watch ☐ *Creative Curriculum*, pp. 82–97 ☐ Participants' daily schedules ☐ *Implementation Checklist*	60
Weekly planning helps teachers organize materials and plan activities.	**Using the Weekly Planning Form** (p. 84)	☐ *Creative Curriculum*, pp. 97–101, 526–529 ☐ Transparency **2F:** Weekly Planning Form ☐ Handout **2F:** Weekly Planning Form	45
In a classroom community, teachers build a positive relationship with each child and teach children how to make friends.	**Promoting Positive Relationships in the Classroom** (p. 86)	☐ *Creative Curriculum*, pp. 102–108 ☐ Handout **2G:** Helping Children Make Friends—Scenario ☐ Handout **2H:** Helping Children Make Friends—Worksheet ☐ *Implementation Checklist*	20–30
Rules help children feel safe and comfortable so they can learn.	**Developing Rules for a Classroom Community** (p. 88)	☐ *Creative Curriculum*, pp. 108–110 ☐ Chart paper	15–30
Teaching children social problem-solving skills will help them get along in school and in life.	**Handling Conflicts Between Children** (p. 90)	☐ *Creative Curriculum*, pp. 110–115 ☐ Handout **2I:** Handling Conflicts Between Children—Scenarios ☐ Handout **2J:** Handling Conflicts Between Children—Worksheet	30
Teachers use a repertoire of strategies to deal with challenging behaviors and promote children's self-control.	**Responding to Challenging Behavior** (p. 92)	☐ *Creative Curriculum*, pp. 116–122 ☐ Handout **2K:** Challenging Behavior—Scenarios ☐ Handout **2L:** Responding to Challenging Behavior—Worksheet ☐ *Implementation Checklist*	30

Elements of an Effective Learning Environment

☐ Handout **2A**

PREPARATION

Duplicate handout 2A. Cut it apart so that each participant will have a copy of one of the three sections. You may elect to have participants read and discuss each classroom scenario rather than present skits.

INTRODUCTION

Introduce the workshop:

- The starting point for implementing *The Creative Curriculum* is the learning environment.

- In the Curriculum, the learning environment includes the physical environment, the structure including the daily schedule and routines, and the social/emotional environment.

- To design an effective learning environment, a teacher reflects on all the components of the framework:

    How do I use my knowledge of child development and children's individual needs and interests to design classroom space, the daily schedule, and the social atmosphere to address goals for children?

    What content is appropriate for preschool children and how should it be reflected in the environment?

    What is my role in planning this environment?

    How can I involve families in creating the learning environment?

- The purpose of this activity is to experience three different types of environments and identify elements that make an environment effective for learning.

ACTIVITY

Form three equal groups and give each group copies of one of the scenarios, i.e., the first group (group 1) receives the description of classroom 1.

Give the following instructions:

- Find a place where you can get together to plan a skit representing the scenario described in your handout.

- Take about 5–10 minutes to get ready to present your skit to the rest of the group.

Pull everyone back together for the dramatizations. After each skit, ask:

- How would you describe the learning environment in each classroom?

- How do various elements of the environment affect children's learning and behavior?

- What messages are sent to children in each situation?

SUMMARY

Summarize with the following points:

- The learning environment includes

    the physical environment

    the structure of the day

    the social and emotional atmosphere

- When the learning environment meets children's developmental needs to belong and feel safe and comfortable, children become independent and confident learners.

WORKSHOP

Setting Up and Maintaining the Classroom

□ Blank transparency or chart paper
□ *Creative Curriculum,* pp. 63, 81
□ Handout **2B**

◖ **PREPARATION**

Ask participants to bring or make floor plans of their own classrooms to use as they reflect on the classroooom's physical environment.

◖ **INTRODUCTION**

Introduce the workshop:

- The learning environment is the starting point for implementing the Curriculum.

- The physical environment sets the stage for learning and affects children's behavior.

Ask participants to think about a store where they hate to shop—a store that drives them crazy!

Have them visualize the store: what it looks like, how it smells, what they hear, and how they act and feel when they are shopping there. Ask them to think about what frustrates them as a shopper and what features of the store they really dislike.

Allow a few minutes for discussion at tables. Then ask the group members to share their ideas as you record them on a chart or transparency.

> **Possible responses:** *dirty, cluttered, disorganized, unattractive displays, crowded, poor lighting, disgusting odors, narrow aisles, loud music, salesclerks—none to be found, follow you around, or rude and insensitive, limited selection of merchandise, don't have what I want or my size, merchandise is broken or it is too high, keep moving things around, long waiting lines, cluttered, no return policy, the hours do not fit my needs.*

Ask:

- Do these characteristics affect the way you feel and behave?

- Do any of these characteristics apply to preschool classrooms?

Go back through the list drawing parallels between each item and the classroom environment. Discuss how poorly organized environments can make us angry, frustrated, and inefficient, whether we are shopping in a store or working in a classroom.

◀ ACTIVITY

Distribute the handout and lead a discussion:

- The floor plans show a classroom with the same furniture arranged in two different ways.

- What behavior would you expect to see in the classroom on the left?

  Possible responses:

  Too much open space encourages running.

  Block area is too open and structures will be knocked over.

  Quiet areas are near noisy ones.

  Areas are not clearly defined so children will have trouble making choices.

- Room arrangement can promote the development of certain behaviors and skills such as those listed on the bottom of the handout.

Ask participants to examine the floor plan on the right. Have them work with a partner to generate a list of ways that the physical environment supports these behaviors and skills.

Invite participants to share some of their ideas.

Summarize the discussion with the following points:

- Children can see what choices are available and select the interest area they want.

- Children are able to concentrate more easily in clearly defined spaces.

- Running is less of a problem because there are no long open spaces.

- The interest areas encourage small groups of children to work together.

- Distractions have been minimized.

- Children are more likely to take care of materials because they are organized logically and everything has a place.

- The organization of materials encourages children to use classification and reading skills as they select materials and put them away.

Point out the floor plan on page 63. Call participants' attention to the following sections in the chapter: "Guidelines for Setting Up Interest Areas," page 64; "Equipping Interest Areas," page 65; "Displaying and Labeling Materials," pages 65-67; and "A Place for Group Time," page 67. Make any necessary points from the Curriculum that have not yet been addressed.

Give the following instructions on applying what they have learned to their own classroom environments.

- Take out the floor plan of your classroom or draw one.

- Pair up with someone at the table.

- Take turns examining and evaluating one another's classroom environment using information learned and consider recommendations for changes.

SUMMARY

Summarize with the following points:

- Assess how well the physical setting is working for children and for you. Ask yourself:

  What materials do children typically select?

  How are children using these materials?

  What are children learning?

  How do children relate to others while working?

- With this information, you can make the appropriate changes to the physical environment.

- Even if you have organized the classroom carefully, things don't always go according to plan.

VARIATIONS

Variation 1:
Ask participants to think about and share how they set up their kitchens.

> **Possible responses:** *there are different areas (for cooking, washing dishes, etc.); materials are stored near where they are used; there are enough materials for everyone in the family to use; the kitchen is clean; it is set up so that family members enjoy spending time in it, etc.*

Variation 2:
Ask participants to describe a place where they find they can get things done well—they feel comfortable, they can be themselves, they feel like they really belong.

> **Possible responses:** *enough space, adequate lighting, soothing colors, pleasant temperature, smells, or sounds, comfortable furnishings, arrangement of furniture, ample and interesting materials that are easily accessible, people who value and respect me, surrounded by personal belongings.*

Variation 3:
Have participants brainstorm a list of what they hope to see in a classroom environment and what they hope not to see.

NOTES

Messages in the Environment

☐ *Creative Curriculum,*
pp. 76–78
☐ *Room Arrangement*
video
☐ TV/VCR
☐ Handout **2C**

PREPARATION

Ask participants to bring or make floor plans of their own classrooms to use as they reflect on the classroom's physical environment.

Duplicate the handout.

INTRODUCTION

Introduce the workshop:

- Teachers who are aware of the power of the physical environment arrange space purposefully to convey six positive messages to children and families:

    This is a good place to be.

    You belong here.

    This is a place you can trust.

    There are places where you can be by yourself when you want to.

    You can do many things on your own here.

    This is a safe place to explore and try out your ideas.

- During this workshop, you will identify ways in which these messages are already conveyed in your classroom and view the *Room Arrangement as a Teaching Strategy* video to identify any new ideas you might want to try.

ACTIVITY

Distribute handout 2C. Assign one message to each table of participants.

Have participants think of ways in which their current environment communicates this message to the children in their programs and record their ideas in column 2 of the handout.

Show the *Room Arrangement* video. Stop the video after each message to allow participants to record new ideas in column 3.

Invite participants to share an idea they especially liked and want to try.

SUMMARY

Summarize the activity with the following points:

- The physical environment affects how children feel and behave.

- The arrangement of the classroom and selection of the materials convey messages and support goals for learning.

- Preschool children like to have choices, to explore, and to do things on their own. They work better in small groups in well-defined areas. If we want children to grow and learn, and to begin to assume responsibilities for themselves and the classroom, we need to provide an environment that works.

- Teachers must continually evaluate the effectiveness of the classroom environment and make necessary adjustments.

Adapting the Environment for Children With Disabilities

☐ *Creative Curriculum,*
  pp. 72, 76–78

PREPARATION

This workshop is a modified version of the previous one and can be used with audiences who have special needs children, i.e., children who have disabilities, are gifted, or second language learners in their programs.

The activity is written to focus on adaptations for children with disabilities. It can be modified to have participants consider the needs of gifted children and Second Language Learners. Prior to the workshop, spend some time thinking about how the messages might be conveyed for each need being addressed.

INTRODUCTION

Introduce the workshop:

- Teachers who are aware of the power of the environment consider the arrangement of space, presentation of materials, daily schedule, and transition strategies when planning for the individual needs of every child, including those with and without disabilities.

- There are messages we purposely want to convey to all children through the environment:

    This is a good place to be.

    You belong here.

    This is a place you can trust.

    There are places where you can be by yourself when you want to.

    You can do many things on your own here.

    This is a safe place to explore and try out your ideas.

- In this activity, you will consider how one of these messages is conveyed to children with disabilities.

ACTIVITY

Divide participants into six groups. Give each group a message strip.

Give these instructions:

- Have someone from your group read the message aloud.

- Think of a child in your class if you work in an inclusive model program, or your class as a whole if it is a self-contained model. List the ways in which your current environment conveys this message to the child with a disability.

Invite the groups to share one or two points from their discussions.

Now have participants work in pairs. Give these instructions:

- Describe a specific child and the strategies you currently use to convey your group's message to this child.

- Brainstorm additional ways you might communicate this message to that child. Consider new strategies for adapting the schedule, room arrangement, presentation of materials, transitions, and expectations and how they are communicated and upheld.

Refer participants to the chart on page 72. Offer examples such as the ones below if needed.

A child with attention-related difficulties goes to the teacher when he is overstimulated and says, "I need to go to the Quiet Place for a while." This is an area with pillows and stuffed animals. This strategy sends the message, "There are places where you can be by yourself when you want to," and that it's okay to need a quiet time and space.

A child with autism may become agitated, anxious, or act out in response to bright colors and too much visual stimulation. To convey the message, "You belong here," the teacher considers what, where, and how things are displayed, including materials and children's work. One teacher decides to display children's work on a special board that could serve as a room divider and be moved or removed if the room becomes too stimulating.

Allow time for participants to share at their tables and to discuss any observations.

SUMMARY

Summarize the activity:

- Making adaptations cannot be done by recipe, even for children with the same diagnosed disability.

- Meeting the needs of any child is about problem solving and revisiting situations to determine what worked and what didn't.

- Children with disabilities are more like than different from other children.

- The environment is a powerful tool for addressing the needs of all children.

Making Your Space Comfortable and Attractive

□ *Creative Curriculum*, p. 71
□ Handout **2D**
□ Variation-Pictures of two classrooms
□ Variation-*Creative Curriculum*, p. 71

PREPARATION

This activity is best done when participants have access to early childhood classrooms and children are not present. If this is not possible, participants can complete the activity in their own classrooms before returning for the next workshop.

Duplicate handout 2D on card stock and cut it apart. Participants will work in pairs or groups of three so you will need enough cards for each group to have one card.

INTRODUCTION

Introduce the workshop:

- Everyone wants to spend time in places that make them feel comfortable and relaxed.

- Because you and the children spend a large part of the day in the classroom, it should be comfortable and attractive, rather than institutional.

- Teachers who incorporate home-like touches into their classrooms convey the message that "preschool is a good place to be."

ACTIVITY

Ask participants to read the chart on page 71. Then have participants work with a partner or form groups of three people. Give each group a card with the following categories listed:

- light
- softness
- textures

- quiet spaces
- home-like touches
- living things

Have each group choose a recorder. Groups move through the classroom(s) making note of materials, furnishings, and spaces that reflect each category.

After groups return to the training room, invite them to share their observations.

Allow time for participants to brainstorm ways to make their own classrooms more inviting (and reflective of the children's lives) and to generate a list of possible businesses in the community that might be willing to donate materials for this purpose.

SUMMARY

Summarize the activity with brief statements about the "positive messages" that are conveyed to children when the classroom is comfortable and attractive.

VARIATION

Secure two pictures of classrooms. Classroom *A* should be developmentally appropriate but have mostly commercial furniture and materials. Classroom *B* is also appropriate but contains additional home-like touches such as softness, a variety of textures, living things, or quiet spaces.

Give the following instructions:

- Draw two intersecting circles on a piece of paper (Venn diagram).

- Record the distinguishing characteristics of each classroom in the appropriate circle.

- Record similar characteristics in the intersecting space.

Ask the following questions:

- How does Classroom *A* make you feel? Classroom *B*?

- How could Classroom *A* be changed to make it feel more like Classroom *B*?

Refer participants to page 71 and have them reflect on these elements as they think about their own classrooms.

Selecting Materials That Support *Creative Curriculum* Goals and Objectives

☐ *Creative Curriculum*, p. 530
☐ Toys and other learning materials
☐ Chart paper, markers, tape

PREPARATION

Gather a selection of open-ended and self-correcting, structured materials. Use some open-ended, commercial materials (e.g., colored cubes, unit blocks, chain links). Also use natural items, scrap materials, or dress-up clothes (e.g., paper rolls, fabric, empty food boxes, kitchen gadgets, an old steering wheel). Each group will need a mixture of at least 6–8 items.

When working with teachers of children with disabilities, you may want to discuss ways to adapt materials as necessary.

INTRODUCTION

Introduce the workshop by explaining that the goals and objectives of *The Creative Curriculum* are the guide for planning your preschool program. The materials should relate directly to helping children achieve those objectives.

• All materials are not equal. Some are more enticing to children, more durable, and serve multiple purposes while others do not.

• You will examine various materials and discuss how they support and contribute to children's learning and development.

ACTIVITY

Place materials, chart paper, and markers at each table and give the following instructions:

• Explore the materials at your table. Discuss how children might use these materials.

• Determine what knowledge, skills, concepts, and behaviors children might learn as they use these materials and record your ideas.

Ask participants to turn to the "Goals and Objectives at a Glance" on page 530 and determine which objectives can be addressed using each material, and which materials address the objectives better than others.

Invite the groups to share their ideas about one item and then explain:

• Open-ended materials address varied objectives. Children can express their own ideas as they create, construct, and pretend.

• Teachers can support children's learning by providing a variety of materials.

Create buzz groups by having participants form small groups (2–4 people). Provide the stem, "Children misuse materials and resist cleanup because…." Allow the groups to talk for 2–3 minutes.

Discuss the importance of teaching children how to use and care for materials. Make the following points:

- When materials are organized in an orderly and systematic way, children know there is a place for everything and everything has a place.

- Labels help children find what they need and participate meaningfully in cleanup and in caring for the classroom.

Ask participants to share guidelines for labeling materials in the classroom.

Make the following points about the importance of labeling materials:

- Label and identify where most materials belong, using pictures and words.

- Write labels as they appear in books, i.e., avoid using all capital letters.

- Labels should serve a purpose, i.e., indicate where a particular material belongs.

- Labels should reflect the languages of the children. Use a different color for each language and be consistent (e.g., English is always written in black; Spanish in red).

- Teachers must take the time to introduce each material and show children where each belongs.

SUMMARY

Summarize the activity by stating that materials selected for the classroom should

- enable children to learn many and varied skills and concepts in different content areas

- challenge but not frustrate

- be relevant to children's experiences and culture

- be safe, organized, and displayed in an attractive and inviting manner

Tell participants that each interest area chapter in the Curriculum has sections that discuss selecting and displaying materials.

VARIATION

Pose the following scenario for small group discussion and have groups report.

You have received a grant to furnish a new classroom with learning materials. As you look through catalogs, the task seems overwhelming. With a limited budget, how would you approach this task? What types of materials would be best to purchase? Consider the characteristics and functions of materials. Refer participants to the chapters on Toys and Games and Dramatic Play (pages 299–303 and 275–279), and to other interest area chapters. Record your ideas.

Why Interest Areas Are Important

☐ Post-it notes

◖ PREPARATION

Raising awareness of the participants' varied interests during their childhood years helps them to better understand the need to provide for the varied interests of children. The goal is to help participants appreciate the value of interest areas. Be prepared to discuss your personal interests.

◖ INTRODUCTION

Introduce the workshop:

- Most people have some fond memories of childhood—memories of favorite things to do, places to play, people to be with.

- During this activity, you will be asked to reflect on those childhood interests and consider how your experiences affect the learning environment you create for children.

◖ ACTIVITY

Give the following instructions:

- Take about 5–10 minutes to recall the activities you enjoyed the most as a child. Record each one on a separate Post-it note.

- Share your memories with others at your table.

- Next, categorize the activities by putting similar activities together. For example, playing Candyland, working puzzles, or building with Legos might be grouped together. Playing "tag," making mudpies, and building forts would be grouped together.

Give each category a label.

Have each group share one of their categories and some of the activities included.

Ask participants to reflect on these lists and consider the implications for the programs and environments that we plan for young children.

Possible Responses:

Provide places for quiet activities such as the Library, Computers, or Toys and Games and places for more active play such as Blocks.

Provide cozy places where children can be alone or with one other friend.

Schedule time daily for outdoor play.

Include materials that invite children to create and use their imaginations.

Provide time, space, and materials for children to play familiar roles and try out new roles.

Bring in materials that build upon children's interests.

SUMMARY

Summarize the activity with the following points:

- All people are different and have different interests.

- Our interests are what motivate us each to learn.

- By establishing interest areas in the classroom, children have an opportunity to pursue their interests and learn many skills and concepts.

- High quality interest areas enable children to learn no matter what interest area they are in.

- Teachers who are aware of the needs and interests of their children have a basis for building a relationship and motivating each child to learn.

Using the *Implementation Checklist* to Evaluate Your Classroom Environment

☐ *Creative Curriculum*, pp. 62–81
☐ *Implementation Checklist*
☐ Transparencies

PREPARATION

Each teacher or class will need a copy of the *Implementation Checklist*. You may want to prepare transparencies of key points or terms you wish to discuss since this is probably the first time you will be introducing the *Implementation Checklist*.

INTRODUCTION

Introduce the workshop:

- Curriculum implementation is an ongoing process.

- The *Implementation Checklist* is a tool designed to help you determine what you already have in place and where changes might be made.

Refer participants to their copies of the *Implementation Checklist* and explain the following about how the *Implementation Checklist* is used:

- Teachers use the *Implementation Checklist* in an ongoing manner to inform their work. Early in the year, the *Implementation Checklist* may help you to set up your classroom environment. Later in the year, it can help you evaluate your work with children. Individual sections can help you implement what you learn in a training session.

- Administrators and supervisors can use the *Implementation Checklist* to gain information as part of a program's ongoing self-assessment and continuous improvement process, as well as to supervise and evaluate teachers. It can help supervisors support teachers, purchase materials, plan staff development, and improve the overall program.

- Trainers can use different sections to follow up on particular staff development issues, to help teachers reflect on how they are implementing what they have learned.

Show that the *Implementation Checklist* is organized into these five sections:

- I. Physical Environment (pages 1–17)

- II. Structure (pages 18–22)

- III. Teacher-Child Interactions (pages 23–32)

- IV. Assessment (pages 33–35)

- V. Family Involvement (page 36)

Note that each section includes descriptions of what to observe in the classroom. Explain that the examples are given only for clarification—not as requirements. Point out the symbols for items that require an interview or documentation.

ACTIVITY

Review the items in section I. A. and I. C. (items 1–4) of the *Implementation Checklist* (pages 1–2, 14–17). Have participants complete self-assessments of their overall physical environments.

Then have them use the results to create a plan for making specific changes in their classrooms. Refer them to pages 62–81 for additional information. Call attention to the individual sections on each interest area in the *Implementation Checklist*. Inform participants that they will complete a self-assessment of each interest area after the training on the interest area is completed.

SUMMARY

Summarize the physical environment by highlighting the following points:

- The physical environment affects how children feel and behave.

- The arrangement of the classroom and selection of the materials are two powerful strategies teachers use to support children's learning.

- Teachers must continually evaluate the effectiveness of their classroom environment and make necessary adjustments.

- The *Implementation Checklist* is a tool for assessing how well the *Creative Curriculum* model is being implemented.

- Teachers can use the *Implementation Checklist* in an ongoing manner throughout the year to track their progress in putting the Curriculum in place.

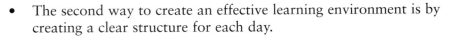

WORKSHOP

Daily Events: What Is Their Value?

☐ Handout **2E**

PREPARATION

This workshop and the one that follows go together. If for some reason you don't plan to do the next workshop ("Using What You Know About Children to Structure the Day"), you may want to have participants read pages 82–92 prior to summarizing this workshop.

Duplicate the handout.

INTRODUCTION

Introduce the workshop with the following points:

- The second way to create an effective learning environment is by creating a clear structure for each day.

- The predictable use of time is a key aspect of what is meant by structure in the classroom.

- The purposes of this activity are to

    examine the importance of establishing a consistent and orderly schedule for the day and

    reflect on the value of daily activities and routines.

ACTIVITY

Have participants think about the things they do within the first hour of rising each morning and jot them down on paper.

Have participants share their routines with a partner and discuss what might happen if things occurred in a different order.

Lead a discussion about the importance of having a consistent daily schedule. Ask:

- How are you affected when your regular routine is altered?

- How do you think children feel when their routine is altered?

- How do children react to an inconsistent schedule?

- How do you think a child with a special need (children with exceptionalities, migrant children, children with varying life circumstances) would be affected? How would this child react?

Discuss the importance of creating a consistent daily schedule. Explain that the events of the day should be shown in pictures and words. Stress that it should be located at the children's eye level and used as a guide to move children from one activity to another. In this way it is a tool to help children follow the sequence of the day.

Invite participants to share how they might prepare children for any changes in the daily routine.

Refer participants to handout 2E. Explain that they are to record the daily activities and routines in column 2 and the length of time taken by each event in column 1.

Next, have them consider the value of each activity or routine. Ask them to use column 3 to answer the questions, "Why is this event important?" and "How does this event contribute to children's learning and development?" For example, at mealtimes, children develop language and vocabulary as they engage in conversations, learn social and self-help skills, and learn about health and their bodies.

Encourage participants to share their thoughts.

SUMMARY

Summarize with the following points:

- Consistent routines are a key part of a well-managed classroom.

- A consistent daily routine helps children feel safe and secure and more in control of their lives.

- Consistent routines also help children to become more independent and self-directed.

- Every event of the day can be used as an opportunity to promote some aspect of children's development and learning.

Using What You Know About Children to Structure the Day

☐ Chart paper, markers, watch
☐ *Creative Curriculum*, pp. 82–97
☐ Participants' daily schedules
☐ *Implementation Checklist*

PREPARATION

Prior to the workshop, ask participants to bring copies of their daily schedules.

Before participants arrive, post seven pieces of chart paper around the room so that there is enough space for a small group of participants to comfortably gather around each one. Write one of the following headings at the top of each page using a different colored marker: Attendance, Large-Group Time, Small-Group Time, Choice Time, Transitions, Mealtimes, Rest Time. Make three columns on each chart, labeling the left "Challenges," the middle "Possible Causes," and the right "Solutions."

INTRODUCTION

Introduce the workshop:

- Some events take place every day:

    taking attendance

    large-group meetings (sometimes referred to a "circle time")

    small-group time (work on a planned experience with a few children)

    choice time (children work in interest areas of their choice)

    mealtimes

    rest time

    transitions

- Each of these events can be a learning opportunity for children if they are well thought out and planned based on what you know about how children develop and learn.

- In this activity, you will think about what often goes wrong during these events and consider ways in which these problems can be minimized or eliminated.

ACTIVITY

Divide participants into seven groups and give each group a different colored marker. Provide the following directions:

- Find the chart with the heading written in the same colored marker as the one your group was given.

- Once at the chart, choose a recorder for your group.

- You will have two minutes at each chart to think about the difficulties you face during this event and record them in the left hand column under "Challenges."

Call "time" after each two–minute interval. Ask the groups to take their markers and move to the next chart. Allow time for them to read the existing list and then add new challenges. Continue in a similar manner until all groups have visited each chart once.

Invite each group to choose one event they wish to discuss further. Have them remove the chart from the wall and return to a table. Allow time for each group to read about their event on pages 82–92.

Next, have participants identify the possible causes of each challenge and strategies or solutions for dealing with it. Have them record their ideas in the appropriate columns.

Remind participants to rely on their knowledge of children's developmental and individual abilities and interests to make decisions about how to handle each challenge.

Have the groups post their charts on the wall when finished. Allow time for participants to walk around, reviewing the charts.

Debrief the activity inviting each group to highlight any key points learned.

Now ask:

- What makes a good daily schedule?

After participants respond make these points:

- A good daily schedule is well balanced and flexible.

- It includes active and quiet times.

- There are large-group activities, small-group activities, and time to play alone or with others.

- It includes indoor and outdoor play times.

- There are times for child-initiated and teacher-directed activities.

Give participants the following tasks:

- Review the "Daily Schedule" on pages 94–95.

- Review "Daily Schedule Guidelines" on page 93.

- Compare your daily schedules with the sample one and the guidelines.

- Think about any changes you might make in your schedules based on what you read in the book.

Allow 10–15 minutes for reviewing schedules and asking questions. Then debrief by asking:

- What changes, if any, will you make in your schedule?

- What made you decide to make these changes?

Review the items in the *Implementation Checklist*, sections II. A.–II. D. (pages 18–21). Have participants complete self-assessments of their program structure and identify areas that need improving or strengthening.

Then, make these points:

- Consistent, orderly events scheduled throughout the day help the day go more smoothly—children know what to expect and this makes them feel safe.

- Consistency doesn't mean you can't be flexible or make changes. It is important to remember to prepare children ahead of time for any changes that may take place in the routine events of the day.

- A good schedule offers children a balance of different types of activities.

- Illustrating the schedule (see page 96) and using it to guide children as they move from one activity to the next promotes both literacy and an understanding of sequence.

SUMMARY

Summarize the workshop:

- Every event of the day offers opportunities for learning.

- Teachers who rely on what they know about young children—their developmental and individual needs and interests—are able to make appropriate decisions about the structure of the day and nature of the experiences they offer.

NOTES

Using the Weekly Planning Form

□ *Creative Curriculum*,
  pp. 97–99, 526–529,
  100–101
□ Transparency **2F**
□ Handout **2F**

PREPARATION

If the workshop is held prior to the opening of a new school year, allocate enough time to review and discuss the section on preparing for the first few days of school (see pages 100–101). Otherwise, you can simply refer participants to this section and discuss the importance of planning for each new group.

Prepare the transparency. Duplicate the handout.

INTRODUCTION

Introduce the workshop with the following questions:

- What kind of planning do you do in your program?

- What is the value of planning?

- What do you consider in writing weekly plans?

Highlight the following points:

- Planning helps you know what materials you will need.

- Decisions are based on observations of children, a topic of study, and your goals for children.

- Plans often change based on what happens each day; planning doesn't mean you can't be flexible.

Walk through the planning forms on pages 98–99 and explain each section. Have participants locate the blank planning form on pages 526–527. Discuss the example of a completed planning form on pages 528–529.

ACTIVITY

Explain that you are going to describe a classroom scenario:

New construction is taking place near your school. Your children are fascinated and are asking many questions:

What are they building and where does the wood come from?

What does that tool do? What do those pipes do?

What does that kind of truck do?

How can the workers pick up those heavy things?

Now give this assignment for work in groups:

> To build on children's interests, use the handout to plan experiences to help children find answers to their questions and gain a deeper understanding of construction. It is not necessary to include a related construction experience in each space on the form.

If time permits, invite the groups to share their ideas.

If you want to go further, you can address changes in the plan.

Make the point that plans may change.

- For example, pretend that during the week you notice a cement truck is at the construction site.

- You may want to change your plans to add experiences related to concrete.

- What are some ideas you might include related to concrete?

  Possible responses: *Weighing chunks of concrete; sidewalk chalk drawings; concrete rubbings*

Review the items in the *Implementation Checklist* on the "Weekly Plan," page 22. Have participants complete self-assessments of their weekly planning and identify items to improve.

SUMMARY

Summarize with the following points:

- Weekly planning helps teachers implement *The Creative Curriculum* in a manageable way.

- The "Weekly Planning Form" provides a structure for planning each week and preparing materials and activities ahead of time.

- The classroom teaching team should review the weekly plan daily to see that everyone is prepared.

- Teachers adjust the weekly plan to accommodate the children's changing needs and interests. These changes should be documented on the "Weekly Planning Form" and shared with families as appropriate.

Promoting Positive Relationships in the Classroom

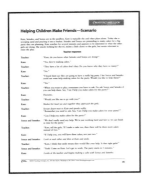

☐ *Creative Curriculum,* pp. 102–108
☐ Handout **2G**
☐ Handout **2H**
☐ *Implementation Checklist*

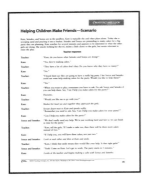

PREPARATION

Arrange space in the room for circles of 8–10 people. Make four copies of handout 2G, and copies of handout 2H for each participant.

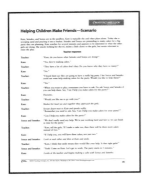

INTRODUCTION

Introduce the workshop with the following instructions:

- Form small groups (8–10 people) and stand in a circle with locked arms, while one person volunteers to remain outside the circle.

- At the signal, the person on the outside of the circle attempts to enter into the circle, while being prevented by the group.

After a few minutes, have participants return to their seats and ask:

- How did you feel and behave from outside or inside the circle?

Lead a discussion about how this might be similar to classroom situations.

> **Possible responses:** *some children are included and some are not; some lack the skills to enter the group; some give up or resort to disruptive behavior; no one was there to provide guidance or support to the outsider.*

Discuss the following points:

- Positive social relationships in preschool create the best environment for learning.

- A *Creative Curriculum* classroom functions as a community—a place where children feel safe and learn how to relate positively to others and how to resolve conflicts peacefully.

- Social problem-solving skills are taught directly by teachers.

- Teachers use a range of strategies for dealing with challenging behaviors and establishing classroom control.

- Positive relationships with teachers ready children's minds for learning.

- Each child needs to feel accepted and appreciated, and have a friend.

- Children who lack friends during their early years are at risk for problems later in life.

Then ask participants how they learn about each child in their classrooms and develop positive relationships.

> **Possible responses:** *observe children to learn about their unique qualities; talk to children respectfully; listen to what they say; be sensitive to children's feelings; and validate their accomplishments and progress.*

Refer participants to pages 102–105. Relate the ideas shared to the suggestions in the Curriculum.

Ask participants to think of children who don't know how to make friends. Then ask them to consider what they know about these children.

Point out the need to teach some children how to make friends and give a brief overview of each skill discussed in the chart, "Skills Children Need to Make and Keep a Friend" on page 106.

ACTIVITY

Ask for four volunteers to participate in a role play demonstrating how a teacher helps a child make friends, and give them handout 2G.

While the volunteers are reviewing their skit, have the rest of the group read "Classroom Strategies That Support Friendships" found on pages 107–108.

Have the volunteers act out the scenario. Ask the others to watch and identify how the strategies in the Curriculum were used. Have them record their ideas on handout 2G.

Discuss what strategies participants noticed and invite them to share other ideas they have tried. Review section III. A. "Building Relationships" of the *Implementation Checklist* (page 23). Have participants complete self-assessments.

SUMMARY

Summarize with the following points:

- *Creative Curriculum* teachers strive to make sure that every child has at least one friend.

- By coaching and teaching children specific skills, teachers can help children overcome the rejection they sometimes encounter.

VARIATION

Adapt this activity to help teachers focus on a child with a special need. Alter the scenario by describing Kate as a child who has language difficulties. For example, Kate is beginning to put two words together, can answer questions, and follow directions with visual cues. Have participants discuss what they would do differently in the sand box scenario.

Developing Rules for a Classroom Community

☐ *Creative Curriculum,*
    pp. 108–110
☐ Chart paper

PREPARATION

No preparation necessary.

INTRODUCTION

Introduce the workshop with the following points:

- Every classroom needs a few basic rules to create a safe community.

- Involving children in the rule-making process conveys a shared responsibility for life in the classroom community.

- When children help create the rules, they are more likely to follow them.

ACTIVITY

Have participants discuss the following questions at their tables:

- What rules do you have in your classroom?

- How did you develop these rules?

- How do you teach them to children?

- How do they work?

Have participants read "A discussion with children about rules" on page 109. You may also invite a small group of participants to role-play the scenario. Lead a discusion about the strategies the teacher used.

> **Possible responses:**
>
> *She made sure the children understood the need for rules.*
>
> *She tied the discussion to feeling safe.*
>
> *She restated children's ideas in positive terms.*
>
> *She identified possible problems so children could come up with rules.*

Discuss these categories for rules in *The Creative Curriculum*:

- maintaining physical safety

- respecting the rights of others

- not hurting the feelings of others

- caring for the classroom

Have participants compare their rules to see if their rules fall into the four categories.

Emphasize that rules should be

- as concrete as possible

- few in number (no more than four rules)

- simple

- stated in positive terms

Have each table create a chart with no more than four rules. Post the charts and comment on the similarities among rules.

SUMMARY

Summarize with the following points:

- Post rules in the meeting area where you can review them with the children.

- When a rule isn't working, ask the children what they think the problem is and engage them in the problem-solving process.

- Remember, children may need to be reminded of the rules and why they were made—to keep everyone safe.

Handling Conflicts Between Children

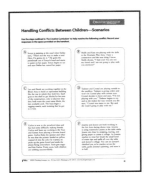

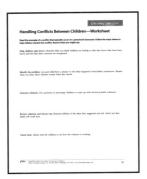

☐ *Creative Curriculum,*
  pp. 110–115
☐ Handout **2I**
☐ Handout **2J**

PREPARATION

Duplicate the handouts.

INTRODUCTION

Open the discussion by asking some questions:

- How often do children come to you to resolve a conflict?

- What kinds of conflicts come up between children?

- What are the advantages of teaching children how to
  solve conflicts?

Refer participants to page 110 and have them read the first three
paragraphs on "Teaching Social Problem-Solving Skills." Then ask:

- Do you agree with the points that are made in
  The Creative Curriculum?

- How do you encourage children to solve problems on
  their own so you don't have to continually mediate?

Review the steps on pages 111–114 for handling conflicts between children:

- "Help children calm down."

- "Identify the problem."

- "Generate solutions."

- "Review solutions and choose one."

- "Check back."

ACTIVITY

Have participants form teams of three. Assign each group a scenario from handout 2I and have each group work together to apply the steps for handling conflicts and record their ideas on handout 2J.

Debrief the activity.

Have participants read pages 114–115 on how to solve problems that involve the whole class. Encourage them to use this approach when a conflict or problem comes up in their classrooms and share the results at a future workshop.

SUMMARY

Summarize with the following points:

- Conflicts are inevitable—they are part of life.

- Teachers who help children acquire the skills to solve social problems when they arise and involve children in solving group problems help them learn how to live in a democratic community.

VARIATION

Adapt this activity to help teachers focus on a child with a special need. For example, ask teachers to consider what they might do or say if one of the children in their assigned scenario has a language difficulty.

Responding to Challenging Behavior

☐ *Creative Curriculum,*
   pp. 116–122
☐ Handout **2K**
☐ Handout **2L**
☐ *Implementation
   Checklist*

◖ PREPARATION

Duplicate the handouts.

◖ INTRODUCTION

Begin by reading, with expression, the following negative statements, found on page 116:

> Haven't I told you a hundred times not to do that?

> I don't care what happened, I'm angry with both of you.

> Don't you know better than that? You should know the rules by now!

> Instead of going outside, I want you to sit in the time out chair and think about what you just did!

> You know we have a rule about sharing. I'm going to just put this toy away and no one will get to play with it. I hope you're both satisfied.

Ask the group members how this makes them feel. After they respond, emphasize these points:

- When adults lose control, they lose the ability to discipline themselves or their children.

- Positive, secure relationships with children require us to maintain control.

- Discipline comes from the word "disciple" meaning "to teach." Our goal is to promote and teach self-control.

◖ ACTIVITY

Distribute the handouts for this activity and assign each group one of the following challenging behavior scenarios: testing limits, physical aggression, biting, temper tantrums, bullying. Have the groups read their situations and discuss using the following questions to stimulate their thinking:

- What might be causing this child's behavior?

- How do you help the child regain self-control?

Have participants use handout 2L to record their ideas.

Allow time for each group to report.

Refer participants to section III. B. "Guiding Children's Behavior" in the *Implementation Checklist* (page 24). Review the items and have participants complete self-assessments.

SUMMARY

Summarize with the following points:

- In a classroom community, children learn how to relate positively to others and to make friends.

- Rules help children feel safe and comfortable so they can learn.

- Teaching children social problem-solving skills will help them get along in school and in life.

- Teachers use a repertoire of strategies for dealing with challenging behaviors and teaching self-control in the classroom.

Different Kinds of Classrooms—Skits

Classroom 1

As you near the classroom, you hear the teacher say, "O.K., boys and girls, you may go play." The children jump up from circle and rush to their favorite places. Within minutes, you hear shrieks and cries from children in the dramatic play area as they tug over a toy steering wheel. You hear one child say, "I need the car to take my baby to the doctor!" The other children reply, "Well we need it to go to the park!" Juwan decides to leave the Dramatic Play Area and proceeds to a nearby shelf. He looks through a stack of boxes and finally pulls a floor puzzle off the shelf. He takes it to the block area and dumps the pieces on the floor. As he looks up, he sees a small group of children pretending to be airplanes. He watches as they prepare to "take off" down the path in the middle of the classroom. Juwan laughs and leaves to joins his other friends, leaving the puzzle strewn on the floor. Suddenly, above all of the commotion, the teacher says, "Freeze!" Some of the children strike a favorite pose, while others continue playing. The teacher continues, "Boys and girls, how many times do I have to tell you? If you can't share the materials, use them in the areas where you found them, or put them back where they belong, I am going to take them all away! Pretty soon, you won't have any toys to play with. Would you like that?" All of the children join in with a loud, "NO!" "And one more thing, this classroom is not an airport, so park those airplanes and find something else to do!" The teacher turns to her assistant, shakes her head and says, "I don't know why I continue to do this job. I never realized how difficult preschool children could be."

Classroom 2

As you enter the classroom, it is very quiet. You see the children sitting in a circle near the teacher in the front of the classroom. The teacher says, "Let's see, we have put the date on the calendar, checked the weather, and reviewed our jobs for the week. Oops, I forgot to take attendance. Let's do that. Is everyone sitting with his legs crossed properly?" The teacher calls every child's name and each responds, saying, "Here." One child shouts, "I don't see Carlos. I saw him playing outside in his yard with his brothers and sisters yesterday." The teacher responds abruptly, "What is our rule about speaking out during morning circle?" The child hangs his head in embarrassment. "Besides, I will know that Carlos is not at school when he doesn't say, 'Here.'" The teacher continues, "Boys and girls, I think we will try something different this morning." A child enthusiastically asks, "Are we going to go outside or go to centers?" The teacher responds, "No." The children sigh heavily. "But, since I have been teaching you nursery rhymes, this morning you will each get to recite your favorite rhyme for the rest of the class. Remember, you need to sit still and listen when your friends are having their turn. Let's begin." After the first two or three children have a turn, the others begin fidgeting, lying on the floor, talking with one another, and playing with nearby toys. The teacher interrupts, "Sit still and listen. It's rude not to listen." The fidgeting continues. Finally the teacher says, "OK, since you can't listen, we will have to stop. I suppose you should have a bathroom break before we start our morning lesson. Boys line up here (pointing with her right arm), and girls line up here (pointing with her left arm)." The children rush to line up, pushing and shoving as they go. The teacher thinks to herself, "How hard can listening and lining up be?"

Classroom 3

When you enter the classroom, you see children talking and working with and alongside one another. At first, you don't see the teachers. One is on the floor in the Library Area looking at books with several children. The other teacher is making her way around the classroom, stopping to interact with different groups along the way. One group of children is in the Toys and Games Area, playing a favorite game, "Memory." Another group is busy at work in the Art Area, painting at the easel, working with play dough, and snipping scraps of paper to make a collage. You hear one child say, "I can't make these scissors work," and another child respond, "When I finish cutting this paper, I'll help you." You approach the Block Area where a small group is working together. You stoop down and say, "Tell me about your work." A child volunteers, "Over there is the barn (points to a construction), and now we're building a corral for the animals so they can run around but not get away." Another child chimes in, "Yeah, we saw one yesterday when we went to the farm. A man put all of the horses into a corral, and we watched them run and play." You say, "I didn't know horses needed to run and play. Why do you suppose that is?" A third child replies, "They're kind of like us. When we run and play our muscles get stronger." At that moment, a familiar song begins to play, and it appears to be a signal to the children to begin cleaning up. One of the boys in the Block Area says to the others, "I wish our other friends could see what we made." Another child suggests, "Let's ask the teacher to take a picture of our building." The teacher takes the picture and explains that it will take a little while for the picture to print. She assures the group that they will get to share it as soon as it is ready. The boys respond in unison with an "O.K." They smile and begin putting their blocks away.

Setting Up the Classroom

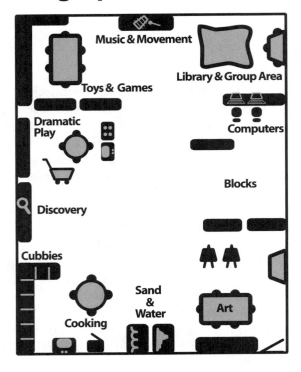 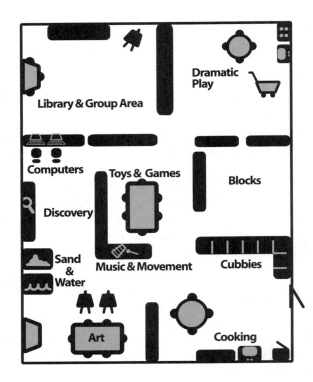

The physical environment and the selection and display of materials can support these behaviors and skills. To encourage cooperation:

_____

_____

To develop independence, make choices, and clean up:

_____

_____

_____

To focus on what they are doing and stay involved in their work:

_____

_____

_____

To acquire skills as they select and use materials:

_____

_____

_____

Messages in the Environment

Messages in the Environment	How My Preschool Environment Conveys These Messages	New Ideas to Try
This is a good place to be.		
You belong here. You are a valued member of this community.		
This is a place you can trust.		
There are places you can be by yourself when you want to be.		
You can do many things on your own.		
This is a safe place to explore and try out your ideas.		

Elements of a Comfortable and Attractive Setting

Light

Softness

Textures

Quiet spaces

Home-like touches

Living things

Light

Softness

Textures

Quiet spaces

Home-like touches

Living things

Light

Softness

Textures

Quiet spaces

Home-like touches

Living things

Light

Softness

Textures

Quiet spaces

Home-like touches

Living things

The Value of Daily Events

Time	Event of the Day	Why It Is Important

Weekly Planning Form

Planning Changes to the Environment

Week of:_____

Teacher:_____

Study/Project:_____

Assistant:_____

Blocks	Dramatic Play	Toys and Games	"To Do" List
Art	Library	Discovery	
Sand and Water	Music and Movement	Cooking	
Computers	Outdoors	Family / Community Involvement	

From *The Creative Curriculum® for Preschool*, 4th Edition.

Weekly Planning Form, continued

Planning for Groups

	Monday	Tuesday	Wednesday	Thursday	Friday
Group Time (songs, stories, games, discussions, etc.)					
Story Time					
Small-Group Activities					
Special Activities (field trips, special events, etc.)					

Notes *(reminders, changes, children to observe)*

From *The Creative Curriculum® for Preschool*, 4th Edition.
©2004 Teaching Strategies, Inc., PO Box 42243, Washington, DC 20015, www.TeachingStrategies.com

Helping Children Make Friends—Scenario

Kate, Setsuko, and Sonya are in the sandbox. Kate is typically shy and often plays alone. Today she is scooping sand and pouring it into a bucket. Setsuko and Sonya are pretending to make cakes for a big party they are planning. Kate watches for several minutes and appears to be interested in what the other girls are doing. She stands holding her shovel, inches a little closer to the girls, but seems reluctant to enter the play.

Teacher response:

Teacher:	"Kate, do you know what Setsuko and Sonya are doing?"
Kate:	"Yes, they're making cakes."
Teacher:	"They have a lot of cakes don't they. Do you know why they have so many?"
Kate:	"No."
Teacher:	"I heard them say they are going to have a really big party. I bet Sonya and Setsuko could use some help making cakes for the party. Would you like to help them?"
Kate:	"Yes."
Teacher:	"When you want to play, sometimes you have to ask. Go ask Sonya and Setsuko if you can help them. Say, 'Can I help you make cakes for the party?'"
Kate:	Hesitates.
Teacher:	"Would you like me to go with you?"
Kate:	Shakes her head yes and together they approach the girls.
Teacher:	Stoops down next to Kate and speaks softly. "Remember you need to ask. Say, 'Can I help you make cakes for your party?'"
Kate:	"Can I help you make cakes for the party?"
Sonya and Setsuko:	"We don't really need any help. We're just working hard and fast so we can finish in time for the party."
Teacher:	"Kate, tell the girls, 'If I make a cake too, then there will be three more cakes instead of two.'"
Kate:	"If I help you, you will have three cakes, not just two."
Sonya and Setsuko:	Look at each other and then at Kate and smile.
Teacher:	"Kate, I think that smile means they would like your help. Is that right girls?"
Sonya and Setsuko:	"Yeah! Come on Kate. Let's get to work. The party starts in 5 minutes."
Kate:	Looks at the teacher and begins making a cake with Sonya and Setsuko.

Helping Children Make Friends—Worksheet

The following classroom strategies for helping children make friends are outlined on pages 107–108 of *The Creative Curriculum*.

- Have discussions about making friends.

- Coach children.

- Pair children to work on a task.

- Interpret children's actions.

- Point out the benefits.

- Minimize rejection.

How were these strategies used in the scenario?

What other strategies could the teacher have used?

Handling Conflicts Between Children—Scenarios

Use the steps outlined in *The Creative Curriculum*® to help resolve the following conflict. Record your responses in the space provided on the handout.

A Sonya is painting at the easel when Dallas says, "That's not the way to make a tree! Here, I'm gonna do it." He grabs the paintbrush out of Sonya's hand and starts to paint on her paper. Sonya begins to cry and says Dallas has ruined her paper.

B Malik and Kate are playing with the dolls in the Dramatic Play Area. I hear a commotion and the next thing I know Malik shouts, "I hate you! You are not my friend and I am not going to play with you anymore!"

C Leo and Derek are working together in the Block Area to build an apartment building like the one in which they both live. Each goes to the shelf to get blocks for his area of the construction, only to discover that they both want the exact same block, the last available arch. The boys begin a tugging match, each insisting that he got to it first.

D Tasheen and Crystal are playing outside in the sandbox. Tasheen is giving orders and won't let Crystal play with certain toys. Crystal decides to leave and says, "I'm not playing with you." Tasheen begins to cry and as she makes her way toward you she says, "Crystal was mean to me. She said she wasn't going to play with me."

E Carlos is new to the preschool class and has had some difficulty making friends. Carlos and Susie are working in the Toys and Games Area playing a favorite board game. Carlos flicks the spinner and when he sees that the pointer landed on yellow instead of red, the color he wanted, he picks up the game board and sends the pieces flying everywhere. Susie gets angry and hits Carlos. Pretty soon, both children are sobbing uncontrollably.

F Jonetta and Juwan are both working in the Art Area during choice time. Jonetta is using watercolor paints at the table while Juwan sits close by snipping, tearing, and gluing paper to create a collage. As Jonetta reaches to rinse her brush the small bowl of water tips and spills all over the table and Juwan's collage. You can see Juwan's clenched jaw as he reaches across the table, grabs Jonetta's painting, and tears it in half.

Handling Conflicts Between Children—Worksheet

Read the example of a conflict that typically occurs in a preschool classroom. Follow the steps below to help children resolve the conflict. Record what you might say.

Help children calm down. Describe what you think children are feeling so that they know they have been heard and feel that their concerns are recognized.

Identify the problem. Let each child have a chance to tell what happened from his/her perspective. Repeat what you hear. Have children restate what they heard.

Generate solutions. Use questions to encourage children to come up with several possible solutions.

Review solutions and choose one. Remind children of the ideas they suggested and ask which one they think will work best.

Check back. Check with the children to see how the solution is working.

Challenging Behavior—Scenarios

Testing Limits

Ms. Tory is three sentences into a book at story time when she is interrupted by a loud thud. She continues reading, but several children look to see what is happening. As she turns the page, she hears giggling, then whispers, coming from a group of children near Derrick. Out of the corner of her eye, she sees Derrick trying to make the other children laugh. When she looks his way, he sits up straight, puts his hands in his lap, and grins at Ms. Tory. She reminds Derrick of the rules during story time. She begins to read again, and 30 seconds later she hears, "Ouch! Derrick kicked me!" Throughout story time, Derrick continues to disrupt the group and keep other children from enjoying the story.

Aggression

Janelle is a friendly, verbal child who thoroughly enjoys preschool. She's very imaginative and particularly likes role-playing in Dramatic Play, building elaborate structures in the Block Area, and riding the tricycle outdoors. Janelle enjoys being the leader during play. The other children usually go along with Janelle, but if they do not, she often hits them. After she hits, she usually pokes out her lip and stomps off saying that no one likes her.

Biting

Juan is just learning English and is going through a non-verbal period. He is a very loving child, giving frequent hugs to his teacher and friends. However, if someone has a truck or a puzzle that he wants, Juan simply bites to get it. At other times, he walks up to a friend, puts his arm around him, and with a big smile on his face sinks his teeth into his cheek. He has bitten the arm of the child sitting next to him at snack time when he didn't get the crackers quickly enough.

Temper Tantrums

When Kate doesn't get her way, she lies on the floor kicking, swinging her arms, and crying. If an adult tries to console her, she stiffens her body and resists being held. She continues to scream and attempts to run away. When she has a tantrum, she often hurts other children and destroys toys and materials. When she is not having a tantrum, Kate is a sweet, caring child.

Bullying

Dallas is small for his age. He takes and hides other children's belongings. He doesn't start fights, but often pinches or pokes other children. Dallas has realized that he can bring children bigger and stronger than he is to tears by making fun of them. He thinks up names that ridicule and encourages others to join him in taunting. He shows no remorse after his victims break down in tears.

Responding to Challenging Behavior—Worksheet

Challenging Behavior	Possible Causes	How I Can Help This Child Gain Control
Testing Limits		
Aggression		
Biting		
Temper Tantrums		
Bullying		

The Teacher's Role

PURPOSE

Learning in a preschool classroom is full of contradictions. It is calm, yet dynamic; predictable, but full of surprises; active and hands-on; but sometimes quiet and reflective. These contradictions make teaching preschoolers exciting and interesting. They also leave some teachers feeling challenged and overwhelmed as they come to realize that what works to introduce, reinforce, or extend learning in one situation may not be effective in another.

Given the nature of the preschool classroom, this workshop series is designed to show participants how knowledge of child development, individual children, and content are used to make decisions about when and how to respond to children to support and guide their learning. Emphasis is placed on the importance of using a variety of teaching approaches and selecting the right approach for each child at the right time. Participants are introduced to the ongoing cycle of observing, guiding learning, and assessing children's progress using the *Developmental Continuum*.

BIG IDEAS:

- All teaching clearly begins with observing children.

- Teachers use a variety of teaching strategies depending on individual and group needs and the content to be addressed.

- Teachers should be responsive to all children.

- Carefully planned interest areas are used to promote development and address content.

The Teacher's Role

WORKSHOPS

🔑 Key Points	⚙ Workshop	📄 Materials	🕐 Time (minutes)
Teachers play many different roles.	**How Is a Teacher Like…?** (p. 112)	☐ Handout **4A:** An Interview With… ☐ Handout **4B:** How Is a Teacher Like…?	20
The goals and objectives of the Curriculum provide a focus for observing and responding to children.	**Observing Children: Why, When, What, and How to Observe** (p. 114)	☐ Transparency **4C:** Observing Children: Why, When, What, and How to Observe ☐ Chart paper ☐ *Creative Curriculum,* pp. 166–168 ☐ Post-it notes ☐ 2 books as props	60
The *Developmental Continuum* is a tool for observing and responding to children.	**Observing and Responding to Children** (p. 118)	☐ Handout **4D:** Observing and Responding to Children ☐ *Creative Curriculum,* pp. 46–58, 530	40
A teacher's approach to working with children is determined by the needs of the children and the skills or content to be addressed. Effective teachers use a wide range of teaching strategies to support children's learning.	**Using a Range of Teaching Approaches** (p. 120)	☐ *Creative Curriculum* video ☐ Handout **4E:** Responding to Children—Scenarios ☐ *Creative Curriculum,* pp. 46-58, 173–198 ☐ Collectibles ☐ *Fish Is Fish* by Leo Lionni ☐ Variations– Handout **4F:** Questions and Comments: Do They Sustain or Interrupt Children's Play?	60–90
Knowing each child's strengths and needs enables teachers to adapt instruction.	**Adapting Instruction for Children With Special Needs** (p. 124)	☐ Transparency **4G:** Points to Remember About Children With Special Needs ☐ *Creative Curriculum,* pp. 179–183 ☐ Paper	20
Setting up interest areas and interacting with children around the materials you provide is a key way to promote children's learning in the content areas.	**Exploring Content in Interest Areas** (p. 126)	☐ Handout **4H:** Exploring the Content Areas ☐ Handout **4I:** Exploring Content in Interest Areas ☐ *Creative Curriculum,* pp. 126–160 ☐ *Implementation Checklist*	60–90

How Is a Teacher Like…?

☐ Handout **4A**
☐ Handout **4B**

PREPARATION

Duplicate the handouts.

INTRODUCTION

Introduce the workshop with the following points:

- The Teacher's Role is the fourth component of *The Creative Curriculum* framework.

- While the teacher's role is part of every chapter and every workshop, this series of activities will focus exclusively on how teachers use their knowledge of child development, individual children, and content to guide children's learning.

- The first activity, "How Is a Teacher Like…?" is meant to help you identify the varied aspects of your role as a teacher.

ACTIVITY

Distribute handouts 4A and 4B.

Assign each table one interview and provide the following instructions:

- Read the interview and discuss how the work of a teacher is similar to the job described. Give specific examples.

- Record your ideas in the appropriate space on the handout.

- Prepare to share your ideas.

Have the groups share key points from their group discussions. Invite them to suggest any other job descriptions that might be similar to the teacher's role.

SUMMARY

Make the following points:

- All teaching begins with observation. As teachers observe and interact with children, they gather information that will enable them to make decisions about when and how to respond best.

- Assessment is an integral part of implementing curriculum and planning for each child.

- Effective teachers know that what works for one child may not necessarily work for another; therefore, they use a variety of teaching strategies depending on individual and group needs and the goals (content) to be addressed.

VARIATION

Place an assortment of props (flashlight, signs, binoculars, magnifying glass, maps, cooking utensils, tools, gardening tools, soil and seeds, light bulb, rubber bands, band-aids, safari hat, etc.) or photos of these props at each table. Ask participants to discuss how each relates to the teacher's role.

Invite groups to share points from their discussions.

Highlight comments about the teacher's role as an observer and guide for learning.

Observing Children: Why, When, What, and How to Observe

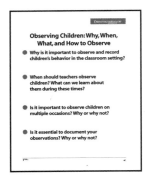

□ Transparency **4C**
□ Chart paper
□ *Creative Curriculum,*
   pp. 166-168
□ Post-it notes
□ 2 books as props

PREPARATION

Create the transparency.

Sketch a push-button (touch-tone) telephone keypad on chart paper, but do not display it.

Prior to beginning this workshop, ask for a volunteer to participate with you in a role-play of two children looking at books. Privately tell your partner that no matter what you do, he or she should concentrate on looking at the book without being distracted. Explain that during the role-play, you will try to distract the other person. You will read your book, turn it upside down, hum a tune, read from back to front, etc.

INTRODUCTION

Introduce the workshop:

- Knowing children begins with observation.

- In this workshop, you will learn why, when, what, and how to observe young children.

Show the transparency, revealing each question one at a time. Allow time for participants to discuss each question with others at their tables. Have them choose an individual to record the big ideas of their discussion.

Lead a brief discussion about each.

- Why is it important to observe and record children's behavior in the classroom setting?

  Possible responses:

  We can't rely on standardized tests or questionnaires. If teachers are to really know young children—how they think, what they know, how they relate to others, or their approaches to learning—a systematic way of observing and documenting their behavior must be in place.

  We can't rely on children to explain themselves or their behavior. They may not know and often cannot tell us why they behave as they do. When an adult asks a child "Why did you do it?" the typical response is "I don't know."

- When should teachers observe children? What can we learn about them during these times?

Possible responses:

> *Arrival, departure, toileting, transitions, wash-up, clean-up, story time, choice time, indoors, outdoors, alone, with other children, with adults*

> *Teachers learn about children's preferences and interests, temperament, comfort level in different situations, and level of competence. Observation and documentation should be a regular, integral part of the classroom day.*

- Is it important to observe children on multiple occasions? Why or why not?

Possible responses:

> *Children do things differently at different times of the day and during different activities. They have different temperaments and interests, or may be more alert at certain times of the day. Observing children on multiple occasions gives a more realistic picture of what they know and can do.*

- Is it essential to document your observations? Why or why not?

Possible responses:

> *It is essential to document observations. Teachers forget, patterns are revealed over time, and parents enjoy hearing personal examples of what their child did.*

> *Without documentation, teachers would have no evidence upon which to base their evaluation of a child's development and learning or to make instructional decisions.*

ACTIVITY

Ask participants whether they feel they are good observers.

Explain that they will participate in an exercise that will help them evaluate their observation skills. Give these instructions:

- Take out a blank piece of paper and a writing tool.

- I'm going to ask you to recall the details of an object you see and use every day.

- The first part of the exercise is to be done individually, with no talking or outside assistance.

- Draw a picture of a push-button (touch-tone) phone keypad.

When you think everyone is finished, have them share their drawings with others and add any new details they forgot. Then show the drawing of the phone keypad on chart paper.

Lead a discussion about the drawings:

- How often has each of us looked at a phone keypad over the course of our lives?

- How well did your memories serve you in this exercise?

- Were you able to draw an accurate picture of a phone keypad?

- Did you remember to include the star and pound keys in your drawings?

- Were you able to recall which letters of the alphabet were found with which numbers—or did you have to figure it out?

- Did you remember that there is not a *Q* or *Z* and that the number *1* has no letters on it?

Make the following points:

- We observe many things throughout our daily lives. Unless we have a focus or know what we are looking for, it is difficult to **really** observe.

- We have said that the goals and objectives of *The Creative Curriculum* are your guide for planning a preschool program. Everything we do is directed toward helping children learn and develop in relation to these objectives.

- Children reveal themselves (what they know, what they think, what they can do, and how they feel) in many special ways. They are developing language; nevertheless, they communicate with us through varied means—their eyes, their bodies, their smiles, their constructions, and their dramatizations.

- Human development is complex and no teacher can observe or assess everything. Deciding what to observe and assess requires us to focus, select, and sample. The goals and objectives of *The Creative Curriculum* provide a framework for us to focus our observations and select samples of work.

Introduce the next activity with these statements:

- It is important that we gather good clues or evidence that will help us get to know children better. Recalling observations from memory often yields faulty results, while focused, firsthand observations yield more accurate results.

- In order to use observations effectively, they must be written down.

Tell participants that they are going to practice observing and recording behavior as they watch a three-minute role-play of two children in the Library Area during choice time.

Have each person take several Post-it notes and ask them to jot down one observation on each Post-it.

Conduct the role-play, then collect the observations from each table.

Draw two columns on a piece of chart paper. Label one column "Fact" and the other "Interpretation." Read the notes you collected on the role-play and ask participants to tell you in which column each belongs.

Observe where most of the observation notes fall—under "Fact" or "Interpretation."

Have participants restate some of the interpretive statements so that they become more factual.

> **Possible responses:** *Child is restless.* Restated, it might be: *Child moves around while pointing at pictures in book.*

Have participants read the section "Being Objective" on pages 167–168 to see examples of each type of statement.

Invite participants to share comments and conclusions.

SUMMARY

Summarize with the following points:

- Observation is an objective look at what a child does and says.

- Children show us what they know and can do in a multitude of ways in the context of regular classroom activities. We have to know what we are looking for, make time to observe children, and document what we see.

- Firsthand observations yield a wealth of information about a child.

- To be useful, observation notes should be objective or factual.

- Factual observations, collected over time, enable you to draw more accurate conclusions.

- Writing objective observations takes time and practice.

Observing and Responding to Children

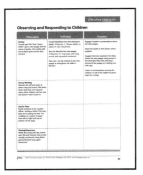

□ Handout **4D**
□ *Creative Curriculum*, pp. 46-58, 530

PREPARATION

Select the workshop you wish to use from the interest area chapters.

INTRODUCTION

Make the following points:

- Observing children and documenting their behavior and language provides a wealth of information that guides instruction.

- The *Developmental Continuum* is a tool for planning instruction and assessing learning.

- Teachers who are familiar with the 50 Curriculum objectives and the developmental steps for each objective are able to organize what they see and think about how to respond and how to support learning.

- The purpose of this activity is to explore the *Developmental Continuum* and learn how to use it as a guide for responding to children.

ACTIVITY

Using one or more favorite workshops in the interest area chapters (e.g., "The Teacher's Role" in Toys and Games or "How Block Play Promotes Development" in Blocks), conduct an activity that addresses the teacher's role. These workshops typically place participants in a play scenario where they assume the roles of teacher/observer and/or player. Participants use the "Goals and Objectives at a Glance" (page 530) to determine which objectives are addressed. They are then asked to consider how they might respond to children in a given situation.

Next, have participants find a partner. Distribute the handout and explain that the top row is an example of the natural process a teacher uses when deciding how to respond to a child.

Go over the first example that is filled out. Discuss the process of observing, reflecting, and responding, and how it should become part of a teacher's thinking throughout the day.

Explain that the first step in the process is to reflect on the observation about the child.

- What did you learn about the child?

- Which objectives and developmental steps seem to be reflected in the behavior?

- Does it show a special interest, a particular learning style, or a challenge?

Ask participants to respond to what they observed. Decide the best way to support learning. Tell them to ask themselves:

- What are the developmental steps related to this objective?

- How can I use this information as I interact with this child?

- What questions can I pose or what comments can I make?

- What materials can I provide?

- How might I involve the family?

Have participants work with a partner to complete the handout, referring to the *Developmental Continuum* as a guide.

Invite participants to share any thoughts they have after completing the handout.

SUMMARY

Summarize with the following points:

- Most observations occur during the course of daily activities as you work with children and as you take note of what they do and say.

- The behaviors you see are likely to relate to many of the *Creative Curriculum* objectives.

- Using the *Developmental Continuum* as a guide enables you to

  organize what you see

  consider how you might respond

  consider how you will plan and interact with individual children and the group

  think about what teaching strategies you will use

Using a Range of Teaching Approaches

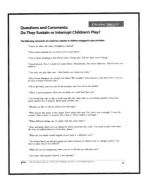

□ *Creative Curriculum*
  video
□ Handout **4E**
□ Handout **4F**
□ *Creative Curriculum*,
  pp. 46–58, 173–198
□ Collectibles
□ *Fish Is Fish* by
  Leo Lionni

PREPARATION

Even if participants have seen the *Creative Curriculum* video, this time they will view it to focus on the varied roles of teachers.

Gather enough collectibles (e.g., bottle caps, keys, shells) for each group to use.

Duplicate the handouts.

INTRODUCTION

Introduce the workshop:

- Learning in the preschool classroom is full of contradictions.

- What works to introduce, reinforce, and extend learning in one situation may be ineffective in another. Therefore, good teaching requires a range of teaching approaches.

- The purpose of this workshop is to learn more about guiding children's learning.

Give the following instructions:

- Think about the teacher who had the greatest impact on your learning. Jot down the strategies the teacher used to help you learn.

- Identify which of these strategies you currently use in your program.

- Turn to a neighbor and share your experience. Brainstorm ways you could improve the learning atmosphere for children in your program.

- Invite participants to share points from their discussions.

Make the following points:

- Every child has unique learning styles, needs, and interests. Learning various skills and concepts requires different teaching approaches.

- In order to meet children's individual needs and address program learning goals, a *Creative Curriculum* teacher uses a full range of teaching approaches and varied levels of involvement.

Point out strategies described in the Curriculum on the following pages:

- Use a range of teaching approaches (pages 173–178).

- Adapt instruction to include all children (pages 179–183).

- Work with children in a variety of group settings (pages 183–187).

- Establish interest areas (pages 187–189).

- Organize studies that engage children in research about topics of interest to them (pages 190–198).

◖ ACTIVITY

Introduce the activity with the following points:

- When you want children to explore and construct an understanding on their own, child-initiated learning is effective.

- In a *Creative Curriculum* classroom, interest areas are the primary settings in which child-initiated learning takes place.

- Work in interest areas requires a range of teacher involvement.

- As you watch the *Creative Curriculum* video, you will notice this range of teacher involvement.

Explain the following:

- Each person will need several Post-it notes.

- As you view the video write down "ing" words that best describe what the teacher is doing to guide and support a child or children. Write each word on a separate Post-it note. For example, "talking" or "playing."

    Possible responses: *questioning, acknowledging, observing, interacting, modeling, teaching, facilitating*

Next, have each table of participants organize their "ing" words to create a continuum of involvement, from the least amount of teacher involvement to the most.

Invite participants to share, then make the following points:

- Teachers plan for child-initiated learning by preparing the environment with rich and interesting materials. However, teachers don't leave learning to chance.

- What works with one child or in one situation may not work in another.

- Effective teachers know when to observe, when to offer encouragement, when to step in with guidance, and when to intervene or facilitate to help children overcome an obstacle.

- And, they know what, when, and how some skills or content must be explicitly taught.

Read the book *Fish Is Fish* by Leo Lionni. Then lead a discussion about direct or explicit teaching. Make the following points:

- Direct teaching is not simply "telling" or "giving" children information. It is any kind of help that makes things clear to children so they do not have to reach understandings by inferring them on their own.

- Just because the frog in the book told the fish about the wonderful things he saw in the outside world, it doesn't mean that the fish really understood them.

- Direct teaching may include modeling and demonstrating, explaining, or helping children to make connections to what they already know.

Have the group read the example of the small-group activity on page 186. Ask:

- What do you notice about this small-group activity?

- What did the teacher do to make it a successful learning experience?

Review the features of a successful small-group experience found on page 187.

Allow each group time to practice conducting a small-group time similar to the one described in the Curriculum. Distribute the collectibles to each table. Give the following instructions:

- Select one person at your table to be the teacher and another to be the observer.

- The teacher is to lead the other participants in a small-group activity using collectibles.

- The observer is to record any objectives or skills addressed during the activity, approaches the teacher used in working with others, and ways in which the others worked together.

Explain that direct teaching can also occur in a large-group setting. Ask participants to read the "teachable moment" example on page 175. Make these points:

- It's too simplistic to think of child-initiated or teacher-directed learning as either/or approaches.

- Both child-initiated learning and teacher-directed learning will require different kinds of teacher interaction with children. One kind or level of involvement is not superior to another.

- An effective teacher observes and interacts with children and then thoughtfully determines the right degree of involvement needed to support learning in each situation.

Distribute handout 4E and assign one scenario to each table.

Have participants read the scenario and think of ways to respond to the children.

Next, have participants identify *Creative Curriculum* objectives related to the scenario.

Locate the objectives on the *Developmental Continuum* (pages 46-58) and reflect on their responses. Consider how this additional information might inform their next steps with the children.

SUMMARY

Summarize with the following points:

- Interruptions of children's play are inevitable; however, the goal is not to intrude, but to follow the children's lead and respond in ways that build on and sustain their play and learning.

- In *Creative Curriculum* classrooms, teachers observe children during child-initiated experiences in interest areas and then consider what teacher interactions will best guide learning and what kind of teacher-directed learning is needed.

- Teachers use the *Developmental Continuum* as a framework for thinking about how they might respond to children.

VARIATION

Questions and Comments: Do They Sustain or Interrupt Children's Play
Distribute handout 4F.

Ask participants to work as a group at their tables. Have them decide which questions and comments would help sustain children's play and how each one would do so. Ask them which questions and comments would **not** be helpful. Discuss together how they made their decisions. After they have finished, ask a representative from each table to choose one item that provoked a lot of discussion and share the issues involved.

Adapting Instruction for Children With Special Needs

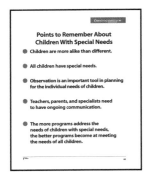

Points to Remember About
Children With Special Needs
● Children are more alike than different.

● All children have special needs.

● Observation is an important tool in planning for the individual needs of children.

● Teachers, parents, and specialists need to have ongoing communication.

● The more programs address the needs of children with special needs, the better programs become at meeting the needs of all children.

☐ Transparency **4G**
☐ *Creative Curriculum,*
　pp. 179–183
☐ Paper

PREPARATION

No preparation necessary.

INTRODUCTION

Introduce the workshop:

Have participants think of a personal label they have been given (e.g. quiet, outgoing, strong-willed, smart, or gifted). Ask them to talk about how this label has helped, hindered, pressured, or limited them. Acknowledge that not everyone will want to share their thoughts. Invite those who wish to do so, to discuss any insights they gained. You might start by sharing your own personal experiences.

Lead a brief discussion about how labels can affect someone's view of a child.

Make the following points:

• Labels sometimes limit our thinking about what a person can do and are therefore not always helpful.

• As you develop a relationship with a child with special needs, as with any other child, you come to know how to respond and which strategies seem to be effective in each situation.

• The purpose of this workshop is to take a closer look at the specific needs of a child in your class, one who may be gifted, who may have a disability, or who is learning to speak English as a second language, and your own needs to determine how you can best support and guide this child's learning.

ACTIVITY

Have participants form groups of four. Distribute a blank piece of paper to each participant and give the following instructions:

- Fold the paper in half.

- Think of a child in your classroom whose situation challenges you. It may be a child who is gifted, has a disability, or is learning a second language. List all of this child's special needs on one side of the paper.

- Next, think about what you need in order to work successfully with this child to guide learning. List your needs on the other side of the paper.

- Refer to pages 179–183 for ideas on working with gifted children, children with disabilities, and second language learners.

- Work with others in your group to brainstorm ways to meet or balance these needs.

Invite one or two participants to share points from the small group discussions.

SUMMARY

Close with brief remarks about each point on the transparency.

- Children are more alike than different.

- All children have special needs.

- Observation is an important tool in planning for the individual needs of children.

- Teachers, parents, and specialists need to have ongoing communication.

- The more programs address the needs of children with special needs, the better programs become at meeting the needs of all children.

WORKSHOP

Exploring Content in Interest Areas

☐ Handout **4H**
☐ Handout **4I**
☐ *Creative Curriculum,*
    pp. 126–160
☐ *Implementation
    Checklist*

PREPARATION

This activity is a brief introduction to content so that teachers may begin thinking about how content can be addressed as part of everyday classroom activities. Volume II of *A Trainer's Guide to The Creative Curriculum* provides an in-depth look at the components of each content area—literacy, math, science, social studies, the arts, and technology—and process skills.

INTRODUCTION

Introduce the workshop with the following suggestions:

• Think about one of the interest areas or activities in your own classroom where the most interesting children's conversations and questions develop. List the characteristics of this area or the situations that seem to encourage children's interactions.

• Think of other areas where these interactions do not seem to occur. Write a description of what you can do to integrate these qualities into other interest areas or activities.

• Share with others at your table.

Invite each table group to share key points from their discussions.

Make the following points:

• Interest areas are the primary settings in which children learn.

• They also provide teachers the opportunity to teach important content as children explore materials that are interesting and appealing.

• The purpose of this workshop is to introduce the six content areas described in chapter 3 and to consider how this content can be addressed appropriately through interest areas.

ACTIVITY

Ask each table group to choose one of the content areas—literacy, math, science, social studies, the arts, and technology—and then give the following instructions:

- Read your respective section in chapter 3 of the Curriculum.

- Discuss the reading with others at your table so that everyone learns about each content area. Use the following questions as a framework for your discussion:

    What are the key components of this content area?

    How can this content be integrated into interest areas?

- Use handout 4H and handout 4I to note your ideas.

- Review sections I. C. and III. C. 2–7 of the *Implementation Checklist* (pages 14–17, 26–31) for your content area as well as section III. C. 1 (page 25). Discuss the items with others in your group.

Regroup participants so that new groups are formed with a representative from each content area. Explain the following:

- Each of you is now considered an "expert" in one content area.

- Your job is to share what you have learned about your content area with others in your new group describing the key components, ideas for integrating the content into interest areas, and suggested resources.

- The rest of you will take notes on your handouts, ask questions of the expert, and share any related ideas.

SUMMARY

Summarize with the following points:

- Setting up interest areas and interacting with children around the materials you provide is a key way to promote children's learning in the content areas and address developmental goals.

- When you share these strategies, and the learning that is taking place in your classroom, with families and others, you are more likely to gain support for children and your program.

An Interview With...

An Interview With a Gardener

As a gardener, I am concerned with the well being of plants. Because of the diversity of plants, I have to have a wide range of niches in which to put the plants. There are plants that need cooler temperatures while others need a warmer climate. Some like a moist or wet soil while others prefer it drier. Therefore, my job is to work with Mother Nature to provide the conditions that will promote optimal growth in the plants.

There are some plants that need to be nurtured for five to seven years before they are large enough to plant in the ground. Each day, I look at the plant and make any necessary adaptations. I have learned to be patient and flexible. If I try to force the growth process in these types of plants, I won't get the best results.

Plants let me know how they are doing. If their color is not good, I may add fertilizer, move them from the sun to the shade, or I might even try talking to them. I know that if I pay attention to what they are trying to tell me, I will enjoy the fruits of my labor.

An Interview With an Air Traffic Controller

As an air traffic controller, I am interested in maintaining the safety of the flying public. At a large airport, there are hundreds of planes that take off and land each day. My job is to make sure that every one of those planes does so safely. That means I have to be able to look at the entire situation (each pilot's needs) and then make a quick decision.

For example, there may be three planes approaching the airport at about the same time. I have to ask myself "Which plane should have priority at this time; Aircraft A, Aircraft B, or Aircraft C?" I communicate with the pilots and find out what their needs and expectations are. I find out how far each plane is from the airport, the direction they are coming from, or if there is any special need a pilot might have.

I also tell the pilots what our requirements and limitations are. For example, if the weather has been bad, there may be planes backed up and waiting to take off or there may not be a gate available for planes to park. In these instances, I have to find out if the pilot has enough fuel to circle the airport for a while. By maintaining open lines of communication, we are able to get our jobs done safely and efficiently.

An Interview With an Athletic Coach

Some people think my job is to win games. But actually, my job is to have players get better at what they do. I am concerned with helping players become better physically and mentally so they are prepared for the next league.

I usually have 25 different players on my team and that means I have 25 different relationships. I try to assess each player, their personality, what makes them tick, and what's going on in their mind. Based on my assessment, I try to motivate each one to come out to the field and work to better themselves.

An Interview With an Architect

Most people think of an architect as someone who simply draws plans for a building. Actually, several things need to happen before I actually take the pen to paper and we start construction.

The first thing I usually do is meet with the client to gather information or conduct a needs assessment. I need to know things such as:

- what size building he needs and wants
- what kinds of activities he will conduct (that determines the size of the rooms in the building)
- what style of architecture he prefers
- the need for special features or if there are certain requirements he has
- his expectations of me
- the timeline for completing the project
- what his budget looks like

I look at the physical site and make a determination of whether I am able to do everything he has asked for at that location. I have the land surveyed and do a few other things, and then I draw the plan. After I complete the plan, I then meet with the client for him to review the plans and get his feedback. Of course, there are times when I need to make adjustments or get a little more clarification about some aspect of the design.

On occasion, during construction, I go to the site and an opportunity presents itself to do something in a better way than what was originally planned. For example, a tradesman might say, "Did you think of doing it this way?" Or "What if we do this?" We try it and it turns out to be a better idea than the original one and sometimes we even save some money. That makes the client and me really happy!

How Is a Teacher Like...?

A Gardener?

An Air Traffic Controller?

A Coach?

An Architect?

Observing Children: Why, When, What, and How to Observe

● **Why is it important to observe and record children's behavior in the classroom setting?**

● **When should teachers observe children? What can we learn about them during these times?**

● **Is it important to observe children on multiple occasions? Why or why not?**

● **Is it essential to document your observations? Why or why not?**

Observing and Responding to Children

Observation	Reflection	Response
Arrival Crystal says: "Ms. Tory! Guess what? I got a new puppy and his name is Sparky. He's white with some black spots and he licks my face."	Crystal transitions into the classroom easily. *(Objective 1, Shows ability to adjust to new situations)* She can describe her new puppy. *(Objective 39, Expresses self using words and expanded sentences)* How can I use her interest in her new puppy to strengthen her skills in literacy?	Engage Crystal in conversations about her new puppy. Show her books in the Library about puppies. Suggest that she represent her ideas about her new puppy using props in the Dramatic Play Area, drawing a picture of her puppy, or creating one with clay. Listen to conversations among the children to see if this might be good topic for a study.
Group Meeting Setsuko sits still and looks at others sing and march. She looks down and does not respond when other children ask her why she doesn't want to join in.		
Choice Time Derek pretends to be a police officer writing a ticket: "Pull over, lady. You're going too fast." He scribbles on a piece of paper from left to right and top to bottom of the page.		
Closing/Departure While discussing the day, Juwan says "Me and Tasheen dug a hole outside and found a bug. We're gonna find that bug again tomorrow."		

Responding to Children—Scenarios

A

Leo and Kate are busy in the Block Area putting a ramp in various positions to form an incline to roll vehicles down. You've noticed that they have tried leaning the ramp against the wall, on the shelf, and against a chair.

B

Carlos is in the Dramatic Play Area where he puts on a cape and announces that he is Batman. He proceeds to climb on a nearby chair and jump off.

C

Susie takes a milkweed leaf that had been collected on a nature walk from the Discovery Area and places it under the computer microscope. With great excitement she exclaims, "Those white things are bugs!"

D

Shawn is in the Toys and Games area diligently putting together puzzle-like dominos. On one end of each domino is a numeral and on the other end is a set of objects. After she matches the pieces, she lays the domino in its original box, focusing on keeping the matched pieces together.

E

Janelle is at the easel painting pictures of swirling colors. You hear her making whirring sounds and she says, "You better watch out. Oh no, here comes a tornado!"

F

Ben spends the entire outdoor time in the sandbox repeatedly filling cups with sand and pouring them into a bucket. Then he takes the bucket and dumps it in another area.

G

Tasheen spends most of her time on the playground playing "monster" and trying to scare the other children.

H

Dallas and Zack carefully examine the shells in the Toys and Games Area. They put the shells into two piles, then three, and then four.

Questions and Comments:
Do They Sustain or Interrupt Children's Play?

The following comments are made by a teacher to children engaged in play activities:

"I have an idea—let's play firefighters, instead!"

"How many animals do you have? Let's count them!"

"You've been working in the block corner a long time. Tell me what you're doing."

"Knock-knock. Yes, I would love some dinner. Mmmmmm, this tastes delicious. Tell me how you made it."

"You may not play that way – that breaks our classroom rules."

"Hey, Power Rangers, be careful over there! We wouldn't want anyone to get hurt! How can you be sure to keep everyone safe?"

"I'll be the baby, and you can be the mommy and you can be the daddy."

"That's a good question. How do you think we could find that out?"

"Let's build this side so that it looks just like the other side, so everything matches. Does that piece match? No, it doesn't. Better pick another one."

"Would you like to tell me about your drawing?"

"Who knows the name of this shape? How about this one? No, that's not a triangle. Count the corners. Does it have three corners? No, it has four. That's called a rectangle."

"What different things can we make with the sand today?"

"Boys and girls, that's not our theme for those materials this week. You need to play with them the way we talked about in circle time, please."

"What do you think would happen if you tried it a different way?"

"You better hurry up and get going over there because it's almost time to change centers! You have to play fast at our school!"

"What do you see happening when you try to fill this jar with this one?"

"Let's play with puzzles instead. I love puzzles."

Points to Remember About Children With Special Needs

● **Children are more alike than different.**

● **All children have special needs.**

● **Observation is an important tool in planning for the individual needs of children.**

● **Teachers, parents, and specialists need to have ongoing communication.**

● **The more programs address the needs of children with special needs, the better programs become at meeting the needs of all children.**

Exploring the Content Areas

Content Area	Key Components
Literacy	
Math	
Science	
Social Studies	
The Arts	
Technology	

Exploring Content in Interest Areas

	Blocks	Dramatic Play	Toys & Games	Art	Sand & Water
Literacy					
Math					
Science					
Social Studies					
The Arts					
Technology					

Exploring Content in Interest Areas, continued

Library	Discovery	Music & Movement	Cooking	Computers	Outdoors

NOTES

The Family's Role

PURPOSE

Teaching begins with getting to know children. That also means getting to know families. Understanding the important role families can play in a preschool program helps teachers build positive, respectful relationships that support children's learning and development.

These workshops invite participants to explore ways to create a welcoming environment where all families feel that they belong. Participants will examine various ways to communicate with families and partner with them on children's learning. Finally, they explore issues surrounding misunderstandings that can occur between home and school. Together, these workshops provide a comprehensive overview of the family's role in a *Creative Curriculum* classroom.

BIG IDEAS:

- Every family is different and worthy of respect.

- Children's families are an integral part of the program.

- Family involvement takes many forms.

- Teachers and families are partners in promoting children's learning.

- Differences are an opportunity for dialogue.

The Family's Role

WORKSHOPS

Key Points	Workshop	Materials	Time (minutes)
Each of us has different levels of comfort in our work with families.	**True Confessions** (p. 144)	None	20
The more aware teachers are of their personal views and beliefs, the more sensitive they can be to different viewpoints.	**Gaining Self-Awareness** (p. 146)	☐ Handout **5A:** Gaining Self-Awareness ☐ *Creative Curriculum*, pp. 212–213	15
Teachers begin building partnerships by getting to know and appreciate each family.	**How Well Do You Know Your Families?** (p. 148)	☐ Handout **5B:** How Well Do You Know Your Families? ☐ *Creative Curriculum*, p. 212 ☐ Transparency **5C:** Appreciating Differences in Families	30
The environment you create can send positive messages to families that make them feel welcome in the preschool program.	**Making Families Feel Welcome** (p. 150)	☐ Handout **5D:** Conveying Positive Messages to Families ☐ *Creative Curriculum*, pp. 218–222 ☐ Chart paper ☐ Markers	30
Good communication is essential for building partnerships.	**Communicating Effectively With Families** (p. 152)	☐ Small object, chart paper, marker ☐ Handout **5E:** Communicating Effectively With Families ☐ *Creative Curriculum*, pp. 223–224	30
When teachers share information about the Curriculum, families understand more about what the children are learning and how to support this learning.	**Sharing the Curriculum With Families and Others** (p. 156)	☐ Handout **5F:** Sharing the Curriculum With Others	15-30

The Family's Role

WORKSHOPS

🔑 Key Points	⚙ Workshop	📋 Materials	🕐 Time (minutes)
When teachers recognize that every family has something to offer the program, they can find ways to reach every family.	**Involving Families in Your Program** (p. 158)	☐ *Creative Curriculum,* pp. 225–230 ☐ Handout **5G:** Involving Families in My Preschool Program ☐ *Implementation Checklist*	30
Much can be gained when families are viewed as partners in the education of their children.	**Conducting Conferences With Families** (p. 160)	☐ Chart paper ☐ Markers ☐ *Creative Curriculum,* pp. 231–234	30
Differences are an opportunity for dialogue.	**Dealing With Misunderstandings** (p. 162)	☐ Handout **5H:** Dealing With Misunderstandings ☐ *Creative Curriculum,* pp. 235–241	30
Challenging situations require a process to resolve differences constructively.	**Resolving Differences Constructively** (p. 164)	☐ Handout **5I:** Resolving Differences Constructively ☐ *Creative Curriculum,* pp. 231–240	20

True Confessions

PREPARATION

Make sure you have space for participants to move about comfortably.

INTRODUCTION

Introduce the workshop:

- The Family's Role is the fifth component of the framework.

- Everyone feels a different level of competence when working with families.

- This workshop is designed to help you identify, in a playful way, how you feel about your work with families.

ACTIVITY

Give these instructions:

- I'm going to make a series of statements. Then I'll give four possible answers, and designate one corner of the room for each answer.

- Move to the corner of the room that represents how you would respond.

- Talk among yourselves about why you chose that response.

- When it comes to working with families, I am like a

    ship   helium balloon

    bicycle   runaway train

- If I were to describe how I relate to families, I would say I am like a

    pit bull   chihuahua

    cocker spaniel   bassett hound

- When parents are in my classroom, I feel like I'm

    at a symphony concert   in a mystery novel

    in a storm at sea   at the zoo

- When it comes to handling conflicts with parents, I'm

    a fish out of water   a beaver

    an ostrich   a butterfly

- The tool I need most to help me work with families is a

    hammer   plunger

    wrench   glue gun

Have participants return to their tables and discuss any insights they gained from this activity. Invite people to share with the full group if they wish.

Conclude the activity with remarks about how each of us has feelings about our work with families. The information offered in the Curriculum may help address some of the concerns they have.

SUMMARY

Summarize with the following points:

- When home and school are connected in positive and respectful ways, children feel secure and much can be accomplished.

- Teachers who value the family's role focus on developing a relationship with every family so that they can work together to support a child's development and learning.

- The Curriculum can guide your efforts in

    getting to know families

    making families feel welcome

    communicating with families

    partnering with families on children's learning

    responding to challenging situations

Gaining Self-Awareness

☐ Handout **5A**
☐ *Creative Curriculum,*
   pp. 212–213

PREPARATION

Duplicate the handout.

INTRODUCTION

Introduce the workshop:

- Knowing children means knowing families. Each family differs in its structure, personality, temperament, life experiences, and cultural differences.

- Teachers who get to know families and appreciate their differences begin building partnerships that support children's learning and development.

- Knowing families enables teachers to communicate with and involve them in the program in ways that meet their needs and the needs of their children.

- Gaining self-awareness is the place to start.

ACTIVITY

Distribute handout 5A and give these instructions:

- Think about the messages you may have received growing up and the experiences you had in your own family and community.

- Respond to any of these questions in which something comes to mind immediately.

- Share your thoughts with the person sitting next to you, and discuss how personal experiences might influence a teacher's thinking and actions toward families.

Lead a brief discussion about how personal views can affect our ability to build effective partnerships with families. Invite participants to share any insights they gained from this activity.

Point out the differences discussed on page 212.

SUMMARY

Summarize with the following points:

- The more aware we are of our own beliefs and values, the more we can recognize and learn to respect those that are different.

- Learn as much as you can about and from the families in your program. This will help you understand how and why families respond as they do.

VARIATION

Focused Writing

Tell participants to turn to page 213 and read the section "Gaining Self-Awareness."

Ask participants to jot down the issues that come to mind for any of the questions. Have them choose one and write about how it influences their work with families.

WORKSHOP

How Well Do You Know Your Families?

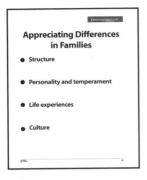

☐ Handout **5B**
☐ *Creative Curriculum*, p. 212
☐ Transparency **5C**

PREPARATION

This activity is similar to the workshop on "Individual Differences." However, the focus is on using what you know about families to determine how to relate to and involve each family in the program. Duplicate the handout. Prepare the transparency.

INTRODUCTION

Introduce the workshop:

- Just as you get to know each child and use what you learn to develop a relationship, you begin building partnerships with families by getting to know and appreciate each family.

- This activity will help you assess how well you know these families.

ACTIVITY

Refer participants to the handout and give these instructions:

- Write the name of each family served in your class in column 1, labeled "Family's Name."

- Reflect on the following questions and discuss your response with others at your table.

    Did you remember all of the families' names?

    Which ones were easier or more difficult to remember? Why?

Show the transparency and briefly discuss key points about the differences listed (see page 212). Give these instructions:

- In column 2, record something unique about each family. It may be related to the differences just discussed or something else.

- Discuss ways in which you learned about these characteristics.

Stress that knowing each family's unique characteristics and circumstances enables teachers to relate to each family in ways that make them feel valued, respected, and a welcome part of the preschool program.

Ask participants to think about how they have or might use what they know about a family to build or strengthen a relationship and support children's learning and development. Have them record their ideas in column 3.

If necessary, offer an example such as the following:

A single father and his children live with an extended family. The father works two jobs and is unable to participate in school functions or parent conferences.

Then suggest that knowing this, a teacher might do these things:

- Invite another family member to attend a school function in place of the father.

- Send home photographs of the child involved in various activities at the school.

- Offer to have a conference with the father at a time that suits his schedule.

Remind participants to consider how this particular information might affect the way they communicate with families, involve them in their programs, or approach and respond to families.

Invite a few people to share some of their ideas.

SUMMARY

Summarize with the following points:

- Knowing children means knowing families.

- Every family is different.

- Knowing and appreciating what is unique or different about each family helps you to build relationships and support children's learning and development.

VARIATION

Create "buzz groups" by having participants form groups of three. Explain that each person in a group will have exactly one minute to complete the sentence, "What I appreciate most about families is…"

Invite groups to share. Then lead a brief discussion about the differences among families listed on page 212 and the implications for teachers' work with families.

Using "buzz groups" again, have participants complete the sentence, "The most successful thing I've done to get to know families is…"

Invite the groups to share their most successful strategies. Remind participants to record any new ideas they may want to try.

Make the following points:

- Just as every child is different, every family is different.

- Teachers who understand and appreciate these differences relate to families in varied and more responsive ways.

Making Families Feel Welcome

☐ Handout **5D**
☐ *Creative Curriculum,*
   pp. 218–222
☐ Chart paper
☐ Markers

PREPARATION

Duplicate the handout.

INTRODUCTION

Begin this workshop by elaborating on the following points:

- Families who feel welcome in the classroom are more likely to return and to become involved in the program.

- To feel welcome, families need to trust you. Trust is built over time as teachers and families engage in positive, respectful exchanges.

- All families come to school with certain feelings and expectations—positive, negative, and neutral. Family members who have had positive, respectful experiences with teachers and schools develop trust that allows them to feel comfortable and welcome in school.

- A *Creative Curriculum* teacher strives to convey positive messages to families to help them feel they belong and have a role to play.

ACTIVITY

Ask participants to think of needs or concerns parents typically have about a preschool program.

Record their ideas on a chart. For example, a parent might be concerned that her child doesn't rest well in unfamiliar places, or she needs to know what her child will be learning during the week.

Then lead a discussion about ways each need could be met in the preschool program.

Emphasize the fact that meeting the needs and concerns of families helps to build trust between home and school.

Next, have participants think of a time when they entered a new environment or social situation. Have them recall some of the thoughts, feelings, or questions that came to mind.

Relate their experiences to those of parents or other family members entering a child in a preschool program for the first time.

Have participants review handout 5D. Explain that, in this activity, they will think about how to convey positive messages to families through preparing their environments, introducing their programs, and reaching out to family members.

Have participants complete column 2 of the handout. Ask them to read pages 218–222 to compare their ideas and to record any new ideas they would like to try.

Invite participants to share new things they will try upon returning to their classrooms.

SUMMARY

Summarize the activity with the following points:

- Positive messages help build trust between teachers and families. They make families feel that they are welcome in the preschool program and that they have a role to play.

- Trust between teachers and families grows when teachers meet families' needs and respond to them in positive, respectful ways.

- Take time to assess whether your environment conveys the messages you intend. Let families know their ideas and contributions are always welcome.

Communicating Effectively With Families

- ☐ Small object, chart paper, marker
- ☐ Handout **5E**
- ☐ *Creative Curriculum*, pp. 223–224

PREPARATION

This activity is much like the "hot/cold" game many of us played as children. To prepare for this workshop, decide upon some nonverbal means of communication for participants to use (e.g., snapping fingers, tapping two pencils, or rubbing or clapping hands together).

Select an object to hide (e.g., a small toy, a bead, a piece of hard candy).

Duplicate the handout.

Ask for a volunteer who will search for the hidden object.

INTRODUCTION

Introduce the workshop:

- Families and teachers have much information to share.

- Regular, positive communication helps families stay informed about what their child is learning and what you have learned about their child.

- When children observe respectful and genuine interactions between their families and teachers, they see that their two worlds—home and school—are connected.

- The purpose of this activity is to examine the essential elements of communication and the role it plays in establishing and maintaining relationships with families.

ACTIVITY

Explain these procedures:

- A volunteer will step out of the room while an object is hidden from view.

- Those of you remaining will "communicate" with the volunteer about the location of the hidden object.

- Slow/soft communication indicates a greater distance from the object while an increase in the pace and volume indicates a closer proximity to the object.

Have the volunteer leave the room and proceed with the activity.

After the volunteer locates the hidden object, ask participants to identify the essential elements of communication revealed through this activity. Record their ideas on chart paper.

Possible responses:

There was a shared goal.

Both parties had to be willing to participate.

There was a common means of communication.

The language had to be consistent.

Both parties watched and/or listened to one another then responded.

In times of uncertainty, the message may need clarification.

Extra support was given when needed.

Relate these ideas to communicating with families as a means of building and maintaining relationships. Discuss the influence culture has on communication styles and subject matter.

Next, refer participants to the handout and give these directions:

- Answer the first three questions individually.

- Share your ideas with others at your table.

- Return to the list of challenges and brainstorm solutions or strategies for overcoming each.

Call attention to pages 223–224 for suggestions on how to make the most of daily exchanges and various ways to communicate with families.

SUMMARY

Summarize with the following points:

- Both teachers and families have much information to share.

- Good communication is essential to building relationships with families.

- It is important to communicate in ways that meet the needs and ability levels of family members, particularly those whose primary language is not English.

VARIATIONS

Variation 1:
Give the following directions:

- Recall a negative experience you had either as a parent dealing with a professional, a patient with a doctor, or a client with another professional.

- Describe some of the behaviors of that particular professional that made you feel uncomfortable or that inhibited communication.

- Recall a positive experience with another professional.

- Describe the behaviors that promoted comfort and communication.

Ask participants how these behaviors apply to the ways in which they work with families.

Variation 2:
Have participants form small groups.

Give the following directions:

- You have recently been assigned to replace a preschool teacher who has been considered a mainstay at a close-knit neighborhood school or center for many years. You are committed to developing positive relationships with families.

- Using the information presented in Chapter 5, write a letter to families letting them know something about you and your plans for including them in your program during the upcoming year.

NOTES

Sharing the Curriculum With Families and Others

☐ Handout **5F**

PREPARATION

Duplicate the handout.

INTRODUCTION

Introduce the workshop:

• Families feel more comfortable leaving their children in a preschool program when they are informed about the structure of the classroom day and the kinds of experiences children will be offered.

• Parents also want to be assured that their children are learning.

• When teachers are able to describe what children are learning and their approaches to teaching children, they are more likely to gain support from families and others.

Ask:

• How many of you have said, or heard it said, that "children learn through play?"

• Does this statement capture all of the learning that occurs in an active classroom? Why or why not?

Stress the importance of being able to explain to families and others "what" and "how" children learn through play.

ACTIVITY

Refer participants to the handout. Give these instructions:

• Look at each picture and think about what children might be learning as they engage in each activity pictured.

• Write a brief comment that describes the learning on the lines below each picture.

Offer an example if necessary. Participants may work alone, with a partner, or as a table group to complete the task.

Invite participants to share their ideas.

Ask participants to suggest ways to share *The Creative Curriculum* with families and others.

Possible responses:

Host an open house.

Offer a guided tour of the classroom.

Share photographs of classroom activities.

Create displays of children's work with a description of what they are doing and learning.

Distribute copies of A Parent's Guide to Preschool *to each family.*

Send home the "Letter to Families" from each interest area chapter.

If you wish, ask each group to choose an interest area and write a sample "Letter to Families" about the area. Then compare it to the letter in the interest area chapter.

SUMMARY

Summarize with the following points:

- As professionals, you should be able to explain what children are learning and your approaches to teaching.

- There are various ways to share the Curriculum.

- Keeping families and others informed about program practices and activities helps to build partnerships and gain support for your program.

VARIATION

TV Talk Show Activity

Each table role-plays a panel of early childhood experts answering parent questions from the audience.

Read a question from the audience. Allow time for each group to discuss it. When a group thinks it has the best response, it should signal and share it with the larger group. Sample questions might be:

1. How will my child learn the basic math skills he will need in kindergarten?

2. Leo is really smart and recognizes all the letters of the alphabet. I bought him one of those workbooks on phonics, but he doesn't get it. Does he need to be tutored? Can I send it to school for you to use with him?

3. Zack writes his name with the "Z" backward. What should I do?

4. Can you test my child to see if she is ready for kindergarten?

5. Why don't you send worksheets home for me to use with my child?

6. We want to get some materials for Carlos to help him improve his English. What kinds of things should we buy?

Involving Families in Your Program

☐ *Creative Curriculum,*
pp. 225–230
☐ Handout **5G**
☐ *Implementation
Checklist*

◖ PREPARATION

Duplicate the handout.

◖ INTRODUCTION

Introduce the workshop:

- Families are already partners in supporting their child's learning.

- Children whose families are involved in their children's education perform better academically and have a better attitude toward school.

- Family involvement can take many forms. The more options you provide for families to contribute to the program, the more likely you are to succeed in reaching every family.

◖ ACTIVITY

Have participants form small groups. Then pose the following scenario:

Your group has been asked to assist the staff at a local school or center in improving and increasing family involvement. Give each group these tasks:

- Identify any issues that may be inhibiting the quality and quantity of involvement.

- Suggest strategies the school could use to increase involvement and make it more meaningful.

Have participants read the chart on page 226, "Ways for Families to Be Involved."

Next, have participants think about the strengths, interests, and abilities of each family in their classes. Using the handout, have participants work individually or with a co-teacher to identify the families in their classes and a way for each family to be involved.

Refer participants to the "Family Involvement" section of the *Implementation Checklist* (page 36). Review each item.

Then have participants complete self-assessments of their family involvement practices. Have them identify areas that need improvement and make plans for change as necessary. Invite them to come to the next workshop and share their progress and successes.

SUMMARY

Summarize with the following points:

- For numerous and varied reasons, family members are not always able to participate in their children's daily school programs.

- Take the view that family involvement is more than attending parent meetings, volunteering in the classroom, or helping with fund-raising events.

- Every family has something to offer. The more options you provide for families to contribute to your program, the more likely you are to succeed in reaching every family.

Conducting Conferences With Families

☐ Chart paper
☐ Markers
☐ *Creative Curriculum,*
   pp. 231–234

PREPARATION

No preparation necessary.

INTRODUCTION

Introduce the workshop:

- Conducting conferences provides time for an in-depth exchange of ideas and for problem solving when needed.

- Conferences are an excellent time for teachers to learn more about a child and to help families understand the program's goals as well as how their children are progressing.

- Conferences provide time to set new goals for children and to plan with families how to meet those goals.

ACTIVITY

Have participants form small groups and brainstorm on chart paper a list of positive practices for planning and conducting conferences. They should consider planning, conducting, and closing the conference.

Possible responses to preparing for the conference:

Send home an invitation. Offer several options for times to meet and provide adequate notice.

Plan the physical environment (e.g., where you will sit, where parents will sit).

Review the Child Progress and Planning Report.

Gather samples of the child's work, including photographs.

Possible responses to conducting the conference:

Set a professional, caring tone.

Begin with a positive comment that shows you know the child.

Greet the parent warmly and enthusiastically.

Use effective listening and communication skills (ask open-ended questions, pay attention to body language, take notes, and listen without interpreting.)

Find out parents' important goals.

Possible responses to closing the conference:

Leave the parents with a positive, confident feeling that they have met with a teacher who really cares.

Set some goals and develop strategies that encourage a child's development and learning in the program and at home.

Summarize your discussion and restate the actions you have each agreed upon.

Have groups report and share their charts.

SUMMARY

Summarize with the following points:

- Conferences are an opportune time for meeting with families to share information and plan.

- The more prepared you are for conferences, the more positive the experience will be for both you and families, and the more you will be able to accomplish.

- Starting off the conference with something positive shows that you know what is unique and special about a child and puts a family at ease.

- Involving families in planning next steps for their children conveys the message that this is a true partnership.

VARIATION

Have participants form small groups. Ask them to read the section, "Meeting with Families to Plan and Share Information," on pages 231–234 and create a scenario of a successful parent conference.

Ask for volunteers to act out their scenario for the whole group.

Invite participants to provide feedback about the positive aspects of what they saw during the role-play.

WORKSHOP

Dealing With Misunderstandings

◖ **PREPARATION**

Duplicate the handout.

◖ **INTRODUCTION**

Introduce the workshop with the following points:

- In spite of your efforts to build positive partnerships, misunderstanding will occur.

- There will be times when a family's wishes or values conflict with your own.

- By learning as much as possible about each family and understanding beliefs and practices that may differ from yours, you gain insight into the causes of misunderstandings.

- These insights help you resolve differences in ways that build trust and respect.

☐ Handout **5H**
☐ *Creative Curriculum,*
    pp. 235–241

◖ **ACTIVITY**

Distribute handout 5H and go over the situation in the first row, inviting ideas on how to handle the situation in ways that promote a partnership.

Possible responses:

Consider the values a family might have in deciding on what objectives to focus on in a conference; then focus on the child's progress on those objectives first. Take time to find out the family's hopes and dreams for their child, and what they want their child to be learning.

Have each group read the remaining examples and discuss how they might handle those situations in a positive way. Give these instructions:

- Examine the situation from the perspectives of the teacher and the family.

- Generate an approach that expresses a "partnership view."

- Record your ideas in the last box in the row.

Invite participants to share their responses with the whole group.

If time permits, have each group divide the reading on "Responding to Challenging Situations" on pages 235–241 and share the information learned.

◀ SUMMARY

Summarize with the following points:

- Every family is different and is worthy of respect.

- Families are vital partners in promoting children's development and learning, and play an essential role in a *Creative Curriculum* classroom.

- Recognizing what beliefs and practices are behind a family's actions enables teachers to respond in respectful ways.

Resolving Differences Constructively

☐ Handout **5I**
☐ *Creative Curriculum*,
  pp. 231–240

This workshop may be used instead of or in addition to the previous workshop, "Dealing with Misunderstandings."

PREPARATION

Duplicate the handout.

INTRODUCTION

Introduce the workshop:

- Some differences are hard to reconcile because they conflict with your program's philosophy and your own strong beliefs. Spanking may be one example.

- *The Creative Curriculum* outlines a four-step process for helping you resolve these kinds of differences constructively.

- The purpose of this activity is to give you an opportunity to practice resolving a conflict using this process.

ACTIVITY

Distribute handout 5I and note each step at the top of the page. Have participants read pages 239–240. Then lead a brief discussion about each step.

Have participants work in pairs and give the following instructions:

- Determine who will be the parent and who will be the teacher.

- Read one of the scenarios and assume your respective role.

- Use the suggested steps to resolve the difference.

- Choose a different scenario and switch roles.

Invite comments and questions.

■ SUMMARY

Summarize with the following statements:

- Some differences can be resolved through compromise while others must be addressed directly.

- Listen to parents, validate their concerns and wishes, explain how you will address them, and assure them that you will follow-up with them on the issue.

- In doing so, you can gain their trust and respect without violating any values, goals, or principles of your program.

Gaining Self-Awareness

How did you become aware of your personal identity—nationality, culture, and ethnicity?

What early messages did you receive about other groups?

How did you define a "family" when you were growing up? Has your definition changed today?

What messages did you receive about your family's socio-economic status?

Were girls treated differently from boys in your family? What do you think your family's expectations were for you?

How and when were you encouraged to express your ideas and feelings?

Was it acceptable to be noisy and active in your home, or were children expected to be seen and not heard?

How was discipline handled?

Was independence encouraged?

How Well Do You Know Your Families?

Family's Name	Something Special I Know About This Family	How I Can Use This Information to Build a Relationship and Support Children's Learning

©2004 Teaching Strategies, Inc., PO Box 42243, Washington, DC 20015, www.TeachingStrategies.com

Appreciating Differences in Families

● **Structure**

● **Personality and temperament**

● **Life experiences**

● **Culture**

Conveying Positive Messages to Families

Messages	What I Currently Do	What I Want to Try
We want you to feel welcome here.		
You and your child are part of our classroom community.		
We want you to know what your child is learning.		
We are interested in your ideas and suggestions.		
We want you to contribute to the preschool program.		

Communicating Effectively With Families

1. What has been your most successful means of communicating with families?

2. Why do you think it is effective?

3. What has been your biggest challenge when it comes to communicating with families?

4. How can those challenges be addressed?

Sharing the Curriculum With Others

Sharing the Curriculum With Others, continued

E

_____

_____

_____

_____

F

_____

_____

_____

G

_____

_____

_____

_____

H

_____

_____

_____

_____

Sharing the Curriculum With Others, continued

I

_____

_____

_____

_____

J

_____

_____

_____

_____

K

_____

_____

_____

_____

L

_____

_____

_____

_____

Involving Families in My Preschool Program

Family's Name	Ways in Which This Family Can Become Involved

Dealing With Misunderstandings

Miscommunication—Different Perspectives

Situation	The Teacher's View	The Family's View	A Partnership View
Sonya's teacher describes how pleased she is that Sonya has begun to speak up more in class and share her ideas. The parents say nothing when they leave the conference.	Talking in class is an important goal for all children. Initially, Sonya rarely spoke up in a group, so the change is an exciting development. She will learn more if she participates actively and puts her ideas into words to express what she knows.	Speaking up in a group means Sonya is boasting and we do not approve of this behavior. We want our daughter to be respectful and quiet so she can learn.	
After conducting a workshop on ways that parents can help their children learn at home, and providing written suggestions, teachers find that several parents do not follow through.	Parents who don't spend time on activities with their child at home just don't care very much about their success at school. The more families are involved, the better children will do in school.	It's the teacher's job to teach my child, not mine. I don't know how to do what the teacher is asking.	
After careful observations over time, a teacher is concerned that a child's language is delayed and suggests an evaluation. The parents fail to make an appointment with a specialist.	If a real problem exists, it should be identified as early as possible. Parents should want to get all the help they can get for their child.	In life, we must accept what we are given. Why interfere?	
Carlos's mother unzips his coat and hangs it in his cubby along with his mittens and boots. The teacher says, "Carlos, you can unzip and hang up his own coat, can't you? Tomorrow, show your Mom how you can do things for yourself."	Self-help skills and developing independence are important objectives for children. Carlos's mother is treating him like a baby.	Helping my child is one way I show him how much his family loves him. I want to care for him, especially just before I have to say good-bye for the day. There's plenty of time for him to learn to take care of himself.	

From *The Creative Curriculum® for Preschool*, 4th Edition.
©2004 Teaching Strategies, Inc., PO Box 42243, Washington, DC 20015, www.TeachingStrategies.com

Resolving Differences Constructively

Take the following steps to resolve differences constructively.

1. Seek first to understand the family's position.

2. Validate the family's concerns and wishes.

3. Explain how your program addresses their concern.

4. Make a plan to check with one another to assess progress.

Scenario 1:

Juwan is a lively little boy, the youngest of three children in his family. Both of Juwan's parents work outside the home and have a long commute to work each day. Therefore, they leave home very early in the morning. When Juwan's parents return home in the evening, it is all they can do to get dinner prepared for the family and help the older children with homework. Unfortunately, when it is time for bed, Juwan is still going strong. His parents are convinced that napping at school is keeping him from going to bed at a reasonable time. They have requested that you keep Juwan awake when the other children are napping.

Scenario 2:

Kate's parents have established a rule that she gets no snacks unless she eats everything she is served at mealtime. In Kate's preschool program, snacks are offered midmorning, after rest time, and in the afternoon. Kate's parents have requested that you withhold snack from Kate at school unless she eats all of her breakfast and her lunch.

Scenario 3:

Setsuko recognizes all of the letters of the alphabet and her parents believe that she is ready for more advanced instruction in phonics. They have been using workbooks to teach her, but she isn't interested. They would like to send the workbooks to school and have you use them to help her.

NOTES

Blocks

WORKSHOPS

Key Points	Workshop	Materials	Time (minutes)
When children construct, create, and represent their experiences through block play, they grow and develop in all areas.	**How Block Play Promotes Development** (p. 180)	☐ *Creative Curriculum,* pp. 243–245, 256–259, 530 ☐ Wooden unit blocks ☐ Chart paper	30–60
Children are more likely to respect and use blocks constructively when the area is well-organized and equipped.	**Creating an Environment for Block Play** (p. 182)	☐ Handout **6A:** Creating an Effective Block Area ☐ *Creative Curriculum,* pp. 246–252 ☐ *Implementation Checklist*	20
Children benefit the most from their play with blocks when teachers talk with them to help them organize and express their ideas.	**How Teachers Support Children's Learning and Development** (p. 184)	☐ *Creative Curriculum,* pp. 261–266 ☐ *Creative Curriculum* video ☐ Handout **6B:** Supporting Children's Learning and Development	20
The Block Area is a natural setting for exploring mathematical concepts and developing process skills.	**Learning Mathematical Concepts in the Block Area** (p. 186)	☐ *Creative Curriculum,* pp. 134–139, 161–162 ☐ Wooden unit blocks	30

How Block Play Promotes Development

□ *Creative Curriculum,*
  pp. 243–245,
  256–259, 530
□ Wooden unit blocks
□ Chart paper

PREPARATION

If possible, conduct this workshop using the Block Area (and additional space as necessary) of a preschool classroom.

If you are using a training room rather than a classroom, put enough blocks on each table so participants can build with them. Or, prior to the workshop, ask each participant to bring 4–5 unit blocks to use collectively during the training.

INTRODUCTION

Introduce the workshop:

* Blocks are standard equipment in a *Creative Curriculum* classroom.

* When children construct, create, and represent their experiences through block play, they grow and develop in all areas (social/emotional, physical, cognitive, and language).

* Through this activity, you will have an opportunity to discover first-hand the value of block play so that you are better able to support children's development and learning and discuss this learning with family members.

ACTIVITY

Give the following instructions:

* Choose one person at your table to act as observer.

* Find a place where you can work comfortably with the blocks.

* Explore and build with the blocks for the next 10 minutes. You do not have to make anything in particular, just let your structure develop as you work.

* Observers are to record anything group members do or say that relates to concepts or skills discovered through blocks.

When time is up, refer participants to pages 256–259, "Stages of Block Play." Briefly discuss each stage of block play.

Have participants look at their own structures to find examples of the different stages—piling, bridging, enclosing, designing, and making elaborate structures.

Use the questions below to begin a discussion of the value of block play. Invite observers to share points from their observations. Record responses on chart paper.

- What did you enjoy most about using the blocks?

- Why do you think children enjoy blocks?

- What kinds of problems did you encounter while working with the blocks? Were you able to resolve them? How?

Building on this discussion, explain that block play enhances growth and development in all four areas: social/emotional, physical, cognitive, and language.

Assign one area of development to each table group. Have them generate a list of examples of how block play enhances development in this area.

Invite each group to share one or two examples from their discussions.

Have participants turn to "Goals and Objectives at a Glance" on page 530 and identify any objectives that could be addressed through block play not yet mentioned in the discussion.

Call attention to pages 244–245 where selected objectives in each developmental area are listed with examples of what children might do or say to demonstrate their abilities while in the Block Area.

SUMMARY

Summarize the discussion with the following points:

- Children enjoy blocks because of their feel, symmetry, and the open-ended play available. They enjoy the sense of mastery and control that block play provides.

- Blocks stimulate a broad range of opportunities for creative, imaginative, and constructive play, from arranging simple designs to building complex structures.

- Many skills and concepts are developed and enhanced through block play.

Creating an Environment for Block Play

□ Handout **6A**
□ *Creative Curriculum*,
   pp. 246–252
□ *Implementation
   Checklist*

PREPARATION

Duplicate the handout.

Gather a collection of photos that show good examples of the strategies for setting up and equipping the Block Area as described on pages 246–251. Make transparencies of the photos so they can be shared with the entire group at the workshop. Be prepared to discuss the value of each type of block including unit blocks, hollow blocks, and other types of blocks and construction materials.

INTRODUCTION

Introduce the workshop:

- The Block Area can be an exciting and stimulating interest area or it can be an area that teachers prefer to keep "closed."

- Many of the problems that occur in the Block Area can be alleviated through

    the proper arrangement of the area

    the materials you provide for the children

    the procedures you establish for using and caring for blocks

ACTIVITY

Distribute handout 6A. Ask participants to work in their groups to discuss some of the problems they or the children encounter during block play. Have them record their ideas in column 1.

Find out which group has the longest list of problems. Then invite each group to share one or two of the problems identified.

Possible responses:

Constructions are frequently toppled.

Children have difficulty sharing blocks and props.

Children have difficulty cleaning-up.

There is a lot of noise.

Boys dominate the area; girls avoid the area.

Children bring props from other areas into the Block Area.

Children become frustrated when they have to dismantle their constructions.

Children strew the blocks on the floor, but rarely build.

It is hard to accommodate children with disabilities.

Have participants discuss among themselves why a particular problem might be occurring and record their ideas in column 2. Next, ask them to list some possible solutions in column 3. Refer participants to pages 246–252 for solutions to the problems they have listed.

Allow time for the groups to report key points from their discussions.

Show the transparencies you have prepared. Discuss how the arrangement of blocks and related materials foster positive and productive play.

Have participants review the section on "Blocks" found on page 3 of the *Implementation Checklist* and ask any questions they may have.

Then ask participants to complete self-assessments of their Block Areas using the *Implementation Checklist* and identify any changes that need to be made. Ask them to be prepared to share their progress at the next workshop.

SUMMARY

Summarize with the following points:

- Many of the problems encountered in the Block Area can be alleviated through the arrangement of the area and the proper display of blocks and props

- When the Block Area is well organized, children are more likely to use it well and there will be many opportunities for supportive teacher/child interactions.

How Teachers Support Children's Learning and Development

□ *Creative Curriculum*,
   pp. 261–266
□ *Creative Curriculum*
   video
□ Handout **6B**

PREPARATION

Set up the TV/VCR and cue the *Creative Curriculum* video to the "Block Area" segment. Duplicate the handout.

INTRODUCTION

Introduce the workshop:

- Children benefit the most from their play with blocks when teachers help them to organize and express their ideas.

- The first step is to observe what children do so you can determine how best to respond to each child. Then use a variety of teaching strategies to support children's learning.

- In observing children in the Block Area, notice

    what stage of block building the child has achieved

    if the child is aware of different shapes and sizes and able to return blocks to their proper places

    whether the child talks about structures and responds to questions

    what props and materials the child uses in building

- These observations will help you determine when to intervene and what to say to support or extend children's learning.

- One of the most effective ways to reinforce children's block play is to talk to them about their structures.

ACTIVITY

Show "The Block Area" portion of the *Creative Curriculum* video. Have participants note the roles the teachers play in the video and how they interact with the children in the area. Lead a brief discussion after viewing.

Have participants read pages 261–266 for suggestions and examples of what teachers might say and do to support children in their block building efforts. Briefly discuss the reading.

Distribute handout 6B. Have them look at each picture and write a few examples of positive, constructive comments or suggestions they might make to the children pictured.

Invite participants to share their thoughts with the group.

SUMMARY

Summarize the workshop with the following points:

- As you observe and evaluate children's experiences with blocks, you gather information to decide whether they need more time to practice a particular stage or need help to move to the next stage.

- These observations are the basis for planning experiences and determining how best to respond to each child to facilitate further learning.

Learning Mathematical Concepts in the Block Area

☐ *Creative Curriculum,*
pp. 134–139, 161–162
☐ Wooden unit blocks

PREPARATION

If possible, conduct this workshop using the Block Area (and additional space as necessary) of a preschool classroom.

If you are using a training room rather than a classroom, put enough blocks on each table for all to explore. Or, prior to the workshop, ask each participant to bring 4–5 unit blocks to use collectively during the training.

INTRODUCTION

Introduce the workshop:

- The Block Area is a natural setting for exploring mathematical concepts and developing process skills.

- As children handle blocks, they learn about number, patterns and relationships, geometry and spatial sense, and measurement.

- They also develop problem-solving strategies as they plan, build, and assess their structures.

- The purposes of this workshop are to

    explore math concepts inherent in block play

    examine the use of process skills by engaging in a problem-solving experience similar to one children encounter in the Block Area

Note that unit blocks are scaled to a unit size: two squares equal one unit, two units equal one double unit, etc. Point out that there are other mathematical relationships that children discover that are less obvious.

ACTIVITY

Ask participants to find a partner and work on the following task:

- Explore with your unit blocks to see how many ways you can find to show mathematical concepts or relationships with blocks.

- List your ideas on paper.

Allow about 10 minutes for participants to work.

Refer participants to pages 134–139 and have them read about the components of mathematics. Afterwards, have them return to their lists to identify which components they addressed during their block explorations.

Invite participants to share their observations.

Make the following points:

- Everyday experiences with blocks offer children the opportunity to learn about each component of mathematics.

- While children discover many math concepts on their own, teachers can extend children's experiences by helping them identify and name many concepts they discover. For example, "Your building is as tall as the shelf. Those long blocks are holding up the short ones. All of your blocks are rectangles, but they're not all the same size."

Discuss how block play uses process skills, which help children learn many concepts in mathematics and other content areas. Have participants read about this on pages 161–162.

Form five groups. Give each group one of the following problems to solve using blocks:

- Build a ramp leading to a bridge.

- Find a way to make five steps leading into a building.

- Create a house with windows and a roof.

- Build an apartment house with an elevator.

- Make a map of your classroom or neighborhood using blocks.

Allow 10–15 minutes to complete the task. Note what participants say that illustrates a specific process skill being used.

Then, have each group choose a "curator" to explain its task to others, during a walk-about.

Lead a discussion about the problems groups were given and how they used process skills as they worked. Share any comments you noted through your observation of their work.

SUMMARY

Summarize the workshop:

- Unit blocks are standard equipment in a *Creative Curriculum* classroom.

- Blocks are an essential learning material in preschool classrooms. With them, children

    recreate the world around them

    learn many social skills as they work together

    learn many mathematic concepts

    develop language as they talk about their constructions and the building processes they are using

Creating an Effective Block Area

Problems With Blocks	Why This Might Be Happening	Possible Solutions

Supporting Children's Learning and Development

_____

_____

_____

_____

_____

_____

_____

_____

_____

_____

_____

_____

_____

Dramatic Play

WORKSHOPS

🔑 Key Points	⚙ Workshop	📋 Materials	🕐 Time (minutes)
Dramatic play is central to children's healthy development and learning.	**How Dramatic Play Promotes Development** (p. 192)	☐ *Creative Curriculum*, pp. 19–26, 46–58, 271–273, 530 ☐ Handout **7A:** Supporting Children's Development Through Dramatic Play	30
When the Dramatic Play Area is set up and equipped appropriately, it becomes a stage where children can enter and immediately take on a role and pretend.	**Creating an Environment for Dramatic Play** (p. 194)	☐ Handout **7B:** Role-Play Cards ☐ Assorted props ☐ *Creative Curriculum*, pp. 274–276 ☐ *Implementation Checklist*	30
Teachers support children in extending their ideas by changing props and setting to incorporate new experiences and interests of children.	**Creating New Settings for Dramatic Play** (p. 198)	☐ Chart paper, assorted colored markers ☐ *Creative Curriculum*, pp. 276–279	20
The ability to engage in and sustain imaginative play is central to children's learning and development. Teachers may need to take an active role in teaching the skills to make believe.	**How Teachers Support Children's Learning and Development** (p. 202)	☐ *Creative Curriculum*, pp. 282–284, 287–290 ☐ *Creative Curriculum* video ☐ Handout **7C:** Levels of Ability in Socio-Dramatic Play—Scenario ☐ Handout **7D:** Levels of Ability in Socio-Dramatic Play—Worksheet	40

How Dramatic Play Promotes Development

☐ *Creative Curriculum*,
pp. 19–26, 46–58,
271–273, 530
☐ Handout **7A**

PREPARATION

Duplicate the handout.

INTRODUCTION

Introduce the workshop:

- When children engage in dramatic play, they deepen their understanding of the world and develop skills that will serve them throughout their lives.

- For this reason, every *Creative Curriculum* classroom includes a Dramatic Play Area.

- We'll begin by examining the ways in which dramatic play supports social/emotional, physical, cognitive, and language development.

ACTIVITY

Have participants form small groups. Refer them to handout 7A.

Ask each group to choose one of the four scenarios on the handout and prepare a response to present to the whole group. Allow ten to fifteen minutes to complete the task.

Have each group share its response.

Ask participants to turn to pages 272–273 and read "Connecting Dramatic Play with Curriculum Objectives." Discuss some of the examples of what children might do or say in the Dramatic Play Area that would indicate their progress on selected objectives.

SUMMARY

Summarize the workshop:

- The "Goals and Objectives at a Glance" (page 530) will help you identify what children are learning as they participate in dramatic play.

- The *Developmental Continuum* (pages 46–58) helps you pinpoint what each child is able to do so you can support the child in moving to the next step.

NOTES

Creating an Environment for Dramatic Play

☐ Handout **7B**
☐ Assorted props
☐ *Creative Curriculum*,
   pp. 274–276
☐ *Implementation
   Checklist*

◖ PREPARATION

Duplicate handout 7B, so that each pair of "players" has a copy of one of the role-plays. The role-play may be done in small groups of six to eight participants or with the entire group. Gather the necessary props for each set of players as described on the Role Play cards.

Provide assorted props such as bright or shiny fabric, netting, old steering wheel, cordless hair dryer or shaver, plastic tubing or hose, tote bag, briefcase, hats, gauze, large white shirt, etc.

The last section of this workshop involves participants in using the *Implementation Checklist* to assess their classrooms' Dramatic Play Areas. If you do the next workshop "Creating New Settings for Dramatic Play" immediately following this workshop, you may choose to use the *Implementation Checklist* immediately following that workshop rather than as part of this workshop.

◖ INTRODUCTION

Explain that the Dramatic Play Area is an important part of any preschool classroom. It is of particular importance today because of concern that many children are not learning to pretend and imagine because of a lack of experience and encouragement.

◖ ACTIVITY

Ask for two volunteers to role-play a brief scene. Give the volunteers the role-play card and ask them to read the directions and act out the role without talking.

Ask the remaining group members to guess what is happening.

Allow about two minutes for the role-play. Then without commenting, place the props in front of the "players." Allow the role-play to continue until the participants have guessed what is happening.

Ask:

- Was it hard to play the role without props? Why?

- How did the props help?

- What other props might have been fun to use?

Summarize the discussion:

- Dramatic play can be stimulated by the props and materials available to children.

- When interesting and relevant props are available, dramatic play scenes usually last longer.

Next, give each group 3–4 assorted props. Give the following instructions:

- Choose someone to be a recorder.

- Discuss the props, identifying ways in which children might use each.

- Identify any dramatic play themes each prop might stimulate.

Allow about 10 minutes for the activity. Invite the groups to share their ideas about one or two of the props discussed and any observations they made.

Make the following points:

- Realistic props inspire children to act out familiar roles and experiences.

- The more varied and creative the props, the more creative and involved dramatic play is likely to become.

Refer participants to the illustration of the Dramatic Play Area on page 274. Lead a discussion about the location and arrangement of the area as well as the selection and display of materials. Ask:

- Where is the Dramatic Play Area likely to be located?

- What do you notice about the Dramatic Play Area pictured here?

Make sure the following points are addressed:

- Props must be clean, safe, and in good repair.

- Consider the background and developmental abilities of the children in your classroom when selecting props.

  Begin with familiar props and play themes.

  Younger children or those at the beginning stage of dramatic play are likely to rely on more realistic props.

  Older children who are better able to rely on their imaginations in their use of props will need more open-ended materials.

  Consider ways in which the environment and props may be adapted or modified to accommodate children with special needs.

- Provide sufficient quantities of props (e.g., two or three dolls, handbags, pocketbooks, etc.); **but**, remember: too many props can be overwhelming to children and make clean-up difficult.

- Convey the message, "This is just like my home" to children in your classroom by adding props and other materials that reflect their home experiences, culture, and heritage.

- Include props that are traditionally used by both men and women.

- Arrange props in a logical fashion. This enables children to make clear choices, work independently, and spend more time in creative play.

- Offer dramatic play experiences beyond the housekeeping roles.

- Incorporate content-related materials(language/literacy, mathematics, science, social studies, the arts, and technology) into the area. Be prepared to explain how you have done so to others. For example, make sure that literacy-related props are part of any setting, e.g., writing supplies, books, magazines.

Share creative ways of organizing and displaying props and materials in the Dramatic Play Area. Invite participants to share their ideas.

Next, refer participants to the section on "Dramatic Play" on page 4 of the *Implementation Checklist*. Review the items. Then have participants complete self-assessments of their Dramatic Play Areas.

Have participants identify any changes they need or wish to make to their Dramatic Play Areas. Invite them to come to the next workshop prepared to share their progress and/or successes.

◀ SUMMARY

Summarize the workshop:

- When the Dramatic Play Area is set up and equipped appropriately, it becomes a stage where children can enter and immediately take on a role and pretend.

- An attractive and orderly Dramatic Play Area conveys the message that this is a special place to be and the items here are to be taken care of and valued.

Creating New Settings for Dramatic Play

☐ Chart paper, assorted colored markers
☐ *Creative Curriculum*, pp. 276–279

PREPARATION

Identify enough dramatic play topics for the number of table groups you have. Participants will work in small groups so you will need one sheet of chart paper for each group. Write the topic at the top of each piece of chart paper using a different colored marker for each. Some suggested topics are: car care center, construction/builder, flower shop, and hair salon.

INTRODUCTION

Introduce the workshop:

- While home-related props and furniture remain in the Dramatic Play Area throughout the year, teachers can extend children's play by incorporating new settings.

- These new settings allow children to recreate their own life experiences and explore new ideas and concepts they are learning.

- The purposes of this workshop are to discuss when and how to introduce new settings for dramatic play and to identify props children might use in play settings that frequently emerge in an early childhood classroom.

Ask:

- When is it appropriate to introduce a new setting into the Dramatic Play Area?

  Possible responses:

  Children seem bored with the Dramatic Play Area; constructive or imaginative play is minimal.

  Children avoid the area.

  Children have had an intriguing or stimulating experience.

  To relate play in this area to a study topic.

- How do you identify play topics to introduce to the children?

  Possible responses:

  You consider any common experiences of the children in your program.

  You hear children talking about a particular experience they've had (e.g., going to the doctor or dentist, getting new shoes).

  Children ask questions about a topic or event.

  You observe children's initial play attempts centered on a particular topic.

- How do you introduce children to a new play topic and related props?

  Possible responses:

  Schedule a field trip about a topic that seems to be of interest. Display pictures from the field trip and discuss them to help children recall what they saw and did.

  Invite experts to the classroom to talk to the children and conduct demonstrations about a topic.

  Read stories and display posters about a topic. Ask children to talk about and describe their personal experiences with the topic.

  Conduct a class meeting to have children generate a list of desired props and materials. Discuss how they might use them.

Summarize the discussion:

- Dramatic play should extend well beyond housekeeping.

- By observing children, teachers are able to identify new topics of play for the Dramatic Play area.

- Involving children in the process of selecting props related to a particular topic helps to ensure more effective use of those props; and, it gives children the sense that they are directing their own learning.

ACTIVITY

Introduce the activity:

- While topics for dramatic play vary with each new group of children, some come up often enough to merit keeping a box of props in storage.

- This activity is designed to get you thinking about the numerous and varied props related to common topics of play.

Refer participants to pages 276–279 to learn more about various prop boxes.

Give each group a piece of chart paper with a colored marker that corresponds to the heading at the top of the chart. Explain that they will be doing "carousel brainstorming." Describe the process:

- Each group will choose a recorder.

- Each group will have one minute to brainstorm a list of props related to the topic of play recorded at the top of your chart.

- When time is up, rotate the charts clockwise, but keep your original marker.

- You will have a minute to read your new list.

- After I say "go" you may add to the list.

After each group has had a chance to add new ideas for each prop box, return the chart to the original group. Review the charts and post them on the wall; or, recommend that someone from each group type up the list and duplicate it for all participants.

SUMMARY

Summarize the workshop:

- The Dramatic Play Area is the ideal place for children to deepen their understanding of the world as they recreate various life experiences.

- Creating new settings sets the stage for children to learn and explore content as they engage in dramatic play.

NOTES

How Teachers Support Children's Learning and Development

□ *Creative Curriculum,*
   pp. 282–284, 287–290
□ *Creative Curriculum*
   video
□ Handout **7C**
□ Handout **7D**

PREPARATION

Set up the TV/VCR and cue the *Creative Curriculum* video to the "Dramatic Play" segment. Duplicate the handouts.

INTRODUCTION

Introduce the workshop:

- Teachers today are finding that young children do not necessarily engage in dramatic play on an advanced level.

- Because the ability to engage in and sustain imaginative play has so much value in promoting children's development and learning, teachers need to take an active role in teaching the skills to make-believe.

Explain that this workshop has two purposes:

- to introduce and discuss the six skills children need to pretend at a high level

- to consider ways teachers can support and enhance these skills

ACTIVITY

Ask participants to read about the six skills outlined on pages 282–284 and offer clarification about any, if necessary.

Show the "Dramatic Play" segment of the *Creative Curriculum* video. Have participants pay particular attention to the various roles of the teachers. Lead a brief discussion about those roles.

Distribute handouts 7C and 7D. Give the following instructions:

- Read handout 7C. Pick one of the children named in the handout and determine the level of play for that child in relation to each of the six skills.

- Write specific examples of what the child did or said in the appropriate box on handout 7D.

Invite participants to share their results.

Next, have participants read pages 287–290. Have them determine how they might best support Leo, Crystal, and Alexa in their dramatic play.

◀ SUMMARY

Summarize the discussion:

- Knowing these six skills gives you a framework for observing children's play and determining the type of intervention that will be most effective for each child.

- Your ongoing observations will help you make decisions about when it is appropriate to intervene and how to extend learning.

- Teachers support children's play by talking and asking questions about what children are doing, making suggestions to extend their play, participating in play, and by introducing new props.

Supporting Children's Development Through Dramatic Play

1. The mother of a child in your class is going to have a baby. The issue is how that will effect the child in your class. Review the sections on social/emotional development found on pages 18–19 and 23–25 in *The Creative Curriculum*. Describe the range of behaviors this child might exhibit. How could you use the Dramatic Play Area to help this child work through any feelings/issues resulting from this situation?

2. You have been given the task of equipping the Dramatic Play Area with props that will support and enhance the physical development of children ages 3–5. Review the sections on physical development found on pages 20 and 23–25. Describe what you could include in the area and why.

3. You have been challenged by some parents who believe that dramatic play is nothing more than "messing about." Read the sections on cognitive development found on pages 21 and 24–26 in *The Creative Curriculum*. Prepare a response that reflects how dramatic play supports cognitive development.

4. Because of the increased emphasis on language and literacy, your director/principal has insisted that you spend more time "teaching" children about language, reading, and writing. Read the sections on language development found on pages 22 and 24–26 in *The Creative Curriculum* and prepare a response that describes how children learn language and literacy in the Dramatic Play Area.

Role-Play Cards

Role-Play #1

Player A.   You are trying to return a gift to a department store. The salesclerk won't take it back because you have no receipt. You explain again it was a gift, but the salesclerk refuses.

Player B.   You are a salesclerk in a busy department store. You are in a bad mood today. Someone is trying to return a gift without a sales receipt. You won't let him/her.

Props to Add:

- Wrapped box with a gift card
- Sales check
- Pencil
- Telephone
- Pad of paper

Role-Play #2

Player A.   You are riding the bus to your new job for the first time. You don't know where to get off. You try to ask the bus driver for help.

Player B.   You are a bus driver. A passenger who is lost is trying to find out which stop is nearest to her new job. You try to help her.

Props to Add:

- Maps
- Driver's hat
- Watch
- Shopping bag

Levels of Ability in Socio-Dramatic Play—Scenario

Crystal, Leo, and Alexa enter the Dramatic Play Area and head straight for the dress-up clothes. Leo pulls out the police officer uniform and begins to get dressed. Crystal takes out a hat, a piece of colorful fabric, a pair of high heel shoes, and a handbag, then sets them aside in a neat pile. Alexa takes out a dress and begins to put it on. The play continues as follows:

Leo:	"I've got to get dressed for work. What are you going to do?"
Crystal:	"I'm laying out the clothes I'm going to wear to work."
Crystal:	Want me to cook you something to eat before you go to work?" *(Leo nods his head yes. Crystal pretends to crack eggs, mix them in a bowl, and cook them on the stove.)*
Leo:	"Is the food ready yet? I have to hurry up and get to work."
Crystal:	"It will be ready in five minutes."
Leo:	"Never mind. I have to get to the police station." *(Leo grabs a set of keys, starts an imaginary car, and making a circular motion with his hands proceeds to "patrol" the other areas of the classroom. You can occasionally hear a siren.)*
Crystal:	"Want something to eat Alexa?"
Alexa:	*(Shakes her head, no. She moves to the baby doll lying in the crib, picks her up, lays her on her shoulder, and pats her back.)* "Don't cry. It will be OK."
Crystal:	*(Pretends to eat breakfast and then puts the dishes in the sink. She begins getting dressed by draping the fabric around her shoulders.)*
Alexa:	*(Searches for the baby's bottle. Finding it, she sits in the rocking chair and begins to feed the baby.)* "That's what was wrong, huh? You were just hungry."
Leo:	*(Drives to the Block Area, picks up a small block, and holds it to his ear.)* "Ring, ring. Ring, ring. Ring, ring."
Leo:	*(When Crystal doesn't notice Leo, he yells.)* "Hey, Crystal, pick up the phone!"
Crystal:	*(At Leo's urging, Crystal picks up the telephone.)* "Hello. Is that you Leo?"
Leo:	"Yeah. It's me. I'm hungry now!"
Crystal:	"There's no more food. I ate it all. Besides, I'm going to work now."
Leo:	"Want to meet me for lunch at the pizza place?"
Crystal:	"OK, I'll be looking for you. Bye."
Leo:	"Bye." *(Leo and Crystal pretend they meet at the food court—the table in the Dramatic Play Area.)*
Alexa:	*(Lays the baby back in the crib and leaves the area.)*

Levels of Ability in Socio-Dramatic Play—Worksheet

Criteria	Beginning Level	Advanced Level

ROLE-PLAY.
 	
  Role chosen
 	
  How child plays role		

USE OR PROPS
 	
  Type of prop needed
 	
  How child uses prop		

MAKE-BELIEVE		
LENGTH OF TIME		
INTERACTION		
VERBAL COMMUNICATION		

©2004 Teaching Strategies, Inc., PO Box 42243, Washington, DC 20015, www.TeachingStrategies.com

Toys and Games

WORKSHOPS

 Key Points	 Workshop	 Materials	Time (minutes)
When children explore, experiment, discover, and create with toys and games, their problem–solving skills and creativity are enhanced as well as every area of development.	**How Playing With Toys and Games Promotes Development** (p. 210)	☐ *Creative Curriculum* video ☐ *Creative Curriculum,* pp. 161–162, 296–297, 530 ☐ Handout **8A:** Sandola Plants ☐ Collectibles (*Creative Curriculum,* p. 300)	30–45
The selection of materials and their organization will influence whether children choose the area and how they use and care for the materials.	**Creating an Environment for Toys and Games** (p. 212)	☐ Handout **8B:** Evaluating Toys and Games ☐ *Implementation Checklist* ☐ *Creative Curriculum,* pp. 299–303	60
Teachers should be purposeful in observing children's use of toys and games and in deciding when and how to support learning.	**The Teacher's Role in the Toys and Games Area** (p. 216)	☐ Handout **8C:** Scaffolding—What Does It Look Like? ☐ Handout **8D:** Interacting With Children in the Toys and Games Area—The Teacher's Role ☐ Handout **8E:** Interacting With Children in the Toys and Games Area—The Player's Role ☐ *Creative Curriculum,* pp. 178, 306–307, 310 ☐ An assortment of toys and games	45–60

How Playing With Toys and Games Promotes Development

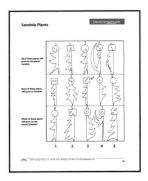

☐ *Creative Curriculum* video
☐ *Creative Curriculum*, pp. 161–162, 296–297, 530
☐ Handout **8A**
☐ Collectibles (*Creative Curriculum*, p. 300)

PREPARATION

Duplicate the handout. Prepare a set of collectibles for each table. Cue the video to the "Table Toys" section.

INTRODUCTION

Introduce the workshop:

- Playing with toys and games, such as manipulatives, puzzles, collectibles, matching games, and games with rules, offers children many learning opportunities.

- In this workshop, you will have an opportunity to think about the kinds of learning that can take place in this area.

ACTIVITY

Refer participants to handout 8A and give the following instructions:

- Review the first two rows to figure out which plants in the bottom row will grow on the planet Sandola.

- When you've figured it out, give me a quiet "thumbs up."

Allow a few minutes for participants to solve the problem. Then ask:

- "Who would like to explain an answer, and how you decided?"

  Possible response: *The answer is numbers 2 and 4 since they have the same three characteristics as all of the plants on the first line:*

   There is something inside the head of each plant.

   There is something on the top of their heads.

   The body of each plant is facing left.

If participants seem particularly challenged, ask:

- What characteristics do the plants in row 1 have in common?

- Which of the plants in row 3 have the same characteristics as the plants in row 1?"

Ask:

- What problem solving and thinking skills did you use in this activity?

- When children work with the materials in the Toys and Games Area, can you provide opportunities for children to develop these skills, and many others?

Place a set of collectibles on each table. Ask each participant to select and examine one object from the set. Have them do the following:

- Look at your object carefully and identify all of its characteristics.

- Find one person who has an object that is like yours in one way (e.g., color).

- Next, choose a different characteristic (e.g., shape instead of color) and find two people who have objects that are like yours in that way, and form a group of three objects.

- Now, see how many ways you can come up with to make new groups with your objects.

Summarize the activity with the following points:

- To complete the tasks, you had to identify similarities and differences and you had to classify or group objects accordingly.

- These are important cognitive skills that children develop and refine when they play with collectibles and other toys and games.

Have participants continue to explore all the collectible items on their tables to see what else they can learn about them, and discover various ways they might use or create with them.

Have participants turn to "Goals and Objectives at a Glance" on page 530 and identify all objectives that might be addressed while children use collectibles. Invite them to share their thoughts.

Refer participants to the examples of how children might demonstrate their growing abilities in relation to the selected objectives on pages 296–297.

Refer participants to pages 161–162. Ask them to read about the process skills discussed and identify how many are used when children work with toys and games.

Show the "Table Toys" segment of the *Creative Curriculum* video and briefly discuss key points.

SUMMARY

Summarize the workshop:

- The Toys and Games Area provides children with many opportunities to cultivate and refine skills in every area of development.

- As children explore, and experiment with toys and games, they use and refine process skills that are related to concepts in math, science, social studies, and literacy.

WORKSHOP

Creating an Environment for Toys and Games

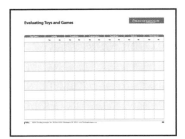

☐ Handout **8B**
☐ *Implementation Checklist*
☐ *Creative Curriculum,* pp. 299–303

PREPARATION

Prior to the workshop, ask participants to read about the four categories of toys and games found on pages 299–300. Ask each of them to bring one toy from each category to share at the workshop. Remind them to label each of their materials with their names or their center's names.

Collect all toys and games from the participants. Mix them up and haphazardly display them or stack them atop a table or shelf in the training room.

If you wish, assemble a collection of "Toys to Avoid" as described on page 302 and add these to the toys and games participants will evaluate.

Duplicate the handout.

INTRODUCTION

Introduce the workshop with the following points:

- The Toys and Games Area offers children a place to engage in a quiet activity alone, with a friend or adult, or a small group.

- It contains an assortment of manipulatives, puzzles, collectibles, and other games.

- The location of the area, the materials you select to include, and the way teachers organize and display them will influence children's decision to use the area and how to care for the materials.

- This workshop will focus on how to create a Toys and Games Area that is enticing to children and maximizes learning.

ACTIVITY

Ask the groups to make lists of favorite toys and games from their childhoods and share why they enjoyed them. You might start by sharing your favorite toy.

Invite each group to summarize points from its discussions.

Next, have the groups generate a list of their children's favorite toys and tell why they think children are attracted to these toys.

Discuss the similarities or differences between the two lists.

Make the following points:

- Children, like you, have different interests and function at different ability levels.

- For this reason, it is important that you have an assortment of toys and games that appeals to a range of children's interests and complexity. (Mention the four categories; point out the chart on page 302 that relates to the levels of complexity of materials.)

- Some toys facilitate creative and imaginative play, while others can have a harmful effect on children's development. (Refer to "Toys and Games to Avoid" on page 302.)

Have participants retrieve the toys and games they brought to the workshop from the area where you displayed them.

Lead a discussion about their experiences in finding their materials. Ask:

- How did you feel when you were trying to find your materials?

- What process or strategies did you use to find your things?

- How were you certain that you had the materials that belonged to you?

Make the following points:

- When materials in the Toys and Games Area are haphazardly strewn about or stacked in random piles, children get frustrated trying to find what they want or need; it is likely that the area will go unused.

- Children will be drawn to the area if it is attractive and uncluttered, and if systems are in place for them to find what they want easily.

Discuss the guidelines for displaying toys and games. Show various ways for organizing and storing materials in the area (see page 303). Invite participants to share any similar ideas.

Refer participants to page 301 and review the criteria for selecting materials for the Toys and Games Area.

Have participants review handout 8B. If you have brought some "Toys to Avoid," distribute them now and give the following instructions:

- You and a partner will critique 8–10 of the toys and games at your table. Try to choose some from each of the four categories described in the Curriculum. The toys you select do not have to be the ones you brought to the workshop.

- In column 1 of your handout, write the name or description of each toy or game you evaluate.

- Determine if the material meets each of the criteria listed on the top row of the handout and check the appropriate box. Write clarifying comments in the last column.

- You will have approximately 15 minutes to complete this task.

Invite participants to share any observations they made about certain materials during this exercise.

To emphasize the value and flexibility of open-ended toys and collectibles, have participants choose one that they've brought. Ask participants to brainstorm ways they could

- adapt it to become a "self-correcting, structured" toy

- use the toy with children at various skill levels

- adapt a material for a child with a specific disability

Invite participants to share their ideas.

Refer participants to the "Toys and Games" section of the *Implementation Checklist* (page 5). Review the items. Then have participants complete self-assessments of their Toys and Games Areas.

Have participants identify any changes they need or wish to make to their Toys and Games Areas. Ask them to come to the next workshop prepared to share their progress and successes.

SUMMARY

Summarize the workshop:

- As you make plans to purchase or select materials for the Toys and Games Area, consider variety and complexity as well as safety, durability, and price. Also, select toys that do not convey stereotypes.

- Be mindful of the ways in which you display and store toys and games since this is key to how children will use these materials, learn from them, and take care of them.

NOTES

The Teacher's Role in the Toys and Games Area

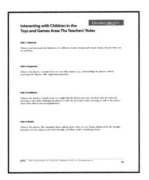

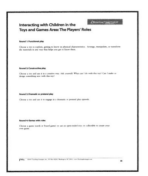

☐ Handout **8C**
☐ Handout **8D**
☐ Handout **8E**
☐ *Creative Curriculum,*
   pp. 178, 306–307, 310
☐ An assortment of toys
   and games

PREPARATION

Before the workshop, place an assortment of toys and games on each table.

INTRODUCTION

Introduce the topic by having participants read handout 8C. Invite participants to share their observations about the role the teacher played.

Possible comments:

> *The teacher observed (materials Tyrone chose, his independent problem-solving efforts).*
>
> *The teacher followed the child's lead.*
>
> *The teacher was patient, not quick to intervene or tell Tyrone how to work the puzzle.*
>
> *The teacher created an accepting environment where he could make a mistake.*
>
> *The teacher reinforced what the child was doing.*
>
> *The teacher asked open-ended questions to extend thinking and problem solving.*

Make the following points:

- By their very nature, materials in the Toys and Games Area provide excellent opportunities for children to build and refine many skills such as math (counting, seriation, matching, patterning, and classification) and problem-solving.

- However, materials alone won't make this happen. Teachers must be intentional about observing how children use materials in the area and then make thoughtful decisions about when and how to become involved in children's play.

Refer participants to page 310 for another example of how a teacher interacts with children in the Toys and Games Area.

- During this workshop, you will

  examine the ways in which children approach toys and games

  explore the range of roles the teacher plays in this area

  consider the kinds of questions that promote problem-solving skills

Review the four ways in which children approach toys and games or have participants read about them on pages 306–307. Name the four ways:

- functional play

- constructive play

- dramatic or pretend play

- games with rules

ACTIVITY

Distribute handout 8D to four participants in each group. Distribute the companion handout 8E to the others at each table.

Give the following instructions:

- Four of you will assume one of the teacher roles—observer, supporter, facilitator, model—on handout 8D. The rest of each group will be "players." The observer will record the interactions between the other three "teachers" and the "players."

- There will be four rounds of play described on handout 8E, each focusing on a different way children approach or play with toys and games.

- Read only the directions for your role or the designated round of play.

- When each round begins, "players" select a toy. The "teachers" will observe what you are doing and then interact with you, according to the roles they have been assigned. For example, during round 1, all of the "players" will be engaged in functional play while three of the teachers interact according to their roles.

- Each round will last approximately five minutes.

Note:
You may choose to have "teachers" and "players" switch roles if you wish to give each participant an opportunity to play the role of the teacher. You may also have the teachers switch roles to practice more than one way of interacting with children.

After the end of four rounds of play, lead a discussion about the role of each teacher. Invite the observers and others to share examples of what was said or done to support, facilitate, or model during each round.

Make the following points:

- Everyday life in the classroom requires different levels of teacher involvement.

- Like a scaffold, a teacher supports a child's learning using a range or combination of approaches.

Continue with a discussion on the value of asking children questions. Discuss the difference between open-ended and closed questions. Then make the following points:

- Because open-ended questions have many right answers, children have less fear of being wrong and are more likely to take risks in their thinking.

- Open-ended questions build and strengthen children's problem-solving skills.

- Open-ended questions encourage children to think creatively (the ability to come up with many and varied ideas, to see many possibilities, or to view objects and situations in new ways).

- Open-ended questions encourage children to think critically or logically (the ability to break a problem or an idea into parts and analyze them; sorting, classifying, and comparing are part of this process).

- Open-ended questions enhance children's language skills—they require children to express themselves and their ideas in phrases or sentences.

Refer participants to page 178 and have them read the different types of open-ended questions teachers can ask children to extend children's thinking.

Ask participants to imagine children using the toys or games on their tables. Have them generate at least one question for each type of open-ended question listed on page 178. Invite participants to share their sample questions.

SUMMARY

Summarize the workshop with the following points:

- Children need high-quality toys and games so they can experiment, explore, discover, and create.

- They also need adults who value the work they are doing in this area and support their learning in thoughtful ways.

Sandola Plants

All of these plants will grow on the planet Sandola

None of these plants will grow on Sandola

Which of these plants will grow on the planet Sandola?

1   **2**   **3**   **4**   **5**

Evaluating Toys and Games

Toy/Game	Safety		Durability		Construction		Flexibility		Values		Comments	
	Yes	No	Yes	No	Yes	No	Yes	No	Yes	No	Yes	No

Teaching Strategies. ©2004 Teaching Strategies, Inc., PO Box 42243, Washington, DC 20015, www.TeachingStrategies.com

Scaffolding—What Does It Look Like?

Scenario:

Tyrone is a 4-year-old in Ms. Tory's preschool class. Ms. Tory has noticed that Tyrone often chooses to work in the Toys and Games Area during choice time. She decides to observe Tyrone in this area to see if the existing materials and experiences are challenging enough for him.

Today, Tyrone chooses interlocking cubes and takes them to the table to work near Crystal. He puts the cubes together and takes them apart several times. Next, Tyrone returns the cubes to the shelf, selects a floor puzzle of the circus, and takes it to an open area on a nearby rug. Ms. Tory's interest is piqued, since Tyrone does not choose to work with puzzles very often.

Tyrone dumps the puzzles pieces on the floor and turns them right side up, spreading them out on the rug. After all the pieces are laid out, he begins the task of putting the pieces together. After five minutes, Ms. Tory notes that Tyrone has only put together three or four pieces (not even half) of the puzzle.

Ms. Tory considers that perhaps Tyrone's skills are at a novice level and the puzzle is too difficult. However, having observed Tyrone in other areas, she realizes that this one observation might not be representative of Tyrone's full potential. She also believes that if Tyrone were to work with Crystal, who is more experienced at doing puzzles, the two of them might be able to complete the entire puzzle. Following Crystal's cues, he would also learn how to approach the task with skill.

Since Crystal has been working rather deliberately with a new manipulative to create quite an elaborate structure, Ms. Tory decides not to interrupt her. Instead she decides to offer some helpful guidance herself. The interaction between Tyrone and Ms. Tory might go something like this:

Tyrone:	I can't make this one fit. *(Tries to insert a piece in the wrong place.)*
Ms. Tory:	Which piece might go down there? *(She points to the bottom of the puzzle.)*
Tyrone:	His shoes. *(Meaning a clown's shoes. He looks for a piece similar to the shoe, tries it, but it does not fit.)*
Ms. Tory:	Can you find a piece that looks like this? *(She runs her finger along the straight edge of the puzzle piece.)*
Tyrone:	That black one. *(He points to a piece and then picks it up.)*

Scaffolding—What Does It Look Like? continued

Ms. Tory: Is the clown's shoe black? *(She asks while pointing to another piece of the puzzle and the scene on the lid of the box.)*

Tyrone: *(Tyrone shakes his head yes. He tries that piece and it fits.)*

Ms. Tory: You got it!

Tyrone: *(Picks up another piece of the clown's shoe and tries it. He looks at Ms. Tory when it doesn't easily fit.)*

Ms. Tory: Try turning it a little bit. *(Demonstrates a twisting motion with another piece.)*

Tyrone: It worked! *(Tyrone proceeds to add pieces to the puzzle, saying to himself when challenged, "Find a red piece that matches," or "Turn it a little.")*

©2004 Teaching Strategies, Inc., PO Box 42243, Washington, DC 20015, www.TeachingStrategies.com

8C

Interacting With Children in the Toys and Games Area—The Teacher's Role

Role 1: Observer

Observe and document the behaviors of a different teacher during each round of play. Record what you see and hear.

Role 2: Supporter

Observe the players. Consider how you can offer support (e.g., acknowledge the players' efforts, encourage the players, offer supporting materials).

Role 3: Facilitator

Observe the players. Consider how you might help the players get more involved with the materials, introduce a new skill, challenge the players to take the next step in their learning, or talk to the players about their efforts and accomplishments.

Role 4: Model

Observe the players. Play alongside them, talking about what you are doing, talking about the thought processes you are using as you work through a problem, and/or wondering aloud.

Interacting With Children in the Toys and Games Area—The Player's Role

Round 1: Functional play

Choose a toy to explore, getting to know its physical characteristics. Arrange, manipulate, or transform the materials in any way that helps you get to know them.

Round 2: Constructive play

Choose a toy and use it in a creative way. Ask yourself: What can I do with this toy? Can I make or design something new with this toy?

Round 3: Dramatic or pretend play

Choose a toy and use it to engage in a dramatic or pretend play episode.

Round 4: Games with rules

Choose a game (cards or board game) or use an open-ended toys or collectible to create your own game.

NOTES

Art

WORKSHOPS

Key Points	Workshop	Materials	Time (minutes)
Creative art is a language through which children express what they know and how they feel.	**How Art Experiences Promote Development** (p. 228)	☐ Handout **9A:** My Early Art Experiences ☐ Handout **9B:** Is This Really Art? ☐ Handout **9C:** Making a House ☐ Chart paper, marker, art materials and supplies ☐ *Creative Curriculum*, pp. 160–161, 530	30–45
The organization of the Art Area is directly related to its effectiveness in inspiring children's creativity and self-expression.	**Creating an Environment for Art** (p. 230)	☐ Transparency **9D:** Taking a Closer Look at Your Art Area ☐ Samples of children's art work ☐ *Creative Curriculum*, pp. 63, 320–323, 332–333 ☐ *Implementation Checklist* ☐ Chart paper, markers	30
The ways in which teachers respond to children in the Art Area contributes to children's enjoyment and appreciation of art and their developing sense of competence.	**The Teacher's Role in the Art Area** (p. 232)	☐ *Creative Curriculum* video ☐ Samples of children's artwork ☐ Handout **9E:** Talking With Children About Their Art ☐ *Creative Curriculum*, pp. 337–340	90
By identifying what challenges some children in art, teachers can find ways to help all children experience success in the Art Area.	**Including All Children in Art Experiences** (p. 234)	☐ Handout **9F:** Including All Children in Art Experiences ☐ *Creative Curriculum*, p. 346	30

How Art Experiences Promote Development

☐ Handout **9A**
☐ Handout **9B**
☐ Handout **9C**
☐ Chart paper, marker, art materials and supplies
☐ *Creative Curriculum*, pp. 160–161, 530

PREPARATION

Assemble materials for groups to complete either the closed or open-ended activity. Use handout 9B to precut enough shapes from construction paper (red, blue, green, yellow) so each participant in Group 1 can complete the picture. Duplicate the handouts.

INTRODUCTION

Introduce the workshop:

- Children's art is fascinating to most adults. Parents are proud of their children's artwork and early childhood educators routinely provide time and opportunities for art experiences in the classroom.

- However, not everyone agrees about the definition of art or what type of art experiences should be offered.

- In this workshop, you will reflect on your own experiences with, and feelings about, art. You will experience firsthand the *Creative Curriculum* approach to art.

Distribute handout 9A and ask participants to take 10 minutes to answer the questions.

Have them share their experiences with someone at their tables.

Invite one or two participants to share with the entire group, or share a personal experience of your own. Summarize with a brief discussion about how personal feelings and beliefs can influence classroom practices.

Discuss the importance of creativity. Make the following points:

- In a *Creative Curriculum* classroom, art is a joyful learning experience; the focus is on process—what children do—rather than product.

- The Art Area is a place where children can go to create and to express what they know and feel.

Then, ask participants to describe a creative person. Record the responses on chart paper.

> **Possible responses:** *Imaginative, inventive; constructive, original, looks at things in a unique way, spontaneous, risk-taker, fanciful, adventuresome, flexible, problem-solver*

Make the following points:

- Creativity is encouraged in all areas of the classroom. By their very nature, art materials provide excellent opportunities for children to explore, experiment, and use their imaginations.

- During this workshop, you will examine various activities to determine their artistic merit.

ACTIVITY

Have participants clear their tables. Designate half the tables as Group 1; the other as Group 2.

Ask for a volunteer at each table to act as the teacher. Give Group 1 teachers instructions from handout 9B and enough materials for each person. Give Group 2 teachers instructions from handout 9B and enough open-ended art materials (e.g., collage, three-dimensional materials, etc.).

Allow participants to work for 10 minutes. Make note of any group comments.

When time is up, lead a discussion about each group's experience. Ask:

- What did you experience?

- What elements of creativity did you use? (Refer to the descriptions of a creative person.)

- Which activity is likely to address more *Creative Curriculum* objectives? Turn to "Goals and Objectives at a Glance" on page 530 and identify a few.

- Which activity encourages greater use of the process skills? Turn to pages 161–162 to review the process skills.

SUMMARY

Summarize with the following points:

- Labeling an activity as art does not mean that the activity has artistic merit. There are many activities that are disguised as creative art. These activities are often teacher-initiated, highly structured, and product-oriented.

- Art experiences in a *Creative Curriculum* classroom are

    personal and original (children are free to express themselves through a variety of media)

    child-initiated (children are intrinsically motivated)

    open-ended and creative (children explore and experiment with varied media; they decide what they will make and how)

    process-oriented (children enjoy the making and doing more than the finished product)

    success-oriented (teachers provide age-appropriate, yet challenging, materials)

- Art experiences encourage children to grow and learn in all areas of development.

WORKSHOP

Creating an Environment for Art

☐ Transparency **9D**
☐ Samples of children's art work
☐ *Creative Curriculum*, pp. 63, 320–323, 332–333
☐ *Implementation Checklist*
☐ Chart paper, markers

PREPARATION

Prior to the workshop, ask participants to bring photos of their Art Areas or floor plans of their classrooms and an inventory of their art supplies.

Prepare the transparency.

INTRODUCTION

Introduce the workshop with a discussion:

- Teachers often experience problems in making the Art Area a successful place for learning.

- What are some typical problems you experience in making the Art Area work well for you and the children?

Record participant responses on chart paper.

Possible responses:

Art activities can be very messy.

It takes too long to clean up the area.

There isn't enough room to store supplies.

There aren't enough materials.

There isn't enough space for art in the classroom.

Children all want to use the easel at the same time.

Parents complain about stains on their children's clothes.

I end up doing a lot of the work.

Explain that the purpose of this workshop is to consider ways to arrange and equip the Art Area to address these issues and inspire children.

ACTIVITY

Show the transparency. Have participants work in pairs to examine their floor plans and discuss the location and arrangement of their Art Areas. Suggest that the questions on the transparency guide their discussions.

Refer participants to pages 63 and 320–321 as you review the guidelines for arranging the Art Area. Relate discussion comments back to issues identified during the opening discussion.

Have participants review their floor plans again to identify any changes to be made.

Lead a discussion about selecting materials using the categories on page 322 as a framework.

Share or display samples of children's artwork using different media if available.

Allow five–ten minutes for participants to review their inventory of art materials. Have them identify new materials to add to the area. Make the following points:

- While the Art Area should be well stocked, it is important to remember that the materials should be sorted, organized, and thoughtfully arranged.

- If children see order and relationships between materials, they are likely to wonder "How can I put these things together?"

Refer participants to the section on "Displaying and Storing Art Materials" on pages 332–333. Show other creative and functional ways to organize art materials and display children's work (e.g., tables, shelves, windowsills, and bulletin boards). Invite participants to share what they do.

Refer participants to the "Art" section of the *Implementation Checklist* (page 6). Review each item. Then have participants complete self-assessments of their Art Areas.

Have participants identify areas that need improvement and make plans for changes as necessary. Invite them to come to the next workshop and share their progress and successes.

SUMMARY

Summarize with the following points:

- The organization of the Art Area affects children's creativity and self-expression.

- If the area is inviting, children will be drawn to it. This is not likely to happen if the area is messy, overwhelming, or barren.

- Art materials can be as diverse as your creativity and funds allow. Begin with the basics and then add more unusual or challenging materials.

- Displaying children's original artwork adds charm and warmth to the classroom, and conveys many positive messages to children.

The Teacher's Role in the Art Area

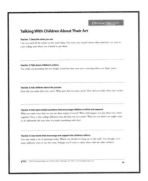

□ *Creative Curriculum* video
□ Samples of children's artwork
□ Handout **9E**
□ *Creative Curriculum,* pp. 337–340

● PREPARATION

Collect samples of children's artwork, representing each of the four developmental stages described on pages 337–338, or, prior to the workshop, ask participants to bring a few samples of children's original artwork. Samples can be from any of the five categories: painting, drawing, cutting and pasting, molding, and three-dimensional art and woodworking.

Set up the five activity stations described in handout 9E, equipped with appropriate materials and supplies for the five categories.

Duplicate handout 9E and cut it apart. Cue the video to the "Art" section.

● INTRODUCTION

Introduce the workshop:

- Through art, children are able to expand their creativity and make meaning of the world around them. Teachers have the opportunity and responsibility to facilitate this process.

- Knowing which materials and experiences to offer children, and how to interact with them to encourage development and learning, are important skills for teachers to have.

- In this workshop, you will explore the teacher's role in supporting and encouraging children's creative ideas in the Art Area.

● ACTIVITY

Begin by showing the "Art" section from the *Creative Curriculum* video. Ask participants to focus on the roles teachers play.

Invite comments and observations about the segment.

Make the following points:

- Supporting children's learning in the Art Area begins with observing and knowing where each child is developmentally.

- There are four stages of development children typically go through in drawing and painting.

Have participants read pages 337–338 on "Stages in Painting and Drawing" and page 339 on "Stages in Using Other Art Materials." Ask them to examine the samples of children's artwork to identify the stage each piece represents. Invite participant comments and questions.

Summarize with the following points:

- When you observe and reflect on what children do and say in this area, you can determine their strengths and challenges. You can then respond in ways to help them develop their skills.

- The *Developmental Continuum* can serve as a guide in this process. (Refer to page 340.)

Give these directions:

- You will have an opportunity to experience some of the materials children typically enjoy.

- You may try several activities or spend all of your time on one activity.

- While you are working, five volunteers will assume the role of a teacher, each demonstrating one of the ways you might interact with children to extend learning.

Ask for five volunteers to play the roles of teachers. Have them choose a slip from handout 9E. Ask them to rotate among the tables, performing their assigned tasks as described on the handout.

Then have participants move to one of the activity stations. Allow 20–25 minutes for the activity.

Ask participants to return to their seats. Lead a discussion about the experience. Ask:

- How did the teacher's role help you feel more competent about what you were doing?

- How did the teacher's role encourage further exploration or learning?

- How did the teacher's role promote problem-solving, critical thinking, or vocabulary development?

- What role did each teacher play?

SUMMARY

Summarize the workshop with the following points:

- The Art Area should be a place filled with materials that children can enjoy on a purely sensory level.

- The way in which you respond can either build a child's confidence and foster a positive attitude toward art, or discourage a child from trying different art activities and enjoying the process.

- Commenting and asking children about their work with art materials convey messages such as:

    I am aware of what you are doing.

    I am interested in your efforts and therefore in you.

    I will help you look closely at your own work.

    I appreciate your growing confidence.

Including All Children in Art Experiences

☐ Handout **9F**
☐ *Creative Curriculum,*
 p. 346

PREPARATION

Duplicate the handout.

INTRODUCTION

Introduce the workshop:

- The Art Area should be a place where all children can experience success and build self-confidence.

- Unfortunately, some children get stuck or seem uninspired in the Art Area. Or, they are particularly challenged by art activities because they are relatively unstructured and involve abstract thinking.

- Teachers who regularly observe and analyze the difficulties these children are having usually find ways to involve and include them in art experiences every day.

- The purpose of this activity is to consider ways in which teachers can respond to children, through interactions or by modifying materials or the environment, so that all children can be involved in, and benefit from, art.

ACTIVITY

Distribute handout 9F.

Have participants work in small groups to identify ways in which teachers might respond to children in each situation. Their responses may be as simple as offering suggestions or words of encouragement, to making modifications to the area or materials.

Have them record their ideas in column 2.

Invite each group to share at least one idea for each situation.

Refer participants to page 346 to read about other strategies.

SUMMARY

Summarize the discussion with the following points:

- The Art Area can present special challenges for some children.

- With modifications, all children can become involved in, and benefit from, art experiences every day.

My Early Art Experiences

1. Did you enjoy art as a child? Why or why not?

2. Describe one of your earliest art experiences.

3. How did your parents and teachers respond to your artwork?

4. How do you currently feel about your artistic abilities?

5. Describe any events since your childhood days that have influenced your feelings and attitudes toward art and your view of your abilities.

Is This Really Art?

Group 1 Instructions:

Give these instructions to your group:

- We're all going to make a picture of a house.

- Watch as I do each step first; then you do it.

Give each participant an 8 1/2" X 11" piece of newsprint, a glue stick, and one red square, one blue triangle, one green rectangle, and one yellow circle.

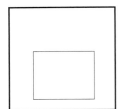

Use a glue stick to apply glue to the outer edges of the red square. Place the square on the bottom center of the newsprint.

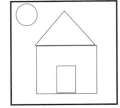

Apply glue to the edges of the blue triangle and place it above the red square to make the roof.

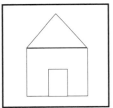

Apply glue to the small green rectangle and glue it in the bottom center of the red square to form a door.

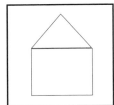

Apply glue to the outside edge of the yellow circle and glue it to the top left hand corner of the page for the sun.

Use a black crayon to make a "V" mark for the bird in the top right corner like this:

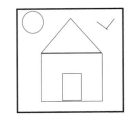

After each person at your table has made a picture, display them for all to see.

Is This Really Art? continued

Group 2 Instructions:

Introduce the materials to your group.

Invite them to explore and use the materials in any way they choose.

As participants work:

- • Make comments to encourage their efforts.
- • Ask open-ended questions about their work.
- • Invite them to talk with you and others about what they are doing.

Making a House

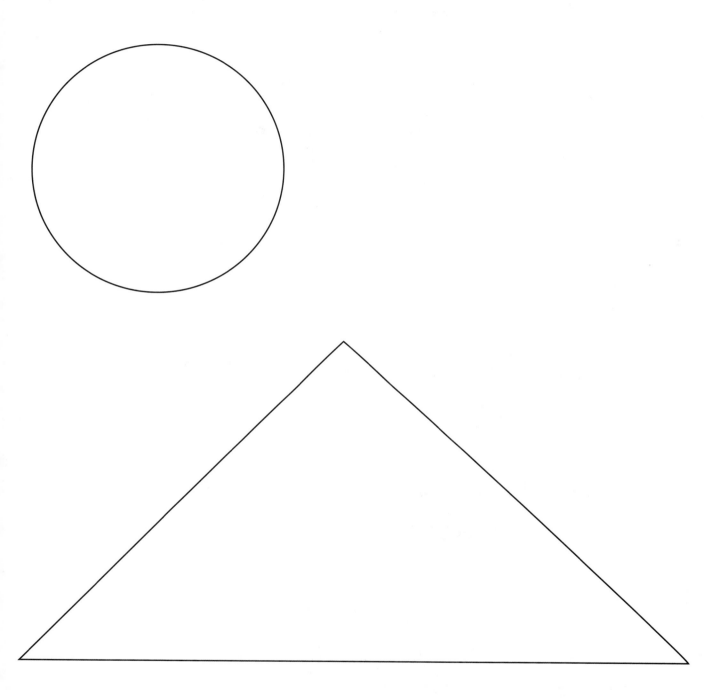

Taking a Closer Look at Your Art Area

- **Would a new child coming into your classroom know where art activities take place?**

- **What other activities take place near the Art Area?**

- **Where do you keep the art materials that children can select and use?**

- **Where do you store extra supplies and teachers' materials?**

- **Do children know where to find art materials and how to return them to the proper place? What systems have you put in place to enable children to work independently?**

Talking With Children About Their Art

Teacher 1: Describe what you see.

I see you used all the colors on the easel today. You were very careful about what materials you used in your collage and where you wanted to put them.

Teacher 2: Talk about children's actions.

You really are pounding that art dough. Look how fast your arm is moving when you finger paint.

Teacher 3: Ask children about the process.

How did you make that new color? What part did you enjoy most? How did you make these tiny circles?

Teacher 4: Ask open-ended questions that encourage children to think and respond.

What are some ways that we can use these scraps of wood? What will happen you mix these two colors together? How is this collage different from the first one you made? What do you think you might want to do differently the next time you make something with clay?

Teacher 5: Use words that encourage and support the children's efforts.

You sure made a lot of paintings today. Which one should we hang up on the wall? You thought of so many different ways to use the loom. Perhaps you'll want to share these with the other children.

Including All Children in Art Experiences

If a child...	Try these strategies...
Has trouble finding and using art materials	
Has difficulty handling materials	
Has difficulty seeing materials	
Is easily frustrated	
Is reluctant or unsure of what to make or do	

NOTES

Library

WORKSHOPS

⚷ Key Points	✳ Workshop	▤ Materials	🕐 Time (minutes)
Sharing books with children not only motivates them to want to learn to read, but also promotes development and learning in all areas.	**How the Library Area Promotes Development** (p. 246)	☐ Collection of children's books ☐ *Creative Curriculum*, pp. 530, 370–371	60
When the Library Area is arranged in an attractive and functional way, children are more likely to read books and to write.	**Creating an Effective Library Area** (This is an alternate activity to "Exploring the Library Area.") (p. 250)	☐ Slides or transparencies of Library Areas reflecting descriptors (*Creative Curriculum*, pp. 355–361) ☐ A selection of various books (*Creative Curriculum*, pp. 356–358) ☐ Handout **10A:** Selecting Books for the Library Area ☐ *Implementation Checklist*	60–90
When the Library Area is arranged in an attractive and functional way, children are more likely to read books and to write.	**Exploring the Library Area** (This is an alternate activity to "Creating an Effective Library Area.") (p. 252)	☐ Books, story retelling props, tapes or CDs, tape recorders or CD players, assortment of writing materials ☐ *Implementation Checklist* ☐ Handout **10A:** Selecting Books for the Library Area ☐ Handout **10B:** Story Retelling ☐ Handout **10C:** Listening ☐ Handout **10D:** Writing ☐ *Creative Curriculum*, pp. 354–361	90
Teachers need to purposefully guide children's language and literacy development.	**How Teachers Support Children's Learning** (p. 254)	☐ Handout **10E:** Skills for Engaging With Books ☐ *Creative Curriculum* video ☐ *Creative Curriculum*, pp. 365–368, 372–374 ☐ A collection of children's writing samples	60
Extending learning through creative experiences is an effective way to help young children to develop many important literacy skills.	**Extending Learning About Literature Through Creative Experiences** (p. 258)	☐ Handout **10F:** Cap Pattern ☐ Books, story props, scissors, scotch tape, stapler, varied art materials and supplies, chart paper ☐ Felt (white, red, blue, gray, brown) ☐ *Creative Curriculum*, pp. 358, 373 ☐ Newspaper, masking tape ☐ *Caps for Sale* by Esphyr Slobodkina	60–90

How the Library Area Promotes Development

□ Collection of children's books
□ *Creative Curriculum*, pp. 530, 370–371

PREPARATION

Choose a favorite book and prepare to demonstrate interactive story reading. Use the suggestions listed in the charts on pages 370–371 to prepare.

Put together a collection of children's books or ask each participant to bring one children's book to the workshop.

INTRODUCTION

Introduce the workshop with some questions. Allow time for participants to reflect on each and share their thoughts with others in their groups. Pose these questions:

• What do you enjoy most about reading books as an adult?

• What do you remember about your early experiences with books as a child?

Invite participants to share thoughts or personal stories from their discussions.

Make the following points:

• Reading is a relaxing pastime for many of us. It provides us with an opportunity to learn new things, escape to other places, and explore new worlds.

• As you reflected on your childhood, you may have recalled titles of favorite books, remembered special times when you and family members, friends, or teachers shared books, or recalled a creative experience you had in connection with a particular story.

• It is likely that these types of experiences are what motivated you to continue reading, since reading habits and motivation to read develop early in life.

• When you share books with young children on a daily basis, you help to instill a love for books and reading.

• When you provide time and space for children to look through books on their own, listen to story tapes, retell familiar stories, or make up their own stories, you further entice and motivate them to become readers and writers; and, you also encourage growth in all areas of development.

Introduce the purposes of the workshop:

- Think about ways in which the Library Area can be used to stimulate children's learning and development in all areas—social/emotional, physical, cognitive, and language.

- Discover effective ways of sharing books to inspire children to explore reading and writing, and to promote language and literacy skills.

ACTIVITY

Have participants form groups of four or five. Give the following instructions:

- Choose a recorder to report on your group's discussion.

- Select one area of development on which to focus.

- Review the objectives under the area of development you selected (refer participants to the "Goals and Objectives at a Glance" on page 530).

- Work with your group to determine how you could use the Library Area to encourage and support children's learning and development in relation to these objectives. Please note that you may not be able to address all of the objectives in each area of development.

Have each group report on one or two different objectives.

Summarize the discussion:

- Teachers who are familiar with the *Creative Curriculum* goals and objectives, along with the steps outlined in the Developmental Continuum, can see how literacy crosses all developmental areas.

- These teachers can use the Library Area to reach many learning objectives.

Recall that the second purpose of the workshop is to discover effective ways of sharing books with children in order to motivate them to read and to promote language and literacy skills.

Make the following points:

- Reading aloud to children is the very best way to inspire a love for books and motivate children to want to learn to read. It also is a key way to promote language and literacy skills.

- Therefore, every *Creative Curriculum* teacher makes time daily to read to children, and with children, from storybooks, informational books, and other sources, such as poetry.

- The Library Area should be filled with beautiful books, props for retelling stories, and writing materials where children can go to "practice" or use the skills they learned during reading time.

- How you read a story or informational book makes a difference. Research has shown that children's language development is positively influenced when adults involve them in the book or story by asking open-ended questions, adding information, and prompting them to make a connection to their prior experiences.

Conduct a demonstration of an interactive story time. Have participants watch for, and make note of, any strategies you use to involve them in the story.

Refer participants to pages 370–371 as you review the strategies reflected in the charts.

Emphasize these points:

- Children should be read to at least twice a day.

- Story time should be an enjoyable social experience for children as well as a learning event.

Invite participants to take turns reading one of the children's books to others at their table using the strategies discussed. Continue as long as there is interest.

Have participants think about strategies for sharing books with children who have special needs, or children who are second-language learners.

Possible responses for children with disabilities:

Use gestures to clarify words for children with hearing or speech difficulties.

Share a story with a child who has cognitive or intellectual challenges prior to sharing it with a larger group.

Keep stories short or use storytelling techniques that allow for greater involvement with children who have social challenges.

Possible responses for children learning English as a second language:

Personalize by pointing out how characters in the book are similar to these children.

Read books that reflect the culture and home language of the children.

Use books with language patterns and simple text.

SUMMARY

Summarize with the following points:

- The Library Area is a place that offers children opportunities to grow and learn in all areas of development—especially in the area of language.

- Reading aloud to children helps them expand their imaginations and creativity and develop vocabulary, listening, comprehension, and many other important language skills.

- The act of reading aloud also shows children that books have information about life experiences (e.g., birth of a sibling, moving, illness, etc.) that might help them think about their own lives.

- When books are read aloud to children, they learn about social responsibilities (e.g., how to be a good friend, how to share and take turns) and about the world around them (e.g., what other people and places are like).

- Reading aloud to children helps to instill a love for books and motivates children to want to become readers.

- You know you have succeeded when children choose to explore and read books by themselves, and to one another, or when they engage in other literacy experiences in the Library Area.

Creating an Effective Library Area

☐ Slides or transparencies of Library Areas reflecting descriptors (*Creative Curriculum*, pp. 355–361)
☐ A selection of various books (*Creative Curriculum*, pp. 356–358)
☐ Handout **10A**
☐ *Implementation Checklist*

PREPARATION

This workshop, and the one that follows, "Exploring the Library Area," are interchangeable. Choose the one that works best for you.

Secure an assortment of books from each category that is described on pages 356–358. Or, prior to the workshop, ask the program sponsor to provide them. Invite participants to bring a favorite storybook to the training as well.

INTRODUCTION

Introduce the workshop with the following points:

- Every *Creative Curriculum* classroom should have an attractive Library Area with soft furniture, beautiful picture books, and a host of other materials that invite children to engage in an array of literacy experiences.

- The Library Area is more than a bookshelf or a place to read stories. It is an oasis that offers children a chance to relax and get away from more active interest areas.

- The purpose of this workshop is to examine ways in which the Library Area can be arranged and equipped so that children choose to spend time there and literacy learning is maximized.

Show slides or transparencies of various Library Areas representing design features described on pages 355–361.

Showcase areas that include spaces for looking at books, retelling stories, listening, and writing.

Review any guidelines for selecting materials for each of these specific activities.

Share strategies for displaying and caring for materials.

Share ways in which the Library Area and materials might be adapted to both accommodate children with disabilities, and to represent children from all cultures.

ACTIVITY

Have participants form groups of four. Put enough books on each table so that every group has at least two books. Invite participants to add their own books to the selections.

Ask each group to choose two books and then read the section, "Selecting Books" on pages 355–358.

Distribute handout 10A, and have participants answer the questions as they review each book.

Invite each group to share a favorite book reviewed, any new observations they made about a familiar or well-known book, or any general observations.

Discuss the value of both storytelling and story retelling to help children grasp the structure of a story and understand its meaning.

Ask if someone would like to volunteer to retell or dramatize a favorite story. Have the audience make note of the skills developed through this activity.

Put one or more storybooks and their related props on each table. Allow time for participants to explore the props and practice retelling the story. Have the groups brainstorm ways to extend the story through writing.

Invite a group, if interested, to retell its story for the entire group of participants.

SUMMARY

Summarize with the following points.

- The Library Area is the hub of literacy learning. Children can develop and refine their speaking, listening, reading, and writing skills.

- By carefully selecting books and by sharing them in a supportive and comfortable setting, teachers can help children learn to love books, acquire many concepts, and develop the skills they need to read.

- By providing props and materials for children to retell stories, teachers help children build comprehension skills, learn about the structure of language, and develop a sense of story.

- And, with writing materials, children can further explore the world of print.

Refer participants to page 7 of the *Implementation Checklist* to review the items for assessing the Library Area in their classrooms. Have them complete self-assessments and identify any areas that need improvement or strengthening.

Exploring the Library Area

□ Books, story retelling props, tapes or CDs, tape recorders or CD players, assortment of writing materials
□ *Implementation Checklist*
□ Handout **10A**
□ Handout **10B**
□ Handout **10C**
□ Handout **10D**
□ *Creative Curriculum*, pp. 354–361

PREPARATION

This workshop, and the previous one, "Creating An Effective Library Area," are interchangeable. Choose the one that works best for you.

Set up four activity stations equipped with appropriate props and materials, such as those described on pages 354–361. They might look like this:

Reading: Provide an assortment of books from each category described on pages 356–358.

Story retelling: Include both familiar and unfamiliar books, and related retelling props (see page 358).

Listening: Set up both appropriate and inappropriate settings for listening to stories. Perhaps include high quality and lesser quality story tapes; one setting with head phones and another without; stories with lively presenters and stories with monotonous voices; an easy-to-operate tape or CD player and one that would be more difficult for children to use, etc.

Writing: Provide an assortment of writing tools and other materials for participants to use (see chart on page 360) as they complete each task.

Duplicate the handouts and place each at the appropriate activity station.

INTRODUCTION

Introduce the workshop with the following points:

- Every *Creative Curriculum* classroom should have an attractive Library Area with soft furniture, beautiful picture books, and other materials that invite children to engage in an array of literacy experiences.

- The purpose of this workshop is to examine ways in which the Library Area can be arranged and equipped so that children choose to spend time there, and literacy learning is maximized.

ACTIVITY

Have participants form four groups. Explain the following:

- There are four activity stations set up to mirror the activities found in the Library Area of the Curriculum.

- At each station, there is an activity sheet with questions to answer and tasks to complete.

- Spend approximately 15 minutes at each station and then rotate to the next. I will give you a signal when it is time to move.

After every group has visited each station, lead a discussion about the ways in which the Library Area is arranged and equipped. Make sure to address

- any guidelines for selecting materials for each of these specific activities

- strategies for displaying and caring for materials

- ways in which the Library Area and materials might be adapted to both accommodate children with disabilities, and to showcase a broad range of cultures and family traditions

SUMMARY

Summarize with the following points:

- The Library Area is the hub for literacy learning. It is an inviting area where children develop and refine their speaking, listening, reading, and writing skills.

- By carefully selecting books and by sharing them in a supportive and comfortable setting, teachers can help children learn to love books, learn many concepts, and develop reading.

- By providing props and materials for children to retell stories, teachers help children build comprehension skills, learn about the structure of language, and develop a sense of story.

- When children follow along to a story read on tape or CD, turn the pages at the appropriate time, or match the story with pictures, they are developing listening and other important skills.

- And, with writing materials, children can further explore the world of print.

Refer participants to page 7 of the *Implementation Checklist* to review the items for assessing the Library Area in their classrooms. Have participants complete self-assessments and identify any areas needing improvement or strengthening.

How Teachers Support Children's Learning

□ Handout **10E**
□ *Creative Curriculum* video
□ *Creative Curriculum*, pp. 365–368, 372–374
□ A collection of children's writing samples

PREPARATION

Gather a collection of children's writing samples that are representative of the various steps described on pages 367–368. Duplicate the samples so that each small group of participants has a collection.

Cue the *Creative Curriculum* video to the "Library" segment. Duplicate the handout.

INTRODUCTION

Introduce the workshop with the following question and have participants discuss it at their tables and record their ideas:

• When it comes to learning language (oral and written), how are children like scientists?

Possible responses:

Gather information (listen and observe others using language)

Form hypotheses (construct rules about how they think language works)

Explore, experiment, test, or try out their new information

Reach a conclusion, seek confirmation

Make the following points:

• Language learning, both oral and written, is a complex process that involves many skills. Like scientists, young children construct their understanding of how language works.

• Left alone, most children don't become literate. They must have many opportunities to interact with adults and others in meaningful situations in order to refine their understanding.

• Some children arrive at school having heard millions of words. These children have extensive vocabularies. Others come with limited vocabularies because they have been exposed to fewer words. Some children enter school with early reading and writing skills, while others are being read to or are handling writing tools for the first time.

- Effective teachers

    know the specific skills children need to learn to read and are familiar with the developmental stages of writing,

    observe children to find out what they already know about literacy

    use what they learn about children to guide their literacy learning in the Library Area

Explain that the purposes of this workshop are to examine some of the skills and behaviors that children acquire as they engage in the reading and writing processes, and to consider strategies that teachers can use to support children's progress.

ACTIVITY

Show the "Library Area" segment of the *Creative Curriculum* video. Have participants watch for ways in which the teachers become involved with children in the Library Area.

Briefly discuss the video. Then make the following general points:

- It is easy to overlook children who are working in the Library Area and to focus attention on children in other more active, noisy interest areas.

- Much can be learned about children while they are in the Library Area—their language and literacy skills in particular. Teachers need to make time each day to visit the area to observe and interact with children.

Reading

Explain that now you are going to focus on reading skills. An appropriate starting point for observations is to look for reading behaviors that children exhibit while engaged with books.

Have participants turn to pages 365–366 and read the section, "Skills for Engaging With Books." Provide clarifying information about each skill as necessary. Emphasize that these skills develop simultaneously rather than in a linear or sequential fashion.

Distribute handout 10E. Have participants work in pairs to discuss each scenario and determine which skill(s) each best represents. Also have them look at the objectives under the "Language" section on page 530 to identify related objectives.

Still working in pairs, ask participants to think about what they would do or say to support or extend children's literacy learning.

Invite participants to share their responses.

Call attention to the strategies for reading with individual children on pages 372–373. Note that reading with individual children, and reading with small groups of children, are opportune times to focus on specific skills.

Writing

Explain that now you are going to focus on writing skills. Read a portion of a familiar story such as *I Know an Old Lady Who Swallowed a Fly*. Have participants think of additional rhymes for the story. Invite several participants to share their ideas and record them on chart paper.

Make the following points

- Research indicates that there is a direct relationship between reading and writing—writing development is facilitated by reading; reading is enhanced by children's experiences with writing (e.g., children see print or writing displayed and used in their environment).

- When children are provided with the materials and opportunity to write, and when they observe teachers participating as writers in the Library, other interest areas, and during other events of the day, they are inclined to explore this connection further.

- It is important for teachers to know and understand children's early attempts at writing so that they can consider how to interact with them to support their efforts, learning, and growth.

- The *Developmental Continuum* maps the steps of writing in objective 50, "Writes letters and words."

Review the steps in writing as described on pages 367–368.

Have participants work in groups. Give each group a collection of children's writing samples to determine what each child knows about writing.

Refer participants to page 374 for a few suggested ways to promote children's writing. Invite them to share other approaches they might use.

Next, have participants identify what they might say, ask, or do to support each child's literacy learning as represented in the collection of writing samples.

Invite the groups to share one or two of their ideas.

SUMMARY

Summarize with the following points:

- Observing children in the Library Area provides you with a picture of each child's interests and skills in literacy related activities.

- With this information, you can plan how you would respond to each child in order to promote learning and growth.

NOTES

WORKSHOP

Extending Learning About Literature Through Creative Experiences

☐ Handout **10F**
☐ Books, story props, scissors, scotch tape, stapler, varied art materials and supplies, chart paper
☐ Felt (white, red, blue, gray, brown)
☐ *Creative Curriculum*, pp. 358, 373
☐ Newspaper, masking tape
☐ *Caps for Sale* by Esphyr Slobodkina

PREPARATION

Make peddler's caps out of felt (white, red, blue, gray, and brown) by using the pattern on handout 10F. Cut 1 white felt circle and use a permanent marker to make it checked. Slit the circle on the dotted line. Overlap the edges and secure them with fabric glue or sew them together. Cut equal numbers of caps from the other pieces of colored felt. Make enough so that every person in the workshop can "steal" a cap from the peddler.

Gather a collection of favorite books that you might use in retelling experiences with children. Either bring these or ask the program sponsor to collect them ahead of time.

Set up an area with varied art materials and supplies that participants can use in their small-group work.

INTRODUCTION

Introduce the workshop:

- Storytelling and story retelling are creative and enjoyable ways to expand children's creativity and imagination.

- They are also effective strategies for enhancing children's literacy learning and overall development.

Explain that the purposes of this workshop are to

- examine the value of storytelling and retelling

- consider various techniques that can be used with preschool children

- discuss the teacher's role in the process

Begin with a storytelling game that involves the whole group. Start the story and then point to someone you would like to continue it. Continue until everyone has had a chance to contribute.

> "It was a cold, dark night. I was walking home from the store when I heard a strange noise behind me. It sounded like…"

Ask participants what children learn from storytelling experiences such as the one just completed.

Possible responses:

When children tell stories themselves, they build important skills for reading.

They use animated and expressive language.

They use details to describe a long series of things that happen to a character in their story.

They often begin with "once upon a time..." or "once there was..."

They describe the characters and setting where the action takes place.

They include a sequence of events.

ACTIVITY

Read the story *Caps for Sale* by Esphyr Slobodkina. Then follow these procedures:

- Explain to participants that you would like to involve them in retelling the story and then discuss the value of the experience.

- Ask for a volunteer to play the peddler. Give the volunteer the caps.

- Ask everyone else to play a monkey.

- Retell the story, acting as the narrator.

Lead a discussion about the skills that children might acquire through story retelling, the roles the teacher might play (see page 373), and strategies for introducing and encouraging story retelling.

Review other ways to retell stories (see page 358) and invite participants to share their ideas.

Have participants form small groups. Ask each group to select a book and think about how they might extend children's learning with that book. Remind them to consider music and movement, cooking, or writing experiences as ways to extend learning as well. They should prepare to demonstrate or share their ideas with the rest of the groups. Allow 15–20 minutes for the activity.

Suggest that materials are available for createing props, as well as chart paper for recording ideas. For more of a challenge, have groups create props using only newspaper and masking tape.

Invite each group to share or demonstrate its ideas.

SUMMARY

Summarize with the following points:

- When children retell a story, they actively participate in a literacy experience that promotes language development, comprehension skills, and a knowledge of story structure as well as other social/emotional, physical, and cognitive skills.

- The Library Area is the ideal place for children to continue exploring language and literacy through retelling experiences.

Selecting Books for the Library Area

Choose one book to read and then answer the questions below.

Title of Book: _____

Author: _____

1. What would children like about this book?

2. Is this book more appropriate for younger preschoolers or older preschoolers? Why?

3. What could children learn through this book?

4. How are children's language and literacy skills promoted through this book?

5. Does this book reflect diversity and/or promote inclusion? If yes, how?

6. Would you include this book in your Library Area? Why or why not?

Story Retelling

Choose a story to retell or re-enact with others in your group. After doing so, answer the questions below.

1. What types of stories would be most appropriate for children to retell? Why?

2. How would you prepare children in your class to retell a story?

3. What are some other strategies you could use to retell the story you selected today?

Listening

With a small group of your peers, choose one story to listen to and then answer the questions below.

1. Which *Creative Curriculum* objectives were touched upon through the listening experience you had today?

2. How would you design the listening station so that children could easily manage things themselves and not intrude upon others in the Library Area?

3. What types of stories are best for younger preschoolers to listen to? Older preschoolers?

4. How could you involve family members in this area?

Writing

1. Choose one of the tasks below to complete. Display your work for others to see.

   • Choose one of the books to read and to respond to in writing using any of the materials available to you. You may illustrate the story as well.

   • Create a greeting card for a friend or relative.

2. Identify meaningful ways you might encourage children to write in the Library Area.

Skills for Engaging With Books

1. The teacher prepares to read the book, *The Grouchy Ladybug* by Eric Carle to a small group of children. Carlos points to the picture on the front of the book and says, "Look at that ladybug. I see lots of ladybugs around my house. Is this book going to be about a ladybug?"

2. Kate and Leo are in the Library Area retelling the story *I Know an Old Lady Who Swallowed a Fly* (Westcott) using a pocket puppet and props. Juwan enters the Library Area and says, "You're not telling it right. She swallows the dog first and then the cat." Kate insists that they are correct and tells Juwan to look in the book. Juwan turns the pages one at a time naming the fly, spider, bird, cat, and then the dog. He looks at Kate and Leo, smiles and says, "uh, oh."

3. At morning meeting, Mr. Alvarez holds up a big book and says, "I'm going to read a story called *Caps for Sale* (Esphyr Slobodkina). Sonya asks, "What are caps?" Mr. Alvarez points to a cap in the picture and says "A cap is a little hat that you wear on your head." Sonya replies, "I've worn a hat before, but not a cap." Derek says, "I wear a baseball cap, but it looks different than that one."

4. Alexa and Susie are in the Library Area during choice time. They chose to read and retell the story *It Looked Like Spilt Milk* (Charles Shaw) using felt pieces. Alexa decides that she will "read" while Susie puts the felt pieces on the board. Alexa opens the book to begin and Susie puts the first felt piece on the board. Alexa takes the piece down and says to Susie, "You have to wait until I read!" Alexa runs her fingers under the text in a sweeping motion, reciting the familiar words of the story. She looks at Susie and says, "Now you can put up the spilt milk piece."

5. While outdoors, Jonelle and Zack discover a variety of insects near a decaying tree stump. Jonelle hurries to get Mr. Alvarez and shows him their discovery. Remembering an earlier experience in using a book to identify birds nesting in a nearby tree, Zack asks Mr. Alvarez if he can get them a book that will tell them more about the bugs they found.

6. Tasheen asks Ms. Tory to read the story, *The Teeny-Tiny Woman* (Paul Galdone), to her in the Library Area. They sit together in the bean bag chair looking at the cover of the book. Tasheen says, "This book has my name in it." "See, here's a "T" and here's a "T" (she points to Teeny and Tiny). That's my name." Ms. Tory reds the title. Tasheen says, "See, I told you, teeny, tiny, and Tasheen. We all start the same."

7. Mr. Alvarez watches Setsuko and Crystal in the Discovery Area as they observe the tree frogs in the terrarium. He listens as the girls talk about how and why they think the frogs jump about so much. The girls move to the Library Area to find the book *Jump, Frog, Jump* (Robert Kalan), a class favorite. They climb on the sofa and together they point at each word on the cover and recite in unison, *Jump, Frog, Jump.* They continue to retell the events of the story in their own words, but point to each word when they come to the repetitive phrase "jump, frog, jump."

8. Ben hurries to Ms. Tory with two books in his hands, *Mama, Do You Love Me?* (Barbara Joosee) and *Is your Mama a Llama?* (Steven Kellogg). He says, "Look Ms. Tory. I found two books about Big Mama. See it says Mama (points to the word Mama on each book). Note: Ben enjoys making cards and writing letters for his grandmother, "Big Mama," who lives with him. Ms. Tory has included "Big Mama" in Ben's collection of favorite words. He refers to it often when writing.

Pattern—
Caps

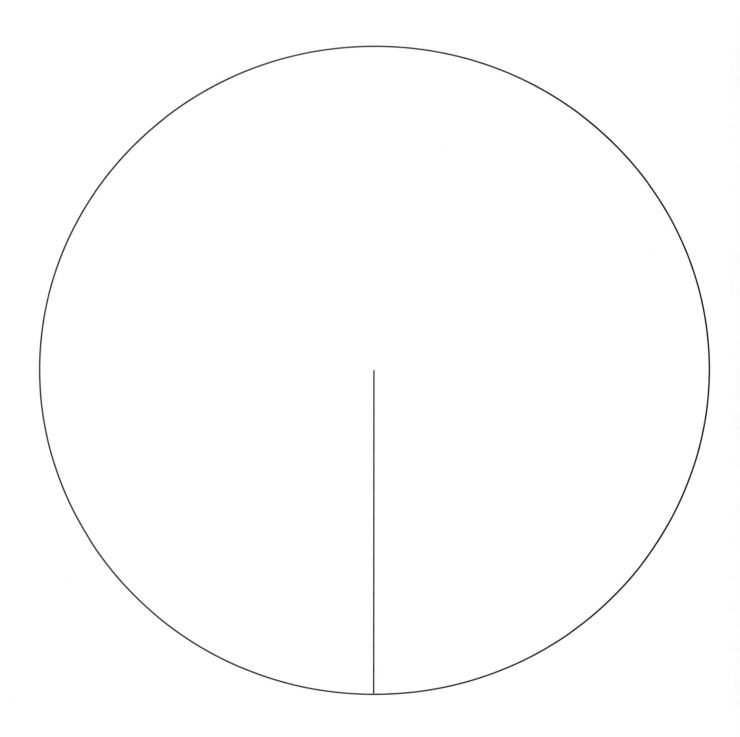

NOTES

Discovery

WORKSHOPS

Key Points	Workshop	Materials	Time (minutes)
The Discovery Area nurtures children's natural sense of wonder about the world around them. It helps children develop important skills and concepts in all areas of development.	**How the Discovery Area Promotes Development** (p. 270)	☐ Children's book ☐ A variety of basic materials for scientific exploration ☐ Handout **11A:** Discovery Workgroups ☐ Chart paper, markers	60
The Discovery Area is the hub of science learning, a place where children will actively investigate the "big ideas" of science.	**Creating an Environment for Discovery** (p. 272)	☐ Materials and tools ☐ Science-related materials, Discovery Trays, Sensory Tubs, or Tubs of Take-Aparts ☐ Paper, pencils, crayons ☐ Handout **11B:** Selecting Materials for the Discovery Area ☐ *Creative Curriculum,* pp. 142–144, 161–162, 384 ☐ *Implementation Checklist*	60
Teachers who are knowledgeable about science content and promote a sense of wonder about the world, can help children learn important skills and content.	**The Teacher's Role in the Discovery Area** (p. 274)	☐ Handout **11C:** Interacting With Children in the Discovery Area ☐ *Creative Curriculum,* pp. 394-401	60

How the Discovery Area Promotes Development

□ Children's book
□ A variety of basic materials for scientific exploration
□ Handout **11A**
□ Chart paper, markers

PREPARATION

Groups will use a variety of basic materials for scientific exploration (see the list on page 386). Include materials and tools related to the three broad content areas of science: life science, physical science, and earth and the environment. Duplicate the handout.

INTRODUCTION

Introduce the workshop with a storybook that has a theme related to something children might wonder about. For example, *Where Do Balloons Go?* by Jamie Lee Curtis or *The Listening Walk* by Paul Showers.

Make the following points:

• Children are born with a sense of wonder and a desire to learn.

• The Discovery Area is intentionally planned to spark children's curiosity, a place where they can seek answers to their questions.

• Now, you will experience the skills, concepts, and dispositions toward learning that children develop as they work in the Discovery Area.

ACTIVITY

Give groups chart paper. Have them list statements or questions that children might ask to show curiosity about the world. Offer these examples:

• I wonder why some rocks are smooth and others are not.

• I wonder what kind of animal lived in this shell.

• I wonder where the salt went when I poured it into the waters.

Invite the groups to share one or two of the items listed on their charts. Pose the following questions:

• What does it mean when children wonder aloud or ask questions?

  Possible responses:

  They are exploring their environment—looking about, noticing things, choosing something specific to think about.

  They are looking for the unknown—being scientists.

  They have made a discovery (e.g., "Hey, I wonder when the butterfly broke out of his cocoon!")

- How is it helpful for teachers to know what children wonder about or are interested in?

    Possible responses:

    It is a starting point for knowing what kinds of materials and experiences to offer and which topics to study in greater depth.

    It provides a basis for building relationships with children and motivating them to learn.

    It sends the message to children that you know and value what is important to them.

Distribute the science exploration materials to each group. Then give the following instructions:

- Explore the materials as if you have never seen them before. See what you can learn about them and what discoveries you can make.

- List the items at the top of handout 11A. Then answer the questions.

- Be prepared to share one of the major discoveries made by your group.

Allow about 20 minutes for the activity, depending on the degree of participant involvement.

Then lead a discussion about how the Discovery Area promotes learning and development using the questions on the worksheet as a guide. Draw parallels between question 1 and process skills; question 2 and social skills; question 3 and the science content areas; question 4 and child development and learning; and question 5 and social/emotional development.

When you get to question 3, have each group share one of its major discoveries.

SUMMARY

Summarize the workshop with the following points:

- Children are already attuned to what is going on in their immediate environment. Wondering and asking questions comes naturally to them and is a hallmark of all good scientists.

- When you create a Discovery Area with intriguing materials, you can support and encourage children's desire to explore, to discover, and to learn. And, you are helping them develop the skills and concepts that they need in school and in life.

- Discovery evokes exciting feelings that can compel a child to look again and want to continue to learn.

Creating an Environment for Discovery

□ Materials and tools
□ Science-related
   materials, Discovery
   Trays, Sensory Tubs, or
   Tubs of Take-Aparts
□ Paper, pencils, crayons
□ Handout **11B**
□ *Creative Curriculum*,
   pp. 142–144,
   161–162, 384
□ *Implementation
   Checklist*

PREPARATION

Prior to the workshop, prepare materials and tools in boxes or on trays. **Materials:** a set of unrelated materials such as a poster of sea shells, a leaf, an animal book, a rock, an x-ray, film, and a pine cone. **Tools:** a selection such as mirrors, magnifying glasses, containers for sorting and classifying, balance scale, magnets, and a flashlight.

Also prepare a Discovery Tray, Sensory Tub, or Tub of Take-Aparts (see pages 388–390) for each table. Duplicate the handout.

INTRODUCTION

Introduce the workshop:

- Discoveries occur throughout the classroom. However, there should be a special place where children do science-related discovery activities.

- In a *Creative Curriculum* classroom, the Discovery Area is the center of activity for science investigations.

- The Discovery Area is not a place where children are directed to learn specific scientific facts. Rather, it is a place where they will actively investigate the big ideas of science and, in the process, learn facts as well as larger concepts.

- The purpose of this workshop is to consider ways to set up and equip the Discovery Area so that children will be excited and challenged as they work as scientists.

ACTIVITY

Ask half of each group to read the section on "Science" on pages 142–144. Ask the other half to read the section on "Process Skills" on page 161–162.

Allow time to share information at each table from their readings.

Give each group a set of unrelated materials and have them answer the questions on handout 11B.

Invite participants to share their responses to the questions.

Next, give each group tools and a Discovery Tray, Sensory Tub, or Tub of Take-Aparts. Have them answer the questions on handout 11B again after using these new materials and tools.

Lead a discussion comparing the two experiences.

Make the following points:

- The Discovery Area should include related materials and objects from each component of science: life science, physical science, and earth and the environment.

- Keep the Discovery Area stocked with basic tools that encourage **interaction** and **creative exploration**. Set up collections of related materials on trays to help children focus their observations or explore a particular scientific concept.

- Offer paper, pencils, and other materials for children to represent and record their discoveries.

- Consider children's interests as you decide which materials to display and when. Allow children to choose from many interesting objects and experiences. Too many items can be overwhelming and invite injuries. Rotate materials to keep children interested and engaged.

- Plan for children's learning by considering these questions:

  What are children interested in?

  What would you like children to experience?

  Do these materials foster creative exploration?

Discuss the location, arrangement, and organization of the Discovery area (refer to page 384).

Make the following points:

- The nature of the experiences may determine the location of the area (discovery can be noisy, and may need natural light for life science).

- Within the area, consider where **quieter** explorations (e.g., observations of collections), more **active** explorations (e.g., magnets, balance scales, mirrors, prisms, Take-Aparts), and **messy** explorations (e.g., water-related activities, color mixing, oobleck, planting) will take place.

- Think about safety—develop rules with the children and review them often. Plan for activities that need adult supervision, and plan ahead to eliminate hazardous situations (e.g., cutting cords off of electrical appliances, removing batteries, putting rubber mats in areas where water explorations take place, providing towels to clean up slippery surfaces).

Review the items from the "Discovery Area" section of the *Implementation Checklist*, page 8. Have participants complete self-assessments of their Discovery Areas, and identify areas that need improving or strengthening. Have participants work with a partner to brainstorm.

◀ SUMMARY

Summarize with the following points:

- A Discovery Area stocked with interesting materials invites children to explore and investigate.

- To create interest and encourage discovery and exploration, include a wide variety of materials and rotate the materials periodically.

WORKSHOP

The Teacher's Role in the Discovery Area

☐ Handout **11C**
☐ *Creative Curriculum,*
   pp. 394-401

PREPARATION

This workshop assumes that participants have already done the previous workshops in which they read in Chapter 3 about the components of science and process skills. If not, have them read these sections along with the others specified in the activity below.

Duplicate the handout.

INTRODUCTION

Introduce the workshop:

* The teacher's attitude toward science and discovery experiences affects children and, in turn, will influence whether they use the Discovery Area to its fullest.

* In the Discovery Area, more than any other interest area, children also have opportunities to develop and refine process skills and learn important scientific concepts. Therefore, the teacher's role in the Discovery Area is significant.

* The purpose of this workshop is to consider ways in which the teacher can respond to children to promote their learning and development.

ACTIVITY

Ask participants to read these sections on the Discovery Area:

* "The Teacher's Role," pages 394-399

* "Frequently Asked Questions About the Discovery Area," page 400

* "Letter to Families," page 401

Next, distribute handout 11C. Have participants read each scenario and work in their groups to answer the questions that follow the scenarios. Ask each group to share some of their responses.

◀ SUMMARY

Summarize the workshop with the following points:

- In the Discovery Area, *Creative Curriculum* teachers focus both on how young children learn (process skills) as well as what they learn (content knowledge).

- By knowing when and how to ask questions, make suggestions, or step back, you can successfully guide children's learning in the Discovery Area.

- If we want children to retain their sense of wonder, they need adults who question and share their sense of wonder as well as their joy and excitement about discovering new things about the world in which we live.

Discovery Workgroups

Collection: _____

_____

1. How did your group investigate the materials? What processes did you use?

2. How did you function as a group?

3. What did you learn about the materials in your collection? What discoveries did your group make?

4. Which *Creative Curriculum* objectives were addressed through this experience?

5. What did you enjoy most about this experience?

Selecting Materials for the Discovery Area

Questions	First Set of Materials	Second Set of Materials
1. Consider the materials in your collection. Do they encourage interaction and creative exploration? Explain your answer.		
2. What component of science would these materials address?		
3. What concept(s) would children likely learn from experience with these materials?		
4. Which process skills will children use as they work with these materials?		

Interacting With Children in the Discovery Area

Leo and Alexa giggle as they study the worms collected from the playground after a spring rain and placed in the Discovery Area. Alexa says she thinks they are baby snakes. Kate watches from a short distance. Finding a craft stick nearby, Leo begins to gently touch the worm he has placed on a shallow tray. Alexa tries to pick up a worm, but asks for help. Leo quickly volunteers. Alexa says, "I don't like worms. They make me feel scared. Ouch, I think one just bit me!"

Zack and Carlos select a Discovery Tray with magnets (horseshoe, bar, wand), a variety of objects that attract magnets (nuts, bolts, washers, nails, paper clips) and some that do not attract magnets (pennies, toothpicks, plastic twist ties, a piece of cardboard, fabric, and wood). Carlos picks up a wand magnet and, while running it over the top of several objects exclaims, "Look, I can make a lot of things stick to this one!" Zack uses a smaller bar magnet to see how many things he can pick up. As he places the bar magnet back on the tray, he notices that another magnet moves slightly. Zack says, "Look Carlos, I can make things move together without touching them. Watch this." Zack places the pole of one magnet next to the same pole of another magnet to attract it.

Ms. Tory makes goop using a mixture of cornstarch and water. She divides the mixture into three bowls and adds food coloring to make one red, one yellow, and one blue. She puts different combinations of colored goop into plastic resealable freezer bags, seals them tightly, and further secures them with duct tape. She then places the bags in the Discovery Area. During choice time, some children notice the new addition. They begin to press on the bags, watching as the colors begin to merge. Sonya smiles and says, "It looks like a rainbow! I see all the colors." Dallas picks up a bag with blue and yellow goop. He says, "I wonder what will happen if I squish these together." The children continue exploring the bags noticing that some get "puffy like pillows." Dallas suddenly exclaims, "I know! I know! Blue and yellow make green!"

Shawn and Setsuko are in the Discovery Area watching the fish in the aquarium. "Look, that fish has three mouths," says Shawn. Setsuko says, "That's the only one in the tank that has three." Mr. Alvarez enters the Discovery Area to listen more closely. Shawn says, "Look Mr. Alvarez, this fish has three mouths, one in the front (points to his own mouth) and two on the side of his head (cups his hands over his ears and making an opening and closing motion).

Interacting With Children in the Discovery Area, continued

What science concepts are children learning?

How could the teacher respond to extend and enhance children's learning?

What open-ended questions or comments might the teacher make in each situation?

Sand and Water

WORKSHOPS

Key Points	Workshop	Materials	Time (minutes)
Sand and water are natural materials that appeal to our senses and promote all areas of development.	**How Sand and Water Play Promote Development** (p. 282)	□ Plastic tubs, water and/or sand, food coloring, liquid detergent, assorted sand/water props, clean-up supplies □ *Creative Curriculum* video □ *Creative Curriculum,* pp. 403–405, 530	30
A functional and attractive Sand and Water Area sets the stage for children to learn and have fun.	**Creating an Environment for Sand and Water Play** (p. 286)	□ Handout **12A:** Taking a Closer Look at Your Sand and Water Area □ *Creative Curriculum,* pp. 76–78, 406–410 □ *Implementation Checklist*	20
Teachers support and extend children's learning in the Sand and Water Area when they offer experiences that encourage children to investigate.	**How Teachers Support Children's Learning** (p. 288)	□ Plastic tubs, water, modeling clay, dried peas or beans □ *Creative Curriculum,* pp. 413–418, 530 □ Chart paper, markers	40–60

How Sand and Water Play Promote Development

□ Plastic tubs, water and/or sand, food coloring, liquid detergent, assorted sand/water props, clean-up supplies

□ *Creative Curriculum* video

□ *Creative Curriculum*, pp. 403–405, 530

PREPARATION

Try to conduct this workshop in a classroom where you can use the sand and water tables. Otherwise, collect enough plastic tubs for participants to use. Gather sand and water props; or, prior to the workshop ask each participant to bring a prop.

Fill the water table and/or plastic tubs with either warm or cold water. Place food coloring and liquid soap next to each tub. Have clean-up supplies available.

If you can, set the mood for the sand and water workshops by playing a tape or CD of ocean or beach sounds.

INTRODUCTION

Introduce the workshop by asking participants to close their eyes and imagine they are at the beach. Then ask:

- How does the beach feel? Look? Smell? Sound? Taste?

- What do you like to do at the beach?

Make the following points:

- Sand and water are natural materials that appeal to our senses. They are relaxing, pleasurable, and soothing.

- Children and adults alike are drawn to sand and water.

- While sand and water play delight the senses, they also can challenge children's minds and enhance every area of development.

Explain that the purpose of this workshop is to promote an understanding of how sand and water play contribute to children's learning and development.

ACTIVITY

Have participants form groups of four or five and gather around one of the water tables or tubs.

Have each group choose one or two people who will not use the materials but rather observe and record what happens during play (e.g., any actions, interesting vocabulary words, concepts or discoveries made, or how the "players" functioned as a group).

Give the following instructions to players, allowing 1–2 minutes for play each time:

- Start with the **plain water** and explore its properties.

- Next, add a few drops of food coloring and explore again.

- Now add the liquid soap.

Ask questions such as:

- How does the water sound? Feel? Look?

- What happened when you added the food coloring? The liquid soap? How did the water change?

Allow 5–10 minutes for this play sequence.

After each step during play, invite the observers to share a few of their written observations.

Next, display an assortment of sand and water props (see the list on page 409.) Invite the groups to choose the ones they want and continue their water play and observations.

Allow another 5–10 minutes for play. Have participants clean up. Then lead a discussion about the experience. Ask:

- Did water alone maintain your interest?

- How did the play change after each step?

- Which props worked best with water?

- What skills and concepts could children learn or develop through water play? Refer participants to the "Goals and Objectives at a Glance" on page 530.

Show the "Sand and Water" segment of the *Creative Curriculum* video. Refer participants to the "Goals and Objectives at a Glance" on page 530. Discuss the way sand and water play encourage development in all areas. Have them identify the objectives that could be addressed through sand and water play.

SUMMARY

Summarize with the following points:

- Children delight in playing with sand and water.

- Exploring these materials alone allow children to discover their many properties.

- When props are added, children experiment even more and further develop their social/emotional, physical, cognitive, and language skills.

- Teachers promote learning and development as they interact with children in the Sand and Water Area.

VARIATION

Repeat the process described here, first having participants explore both fine and coarse sand, and then add water to the sand. Or, have half of the participants explore water and the other half explore sand.

During sand play ask:

- How does sand feel? Look?

- How does your experience change when using coarse sand? How are the two kinds of sand the same? How are they different?

- What can you do with sand?

- What happens to the sand when it is wet?

During water play use the questions mentioned in the activity above.

NOTES

Creating an Environment for Sand and Water Play

☐ Handout **12A**
☐ *Creative Curriculum*, pp. 76–78, 406–410
☐ *Implementation Checklist*

PREPARATION:

Prior to the workshop, ask participants to take photographs of their Sand and Water Areas or have them draw sketches of their areas.

INTRODUCTION

Introduce the workshop:

- Many programs have an outdoor Sand and Water Area. However, sand and water also should be offered as an indoor choice activity.

- An indoor Sand and Water Area gives children more time to use these soothing materials. In addition, some children prefer exploring sand and water in a more controlled environment indoors, rather than in the less structured outdoor area.

- During this workshop, you will examine the arrangement and set up of your Sand and Water Area through the eyes of a child to determine if it addresses children's needs.

ACTIVITY

Have participants take out the photographs or sketches of the Sand and Water Areas in their classrooms.

Distribute handout 12A and give these instructions:

- The statements in column 1 are messages we want children to receive. These messages can be conveyed through the environment.

- Imagine that you are a child in the Sand and Water Area pictured in the photographs or sketches you brought.

- Identify specific ways in which you convey each message to children through the setup of the Sand and Water Area in your classroom. Record your responses in column 2.

- Ask participants to read pages 76–78 and 406–410.

- Have participants work with a partner to present the strategies they currently use to convey each message. Have them record in column 3.

Invite comments and questions.

Refer participants to the section on "Sand and Water" on page 9 of the *Implementation Checklist*. Briefly review the items. Point out that sand and water must be offered as a choice activity daily, but may be offered either indoors or outdoors.

Have participants complete self-assessments of their Sand and Water Areas and identify any changes that need to be made. Ask them to be prepared to share the results of their changes at the next workshop.

SUMMARY

Summarize the workshop:

- While sand and water are two distinct activities, they should be near one another, as one interest area.

- The Sand and Water Area should be attractive and uncluttered. The materials should be accessible so children can select what they want to use.

- Have only a few props out at one time. Too many props in the sand or water table can interfere with play.

- Start with just a few simple props and gradually add and/or rotate props to keep children's interest and introduce them to a range of new possibilities.

- In selecting props, look for ones that are versatile, but don't limit your selection to those that can be used in both areas.

- Sand and water play can be messy. Having child-sized brooms, dustpans, and mops available to children can make cleanup easier for everyone.

How Teachers Support Children's Learning

□ Plastic tubs, water,
   modeling clay, dried
   peas or beans
□ *Creative Curriculum*,
   pp. 413–418, 530
□ Chart paper, markers

PREPARATION:

Place a plastic tub filled with about five inches of water at each table.

INTRODUCTION

Introduce the workshop:

- The purposes of this workshop are to:

   examine the stages children go through as they explore sand and water

   explore ways teachers can respond to children to support their learning and development

- Children approach new materials by using their senses to explore and then manipulating the materials in more purposeful ways.

Ask participants to read about the three developmental stages children go through as they explore sand and water on page 413:

- functional play

- constructive play

- dramatic play

Make the following points about the teacher's role:

- As in other interest areas, teachers observe children to see where they are developmentally and to determine what interests them.

- These observations lay the groundwork for building relationships with children and planning interactions.

- While observing children in sand and water play, think about whether they

   use props for dramatic play or to conduct experiments

   play alone or with others

   play with sand and water both indoors and outdoors

   select the props they want or use those that are already out

- Teachers support children by talking with them about what they are doing, and by planning and facilitating investigations.

ACTIVITY

Explain that the next activity will engage participants in an investigation and help them think about what a teacher might do or say to encourage critical thinking and extend learning.

Give the following instructions:

- Clear your tables and take a piece of modeling clay (not playdough).

- Mold the clay into a shape that you think will float, and make predictions about which shapes may or may not float.

- Test the buoyancy of your shapes using the tubs of water on your tables. If a shape doesn't float, try again.

- Share any discoveries you make with the other people at your tables.

Continue as long as the participants are engaged. While participants are working, make comments (about what they are doing, the processes they are using, or how they are working) or suggestions, ask open-ended questions, offer encouragement, wonder aloud, invite participants to talk about their experiences, ask them to make predictions, and to share their discoveries.

Next, put a bowl of dried peas or beans on each table—enough so each participant will have at least 20. Give these instructions:

- Now, build a boat with your clay that will hold at least twenty beans. Be sure to load your boat before setting it in the water.

- If your boats sink, scoop the beans up quickly and try again.

Lead a discussion about this experience. Have participants share their discoveries, the processes they used during this experience, and any observations about your role.

Call participants' attention to the chart on page 415 to discuss how observation leads to reflection about what children are doing and the objectives involved.

Ask participants to look at page 530 and make a list of the objectives that might have been observed during the activity they just completed.

   Possible responses: *Objectives 10, 19, 20, 22, 23, 24, 25, 26, 27, 34, 39, 43.*

Make the following points:

- A rich activity enables children at different steps in their sequence of development to work on many objectives. Your observations will reveal a wealth of information.

- Reflecting on your observations in relation to the *Creative Curriculum* objectives will help you determine what skills children have and what support and guidance they need.

Tell participants that now they will brainstorm a rich activity. Ask each group to design an investigative experience they could offer in the Sand and Water Area and write it on chart paper. Remind them to consider the needed props and other materials, what they might say to the children as they use the materials, and the questions they might ask.

Allow 5–10 minutes for this activity.

Have each table give the investigation they designed to another table. Ask each group to review the description of the activity and list the objectives that might be observed as children work on this project. Post the charts on the wall for others to review. Call their attention to the investigations described on pages 417–418.

SUMMARY

Summarize the workshop:

- Guiding children's learning in the Sand and Water Area begins with observation.

- In a *Creative Curriculum* classroom, interest areas are the primary setting in which children learn. This is where child-initiated learning usually begins and where teachers observe children to consider what kinds of experiences are needed and what teacher interactions will best guide learning.

- Rich activities provide the best opportunities for learning at many different levels.

- Teachers support children's learning by

    engaging them in conversation about what they are doing

    asking open-ended questions to encourage them to reflect on their actions

    encouraging them to explore, raise questions, and become involved in the process of scientific investigations

Taking a Closer Look at
Your Sand and Water Area

Messages	What I Currently Do	What I Would Like to Do
This is a safe place for me to play. (safety)		
This is a place where I can do things on my own. (independence)		
This is a place where I can explore and try out many ideas. (initiative)		
This is a place where I belong. (individual needs)		
This is a place where I can learn to get along with others. (cooperation)		

Music and Movement

WORKSHOPS

⚷ Key Points	✹ Workshop	📋 Materials	🕐 Time (minutes)
Music and movement naturally delight and interest children, and contribute to all areas of development.	**How Music and Movement Promote Development** (p. 294)	☐ Handout **13A:** Listening ☐ Handout **13B:** Singing ☐ Handout **13C:** Moving to Music ☐ Handout **13D:** Playing Instruments ☐ Handout **13E:** Different Ways to Move ☐ Handout **13F:** Supporting Children's Learning and Development Through Music and Movement ☐ Materials for learning stations (see Handouts 13A through 13E for a list of materials needed at each station)	60–90
In a *Creative Curriculum* classroom, children have the space and time to listen, sing, move to music, play instruments, and imitate movements as a group and on their own.	**Creating an Environment for Music and Movement** (p. 298)	☐ Tape/CD player, recordings ☐ Handout **13G:** Favorite Songs and Movement Activities ☐ *Creative Curriculum,* pp. 426–427, 436–437 ☐ *Implementation Checklist*	45–60
Children engage in music and movement activities in many ways, depending on their interest, temperament, and experience. By observing children during group and independent music experiences, teachers gain valuable information that enables them to respond appropriately.	**How Teachers Support Children's Learning Through Music and Movement** (p. 300)	☐ Handout **13H:** Observing and Responding to Children During Music and Movement ☐ *Creative Curriculum,* pp. 431, 434–439	30

How Music and Movement Promote Development

PREPARATION

Prior to the workshop, notify participants that they will be participating in music and movement experiences so that they arrive dressed to move.

After deciding whether you will be using a tape or CD player, ask each participant to bring a favorite recording on tape or CD. Ask them to also bring enough copies of a favorite song, chant, or rhyme they use during routines or transition times (e.g., arrival, group time, clean-up, departure) to share at one of the learning stations.

Set up learning stations with necessary materials. Each station handout describes two activities. You can decide to have participants do one or both. Duplicate five copies of handouts 13A through 13D and place the appropriate handouts at each learning station. Duplicate sufficient copies of handout 13E for all participants and place them at the learning station for Moving to Music. Duplicate enough copies of handout 13F for each participant.

Play lively music as participants enter the room. Change to quieter, slower music as you begin the workshop.

INTRODUCTION

Introduce the workshop:

- How did you feel when you entered the room and heard the lively music?

- What did you think this workshop would be like, based on what you were hearing?

- Did you think something different when the music changed? Why?

- Music is a language that is used to communicate varied thoughts, ideas, feelings, and stories.

- Can you think of different ways music is used?

☐ Handout **13A**
☐ Handout **13B**
☐ Handout **13C**
☐ Handout **13D**
☐ Handout **13E**
☐ Handout **13F**
☐ Materials for learning stations (see Handouts 13A through 13E for a list of materials needed at each station)

Possible responses:

A mother sings or chants to console her baby.

At a park or on a school playground, a group of children can be heard chanting a popular jump rope rhyme or song.

Driving home after a hard day's work, you play a favorite tape or CD to lighten your mood, calm your nerves, or entertain a tired child.

Our armed forces play "Reveille" to wake up soldiers and "Taps" at the end of the day or when someone is buried.

Two teens "battle" with words or tell a story through a rap song.

Experiences with music are memorable; they touch the emotions and involve the senses; they help people form relationships and bond with one another.

Have participants close their eyes and think of a favorite song from their childhood, adolescence, or adulthood. Ask:

- Where were you when you heard or sang that song?

- What were you doing?

- Who were you with?

- Who taught you the song?

- What makes that song memorable to this day?

- Was there a story associated with the song?

Allow time for participants to share their experiences with their neighbors. Invite one or two participants to share their stories with the entire group.

Make the following points:

- Music naturally delights and interests children just like it delights and interests you.

- When you include music and movement activities in your daily program, not only do you provide an outlet for children's high spirits and creative energy, you contribute to their social/emotional, physical, cognitive, and language development.

ACTIVITY

Have participants form five equal groups to explore music and movement activities. Explain the following:

- Each group will visit five learning stations equipped with materials and instructions for participating in various music and movement activities.

- Each time you arrive at a station, choose someone new to serve as a leader. That person is responsible for giving you instructions and leading you in each activity.

- As you participate in an activity, think about how it might address children's social/emotional, physical, cognitive, or language development.

- You will have approximately 10–15 minutes at each station.

- I will signal when to change stations.

After each group has visited every station, ask participants to name some of the skills and concepts children could acquire through experiences such as these.

Have participants regroup to form groups of four. Distribute handout 13F. Then give the following instructions:

- Read the objectives in column 1, selected from the Curriculum.

- Brainstorm music and movement activities that promote children's growth and development in each of the learning objectives.

- Record your ideas in column 2. Note that the same activity may relate to more than one objective.

Invite alternating groups to share the activities they listed for selected objectives.

SUMMARY

Summarize with the following statements:

- Music and movement experiences are part of everyday life in a *Creative Curriculum* classroom.

- They contribute to children's overall development while bringing joy and delight to all.

NOTES

Creating an Environment for Music and Movement

☐ Tape/CD player,
   recordings
☐ Handout **13G**
☐ *Creative Curriculum*,
   pp. 426–427, 436–437
☐ *Implementation
   Checklist*

PREPARATION

Prior to the workshop, ask participants to make a list of their favorite songs or music and movement activities. Consider asking participants to bring enough copies of some favorite songs or activities to give to others. Put these on a table so participants can pick them up as they exit the workshop. Invite them to bring their favorite tapes or CDs to share with the group.

INTRODUCTION

Introduce the workshop with the following points:

- In a *Creative Curriculum* classroom, children can listen, sing, move to music, play instruments, and imitate movements.

- They typically engage in these experiences by either participating in group experiences or exploring and experimenting with materials independently.

- The music and movement activities you offer at group time will likely inspire a love for music and motivate children to explore it further on their own.

- And, every *Creative Curriculum* classroom includes a specific area where musical instruments, a tape/CD player, and a variety of props are located so children can make, listen, and dance to if they wish.

Explain the following purposes of this workshop:

- Think about ways to create an environment that motivates all children to become engaged in music and movement experiences.

- Consider ways in which the Music and Movement Area can be designed to support and encourage children's independent exploration of music and movement.

Begin a song that everyone knows, or one that you want to introduce to the group. Encourage participants to join in as they become familiar with it.

Lead a discussion about the types of songs and related activities that appeal to children and what children like about each. Point out that pages 436–437 discuss

- simple songs with lots of repetition
- songs with fingerplay
- singing games and action songs
- songs with funny sounds or silly lyrics
- dances and songs of different cultures
- movement games without music

Continue the discussion by asking participants to share ways in which they use music and movement activities in their classrooms.

ACTIVITY

Form groups of 4–6 people. Distribute handout 13G. Give the following instructions:

- Using your list of favorite songs and activities, take turns teaching them to your group.

- Discuss ways that you used these songs and activities with the children in your classrooms.

- Share strategies you use to introduce the song and activities to make them successful.

- Think about problems you encountered and ways you solved them.

- Note on your handout new songs or activities you would like to try in your classrooms.

If participants have brought copies of favorite songs and activities to share with others, remind them to take them as they exit the workshop.

Have participants read pages 426–427. Discuss the guidelines for setting up and organizing the Music and Movement Area. Emphasize the importance of having a space for listening, singing, moving, and playing instruments.

Refer participants to the "Music and Movement" section of the *Implementation Checklist* (page 10). Review the items and have participants complete self-assessments of their Music and Movement Areas. Have them identify any aspects that need improvement.

SUMMARY

Summarize the activity with the following points:

- Singing and moving together is an enjoyable activity that helps everyone feel a part of the group.

- Simple songs are best for preschool children. Often, traditional folk songs are easy to remember and families can help children with familiar words and tunes.

- Take the time to learn and teach some songs and dances of the cultures of your children. It is a great way to involve families and help children gain an appreciation for their own and other cultures.

How Teachers Support Children's Learning Through Music and Movement

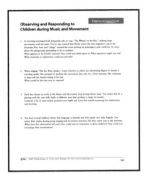

☐ Handout **13H**
☐ *Creative Curriculum,*
   pp. 431, 434–439

PREPARATION

Prior to the workshop, survey participants to find out the type of music they enjoy. Play an assortment or medley of these tunes and observe to see how different people react. Do they listen, sing along, or tap to the rhythm of the tune? Circulate throughout the room, interacting with participants as a teacher might do in a classroom, engaging in conversation about the music, asking questions, or joining participants. Share your observations during workshop discussions when appropriate.

Duplicate handout 13H.

INTRODUCTION

Introduce the workshop with the following points:

- Knowing children's basic patterns of development in music and movement gives you a basis for planning music and movement experiences.

- Because every child is unique, he or she will engage in music and movement activities in a variety of ways depending on individual interests, temperament, and experiences.

- By observing children during group and independent music and movement activities and reflecting on these observations in relation to the goals and objectives, you will be able to respond to each child's interests and skills.

- Your observations will contribute to an overall picture of how each child is progressing in relation to many of the 50 *Creative Curriculum* goals and objectives.

- The goal of this workshop is to provide you with an opportunity to consider how you might interact with children or intervene effectively during music and movement experiences.

Ask participants to read the section, "How Children Engage in Music and Movement" on page 431. Then ask them to discuss with others at their tables how the Music and Movement Area and the experiences they offer children, might change from the beginning to the end of the year.

Invite participants to share their thoughts.

Lead a discussion about the range of interactions between teachers and children during music and movement experiences. Ask participants to think about

- observing children as they respond to music

- talking to children about what they are doing

- reacting to and reinforcing children's explorations

- asking open-ended questions

Refer them to pages 434–439 for ideas about interacting with children.

ACTIVITY

Have groups use handout 13H to answer the questions posed for each scenario. Participants may wish to use pages 434–439 as a reference.

Invite groups to share one idea for each scenario.

SUMMARY

Summarize the workshop with the following points:

- Don't despair if you cannot carry a tune or play a musical instrument. Preschool children don't focus on the voice quality of their teachers—they just want to sing and move!

- Your role is to expose children to music and movement and to create an environment where children can explore.

- Children's explorations, problem solving, and creativity in music and movement is reinforced when teachers respond to what they do. As a result, children begin to see themselves as people who can make and enjoy music, and move to it.

Listening

Activity 1

Materials:

butcher or mural paper, crayons, tape or CD player, and music selections

Procedure:

Cut a sheet of butcher paper large enough for your group to gather around. Play a brief selection of music and ask group members to move their hands and arms to the music. Have them describe the shapes they are creating (e.g., big, round, jagged, etc.).

Next, offer each person a few crayons or markers. Play the music again and have your group move their hands and arms to the music, this time making shapes on the paper. Stop the music and discuss their shapes. Hang your paper on the wall for others to see.

Activity 2

Materials:

assorted containers with lids such as oatmeal tubs, coffee cans, plastic eggs, film canisters, metal band-aid boxes; containers of materials to make sounds such as sand, aquarium gravel, dried peas or beans, buttons, pea gravel, beads, coins; tape or CD player; selections of loud and soft music, chart paper, marker

Procedure:

Gather group members around the table. Have them close their eyes and listen for sounds inside and outside the room that are loud and soft.

Next, show them the various "sound" materials available and ask them to predict which ones they think will make the loudest and softest sounds when shaken in a container. Record their predictions on chart paper.

Invite the members to use the materials to test their predictions. Encourage them to shake their containers in different ways, compare the sounds, and put the "instruments" in order from loudest to softest. Play some music and let the members play along.

Singing

Activity 1

Materials:

tape or CD player, recordings furnished by participants, chart paper, marker, masking tape

Procedure:

Invite group members to take turns playing portions of their favorite songs. Have them introduce the songs and tell why they like each one and how they use them.

Ask each person to write the title and song's author on the chart paper posted.

Activity 2

Materials:

routine or transition songs, rhymes, chants provided by participants

Procedure:

Invite group members to take turns teaching a favorite song, chant, or rhyme used during routine or transition times (e.g., arrival, group time, clean-up, or departure). Have them share copies of their selections if they have them.

Moving to Music

Activity 1

Materials:

See directions on handout 13E, tape or CD player, tapes or CDs

Procedure:

Follow these instructions.

- Divide your group into four smaller groups.

- Distribute the handout and assign each group one section of the handout to complete.

- Ask each group to identify several movement activities in the category assigned and to try the movements themselves.

- Give group #4 the props, tape/CD player, and tapes or CDs

- Allow about 5–10 minutes for each group to work. After they have completed their assignment, have each group lead the others in the movement activities they identified.

Activity 2

Materials:

routine or transition songs, rhymes, chants provided by participants

Procedure:

Explain the following to group members.

- You will be participating in a movement activity with a partner.

- We will begin by selecting partners. When you hear the music, begin moving in any way you like. When the music stops, quickly find a partner.

- For the rest of the activity, you and your partner can move in whatever way you wish as long as you each do the same thing.

- From time to time, I will have you move in certain ways such as, "You and your partner move in very small ways. Move down low. Move backwards."

Playing Instruments

Activity 1

Materials:

selection of musical instruments including those from varied cultures

Procedure:

Lead a discussion on musical instruments. Invite group members to talk about their personal experiences playing or listening to instruments. Ask, "What made your experiences enjoyable or memorable? How can we help children enjoy listening to and playing musical instruments?"

Distribute the instruments. Ask group members to listen for patterns of sounds and rhythms in and outside the room. Then have them repeat the sounds individually, in pairs, in trios, and as a full orchestra. Have each person sound out his or her name with an instrument. Discuss how these activities could be used with children.

Activity 2

Materials:

variety of instruments including teacher-made and those from various cultures, pattern and repetitive books (e.g., *The Three Billy Goats Gruff*, *The Gingerbread Man*) and/or songs (e.g., "The Wheels on the Bus")

Procedure:

Choose a story or song that is familiar to most participants. Review it and discuss its characters, their traits, or actions. Introduce each instrument, playing it as you do so. Have the group members determine how they could use the instruments to retell the story or song. For example, playing a different sized drum to represent each goat in The Three Billy Goats Gruff and a tone block for the "trip, trap, trip, trap, trip, trap" over the bridge.

Next, pass out the instruments to group members to use as you read and retell the story or sing the song.

Different Ways to Move
Directions for Moving to Music Station: Activity 1

Review the example activities for the category of movement that your group was assigned. Identify other activities for this category and record them in the space provided. Then, practice these movements with your group:

1. What are all the ways you can move from one place to another?

      Taking giant steps

      Walking sideways

      Moving like a heavy animal

      Moving like you're as light as a feather

_____

_____

_____

_____

2. What are all the ways that you can move your body without moving your feet?

      Stretch really high

      Slowly unfold from a seed to a tree

      Twist like a pretzel

_____

_____

_____

_____

_____

3. What are all the ways that you can pantomime movements?

      Lift a hippopotamus

      Lift a feather and ask others, "What am I doing?"

      Move like an elephant and ask others, "What animal am I?"

      Move the way a character in a book moves, then describe the action

_____

_____

_____

_____

4. What are the ways you can move your body to match the music being played?

      Move in a happy way to light, lively music

      Move in a serious way to somber music

      Move with deliberate steps to marching music

_____

_____

_____

_____

_____

Supporting Children's Learning and Development Through Music and Movement

Developmental Area and Objectives	Music/Movement Activity
Social/Emotional Development Recognizes own feelings and manages them appropriately	
Respects and cares for classroom environment and materials	
Physical Development Demonstrates basic locomotor skills	
Coordinates eye-hand movement	
Cognitive Development Recognizes patterns and can repeat them	
Explores cause and effect	
Language Development Hears and discriminates the sounds of language	
Understands and follows directions	

Favorite Songs and Movement Activities

Types of Songs and Related Activities	Titles of Favorites
Songs with lots of repetition	
Songs with fingerplays	
Singing games and action songs	
Songs with funny sounds or silly lyrics	
Songs and dances of different cultures	
Movement games without music	

Observing and Responding to Children During Music and Movement

1. At the morning meeting, Derek frequently asks to sing "The Wheels on the Bus," making large movements with his arms. You've also noticed that Derek wears the train engineer's cap in the Dramatic Play Area and "chugs" around the room picking up passengers; and, outdoors, he soars about the playground pretending to be an airplane.

    What appears to be Derek's interest? How could you build upon it? What questions might you ask? What materials or experiences could you provide?

2. When singing "The Itsy Bitsy Spider," Sonya watches as others use alternating fingers to imitate a crawling spider. She attempts to perform the movement, but only for a brief moment. She continues to sing with her hands resting in her lap.

    What would be the best way to respond?

3. Zack has chosen to work in the Music and Movement Area during choice time. You notice that he is playing with the tone bells (bells of different sizes that produce a range of sounds).

    Generate a list of open-ended questions you might ask Zack that would encourage his exploration and learning.

4. You have several children whose first language is Spanish and who speak very little English. You notice their smiles during group singing and movement activities, but they rarely join in the activities.

    What does this observation tell you? How could you be responsive to these children? How could you encourage their involvement?

Cooking

WORKSHOPS

🔑 Key Points	✳ Workshop	📋 Materials	🕐 Time (minutes)
Cooking, a natural part of every child's life, is an ideal way to teach children lifelong healthy eating habits and to promote their knowledge, skills, and creativity.	**How Cooking Experiences Promote Children's Development** (p. 312)	☐ Ingredients (apple, celery, raisins, yogurt), plastic serrated knives, bowls, measuring spoons, paper plates, or cutting boards ☐ Handout **14A:** Fruit Salad ☐ Handout **14B:** Learning Through Cooking ☐ *Creative Curriculum,* p. 530	60
A safe, well-organized Cooking Area where children can explore, experiment, and create offers children a full range of learning opportunities.	**Creating an Environment for Cooking** (p. 314)	☐ Chart paper, markers ☐ Handout **14C:** Cooking in Ms. Lewis's Classroom ☐ Handout **14D:** Washing Hands— Sequence Cards ☐ Handout **14E:** Cooking Icons—Ingredients, Utensils, Processes ☐ *Creative Curriculum,* pp. 446-452, 461-465 ☐ *Implementation Checklist*	60
Thoughtful planning helps to ensure that cooking experiences go smoothly and learning is maximized.	**How Teachers Support Children's Learning Through Cooking** (p. 316)	☐ Handout **14F:** Recipes ☐ Handout **14G:** Preparing and Planning for Cooking in the Classroom ☐ *Creative Curriculum,* pp. 456–467	60–90

How Cooking Experiences Promote Children's Development

- ☐ Ingredients (apple, celery, raisins, yogurt), plastic serrated knives, bowls, measuring spoons, paper plates, or cutting boards
- ☐ Handout **14A**
- ☐ Handout **14B**
- ☐ *Creative Curriculum*, p. 530

PREPARATION

Gather sufficient quantities of ingredients and other necessary materials and equipment for the number of participants attending the workshop.

It would be helpful to conduct this workshop where there is access to a sink, for washing hands and foods. Please note that nuts are used in this recipe. If your school does not permit the use of nuts, you can eliminate them from the recipe.

INTRODUCTION

Introduce the workshop:

- Cooking is an exciting and valuable addition to every early childhood classroom for several reasons.

- Children love doing the same things that grown-ups do.

- Cooking enables children to develop many skills and concepts.

- The focus of this workshop will be on how cooking contributes to children's learning and development. You will be participating in a cooking activity similar to one that might take place in the classroom.

ACTIVITY

Explain to participants that they will prepare an individual serving of Fruit Salad. Refer them to the recipe on handout 14A. Review each step together.

Explain where all ingredients and equipment are located and review safety procedures, including washing hands and foods.

Ask them to clean up their areas and wash their hands when they are finished.

After allowing time for participants to complete the activity, give these instructions for completing handout 14B:

- Reflect on the cooking experience you just had.

- Show examples of skills and concepts children could learn for each of the four areas of development.

Refer to the "Goals and Objectives at a Glance" on page 530 for additional ideas.

Invite participants to share the ideas recorded on the handout.

SUMMARY

Summarize the activity with a discussion about the value of cooking with children by posing the following questions:

- What do children enjoy about cooking?

- How do you think they feel when they are able to prepare their own snack?

- What procedures need to be in place to ensure that cooking is a safe and enjoyable experience for children?

- What were some of the skills and concepts you listed on your handout under Social/Emotional Development? Physical Development? Cognitive Development? Language Development?

Creating an Environment for Cooking

□ Chart paper, markers
□ Handout **14C**
□ Handout **14D**
□ Handout **14E**
□ *Creative Curriculum,*
  pp. 446-452, 461-465
□ *Implementation
  Checklist*

PREPARATION

Ask each participant to bring in a favorite family recipe, preferably one that is nutritious (e.g., salad, snack, bread, vegetable). Duplicate the handouts.

INTRODUCTION

Introduce the workshop by having participants read the scenario on handout 14C and answer the following questions:

• What are Ms. Lewis's goals for cooking activities?

• What learning opportunities are being overlooked in this scenario?

• How can cooking in Ms. Lewis's classroom be improved?

Make the following points:

• Cooking is typically a special activity in most preschool classrooms.

• While Ms. Lewis's cooking activities are a welcome part of her program, they do not tap the full potential for learning through cooking.

• The purpose of this workshop is to examine ways in which the Cooking Area can be set up and organized so that children can explore, experiment, and create on their own, in small groups, or one-on-one with a teacher, parent volunteer, or another child.

ACTIVITY

Ask participants why teachers are reluctant to include a cooking area and cooking experiences in their classrooms. Record participant responses on chart paper.

Possible responses:

It is dangerous.   *It is messy.*

It is noisy.   *The facilities are inadequate.*

Health and safety policies are prohibitive.

I don't have the supplies and materials I need.

It requires too much supervision.

Lead a discussion about how each of these barriers might be overcome. It may be helpful to have participants reflect on their own cooking experiences and the organization of their own kitchens. Share the strategies recommended on pages 446–452 and 463–465 about

- location and set-up of the area

- material and equipment selection

- organization and display of equipment and tools

- health and safety considerations

Refer participants to the "Cooking" section of the *Implementation Checklist* (page 11). Review the items and then have participants complete self-assessments of their Cooking Areas.

Have participants identify any improvements to make to their Cooking Areas. Allow time for participants to discuss or solicit help from others regarding items that seem particularly challenging for them.

Call attention to the format of the recipes presented on pages 461-463.

Have participants work in groups and decide which of their favorite recipes would lend themselves to be used for small-group or independent cooking experiences. If a recipe is to be used independently, have participants reduce the recipe to a single-portion size.

Allow time for participants to plan or make the sequence/step cards for their new recipes using the icons on handouts 14D and 14E.

SUMMARY

Summarize the workshop with the following points:

- The Cooking Area can, and should be, as active and well-developed as the other interest areas in the classroom.

- Once health and safety guidelines are met and basic techniques taught, the Cooking Area becomes a place where children can explore, experiment, and create snacks and other dishes on their own or in a small group.

WORKSHOP

How Teachers Support Children's Learning Through Cooking

☐ Handout **14F**
☐ Handout **14G**
☐ *Creative Curriculum,*
   pp. 456–467

◖ PREPARATION

Duplicate the handouts.

◖ INTRODUCTION

Introduce the workshop:

- The Cooking Area is a natural laboratory, well suited for addressing all content areas and helping children develop and refine many skills and concepts.

- As in other interest areas, the teacher serves as a leader, facilitator, and support system for children working in the Cooking Area.

- To ensure that things go smoothly and safely for everyone and to maximize the learning potential of each cooking experience, teachers must thoughtfully plan.

- Planning includes thinking about children's current abilities and interests andpreferences, the goals you have for their learning, and the strategies (e.g., setting, teaching approaches, mode of interaction) you will use to help them progress.

Explain that, in this workshop, participants will examine a variety of recipes and plan for their use in the classroom. Make these points:

- The **setting** in which each recipe would best be used (e.g., independently in the Cooking Area, in a supervised small group) is an essential consideration.

- The **teaching approaches** you use with the children will vary (e.g., you might consider what skills need to be explicitly taught and how you will do so, or what you will do, say, or ask children in order to promote their learning and development).

- The **content** that could be addressed through the cooking experience—literacy, math, science, social studies, the arts, technology, and process skills—is broad.

ACTIVITY

Have participants read pages 456–467 or suggest that they divide the reading among members of the group and then discuss what they have learned.

Have participants form 10 groups. Explain that each group will select a different recipe from handout 14F and plan for its use in the classroom by completing the questions on handout 14G.

Refer the group to handout 14G and review each question.

Allow about 20 minutes for group work.

Invite each group to share its plan.

SUMMARY

Summarize with the following points:

- Cooking is a natural part of every child's life. It's an ideal way to teach children lifelong healthy eating habits, and to promote children's knowledge, skills, and creativity.

- Children can participate in both independent and small group cooking experiences.

- Through thoughtful planning, teachers can help to ensure that children's experiences with cooking are successful and satisfying, and that meaningful learning is taking place.

Fruit Salad

1. Cut up 1 apple. Put in mixing bowl.

2. Cut up 1 celery stalk. Put in mixing bowl.

3. Add 10 raisins.

4. Crack 2 walnuts into pieces.

5. Add 1 T plain yogurt

6. Mix together. Enjoy!

Learning Through Cooking

For each of the four areas of development, provide examples of things children might learn during cooking.

Social/Emotional Development:

Physical Development:

Cognitive Development:

Language Development:

Cooking in Ms. Lewis's Classroom

Ms. Lewis is a new teacher and has made the decision to include a cooking activity in her classroom every day. She realizes that cooking can be a complex process for young children but believes it will be an enjoyable and worthwhile experience for them. Her plan is to make the experience as simple as possible by using many of the instant products on the market today such as instant pudding or cake mix and by working with only one small group of children each day during choice time. She concludes that in doing so, every child will have a chance to cook at least once during the week and every child will benefit from the finished product each day.

Ms. Lewis introduces the recipe of the day at the end of circle time and identifies the group of children who will prepare it for the rest of the class. She is correct in her assumption that cooking is enjoyable for the children as indicated by the rush of hands in the air and the chanting of "Pick me, pick me!" Seeing their excitement, Ms. Lewis quickly assures the children that everyone will have a chance to cook during the week, but they must learn to wait for their turns.

Washing Hands—Sequence Cards

1

Wet hands.

2

Add soap.

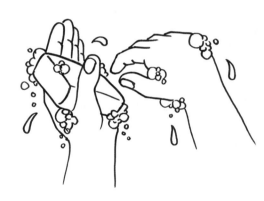

3

Rinse your hands.

4

Dry your hands with a paper towel.

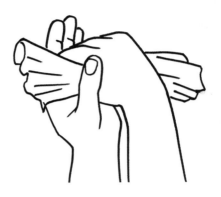

5

Toss the paper towel in the trash.

Cooking Icons—Ingredients

vanilla

spices

bread

carrots

lemons or
lemon juice

lettuce

apple

orange

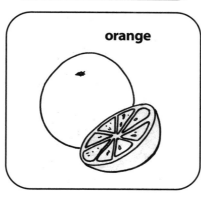

tomato

onion

cheese

banana

Cooking Icons—Ingredients, continued

milk

cooking oil

crackers

potatoes

cornmeal

pears

peach

salt

sugar

flour

eggs

margarine

Cooking Icons—Ingredients, continued

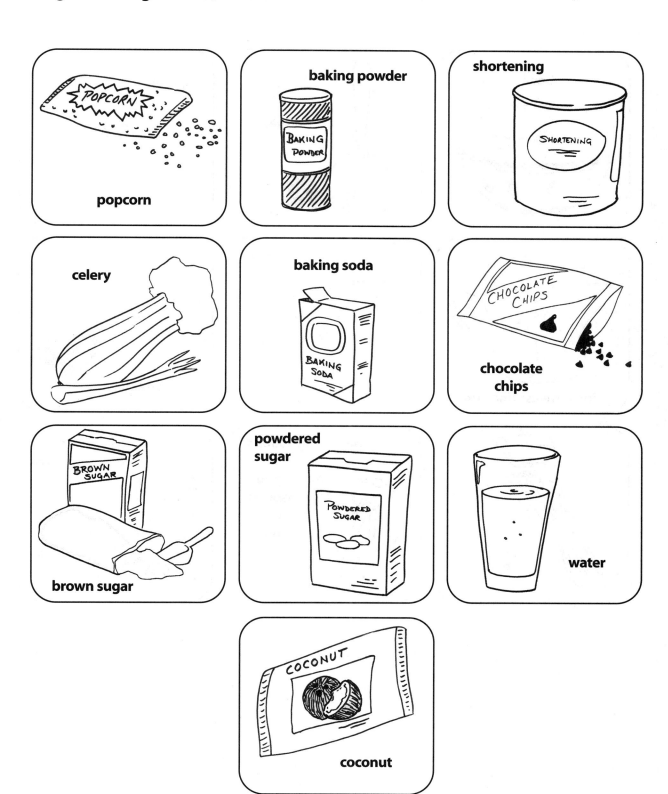

popcorn

baking powder

shortening

celery

baking soda

chocolate chips

brown sugar

powdered sugar

water

coconut

Cooking Icons—Utensils

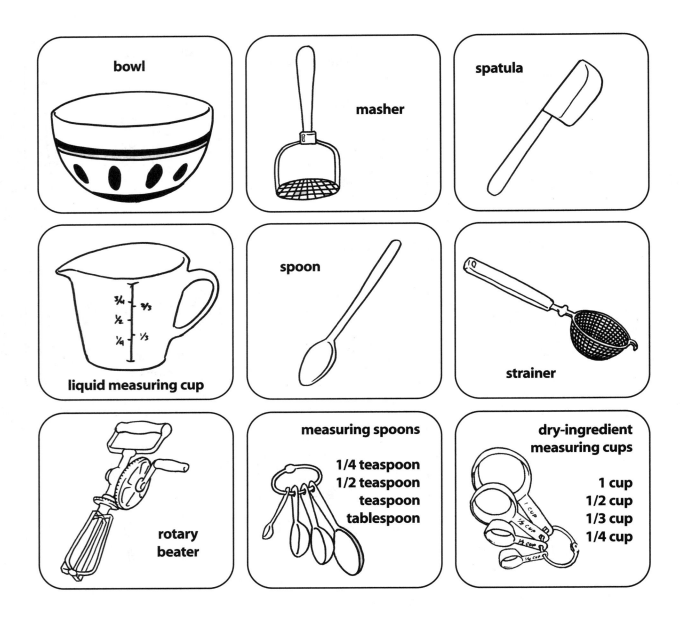

bowl

masher

spatula

liquid measuring cup

spoon

strainer

rotary beater

measuring spoons

1/4 teaspoon
1/2 teaspoon
teaspoon
tablespoon

dry-ingredient measuring cups

1 cup
1/2 cup
1/3 cup
1/4 cup

Cooking Icons—Processes

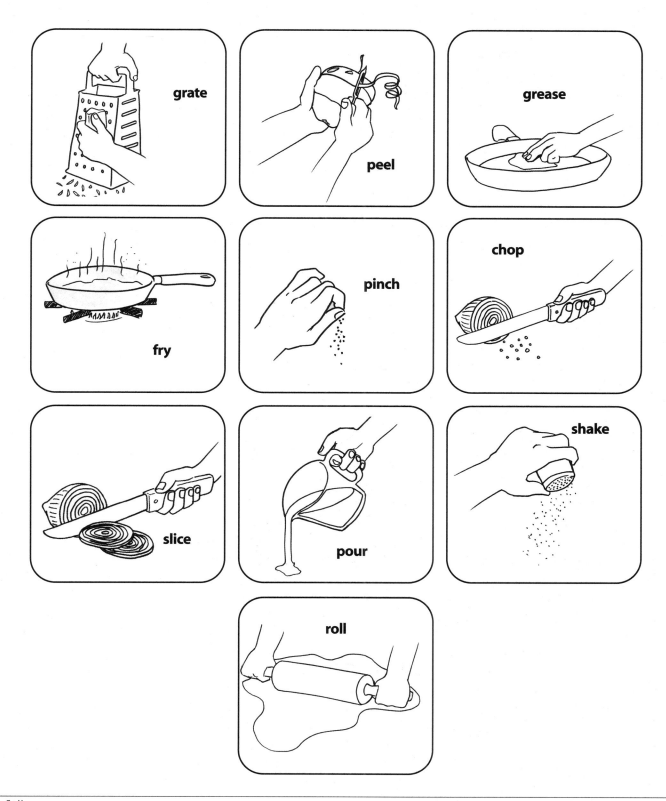

grate

peel

grease

fry

pinch

chop

slice

pour

shake

roll

Recipes

Baggie Ice Cream
(single serving)

Food:
6 tablespoons of rock salt
ice
1/2 cup milk
1 tablespoon sugar
1/8 teaspoon vanilla

Equipment:
large zipper baggie
small zipper baggie

Method:
Fill 1/3 of a large zipper bag with ice. Put rock salt on top of the ice.

Then, in the smaller bag, mix milk, sugar, and vanilla.

Close the bag securely and place it inside the large bag.

Close and shake it for about 5 minutes.

Blueberry Muffins
(makes 12 muffins)

Food:
1 egg
1 cup blueberries, drained
1/2 cup milk
1/4 cup vegetable oil
1 1/2 cups flour
1/2 cup sugar
2 teaspoons baking powder
1/2 teaspoon salt

Method:
Grease the bottoms of the muffin cups.

Beat the egg with the fork. Blend the dry ingredients together and add egg, oil, and milk.

The batter will be lumpy. Carefully blend in 1 cup well-drained blueberries.

Fill the muffin cups 2/3 full of batter.

Bake at 400 degrees for 20-25 minutes or until muffins are golden brown.

Recipes, continued

Cheesy Quesadillas
(single serving)

Food:
1/2 tortilla per child
shredded cheese
cooking spray

Method:
Put shredded cheese on half of the tortilla.

Fold over the other half.

Spray a thin coat of cooking spray on an electric skillet and warm the tortilla until the cheese begins to melt and it has begun to brown.

Flip the tortilla to brown the other side.

Cool slightly before eating.

Coconut-Covered Bananas
(single serving)

Food:
1/2 orange
1/2 banana
shredded coconut

Method:
Cut banana into bite-size pieces.

Squeeze some of the juice of the orange onto a saucer and roll the banana in the juice. (Then eat the orange.)

Then roll the banana in the coconut to coat it well.

Recipes, continued

Lemonade
(single serving)

Food:
1/2 lemon
2 teaspoons sugar
1/3 cup water
colored ice cubes (red or blue)

Method:
Squeeze the lemon and pour the juice into a cup.

Add sugar and water.

Stir.

Add an ice cube to your lemonade.

Fruit Shake
(single serving)

Food:
1 strawberry
1 1" slice of banana
1 orange section
1/4 cup pineapple juice
1 teaspoon sugar or honey
2 ice cubes

Method:
Put all ingredients into a blender and blend briefly.

Pour into a cup.

Recipes, continued

Tuna Fruit Salad
(single serving)

Food:
1 tablespoon tuna fish
1 tablespoon chopped celery
1/8 apple, chopped
3 pineapple cubes
4 grapes
1/2 tablespoon lemon juice
1 lettuce leaf per child

Method:
Toss all of the ingredients in a bowl.

Serve on a lettuce leaf.

Yogurt Parfait

Food:
plain yogurt
blueberries
raisins
banana slices
peach slices
shredded coconut

Method:
Set out the ingredients.

Create a parfait by layering yogurt, fruit, raisins, etc. in a 5 ounce paper cup.

Recipes, continued

Pretzels

Food:
1 1/2 cups warm water
1 envelope yeast
1 tablespoon sugar
4 cups flour
1 teaspoon salt
coarse salt

Method:
Mix together warm water (110-115 degrees F), yeast, and sugar.

Set aside for 5 minutes.

Put salt and flour in a bowl, and add the yeast mix.

Mix together to form a dough and shape into creative twists.

Beat 1 egg and brush onto twists, then sprinkle on coarse salt.

Bake at 425 degrees F for 12 minutes.

Painted Toast
(single serving)

Food:
milk
bread

Equipment:
food coloring
unused fine tipped
paintbrushes

Method:
Pour about 1/2 cup of milk in separate bowls and color each with food coloring.

Put one paintbrush in each bowl.

Give each child one slice of white sandwich bread and allow him/her to paint on the bread.

Toast the bread in a toaster oven.

Recipes, continued

Ants on a Log
(single serving)

Food:
1 stalk celery
cream cheese or
peanut butter
raisins

Method:
Pull off one stalk of celery (the log).

Wash the stalk and trim the celery ends.

Spread cream cheese or peanut butter into the center of the celery.

Add the raisins (ants).

Trail Mix
(single serving)

Food:
1/4 cup each Chex cereals
(corn, wheat, rice)
1/4 cup Cheerios
10 pretzel sticks
1-2 teaspoons raisins
1 tablespoon shredded
coconut
slivered almonds (optional)

Method:
Measure the ingredients and place into a baggie.

Zip the baggie and shake to mix.

Preparing and Planning for Cooking in the Classroom

Recipe: _____

1. Is this a dish that children can make themselves (independently or with supervision) or one that would be better suited to a small group activity? Explain your answer.

2. How would you introduce this recipe to the children?

3. What cooking skills would need to be taught explicitly in order for children to be successful?

4. Describe how you might teach one of the skills children would need to complete this recipe.

5. Which *Creative Curriculum* objectives could be addressed through this cooking experience?

Preparing and Planning for Cooking in the Classroom, continued

6. How would you integrate content through this cooking experience? What might you do, say, or ask to extend the children's critical thinking skills?

Literacy

Math

Science

Social Studies

The Arts

Technology

Computers

WORKSHOPS

🔑 Key Points	⚙ Workshop	📋 Materials	🕐 Time (minutes)
Computers can be a valuable tool in the preschool classroom. Success with computers depends on how they are integrated into the classroom and the software available to children.	**Creating a Computer Area to Support Children's Development and Learning** (p. 338)	□ Computers, software, chart paper, markers □ Handout **15A:** *The Creative Curriculum* Checklist for Selecting Developmentally Appropriate Software □ *Implementation Checklist* □ *Creative Curriculum,* pp. 477–481	90
The way in which teachers support children's use of computers will influence whether their experiences are successful or frustrating and whether computers are used appropriately or inappropriately.	**How Teachers Support Children's Learning in the Computer Area** (p. 342)	□ Handout **15B:** Interacting With Children in the Computer Area □ *Creative Curriculum,* pp. 485, 487–488	30–45

Creating a Computer Area to Support Children's Development and Learning

☐ Computers, software, chart paper, markers
☐ Handout **15A**
☐ *Implementation Checklist*
☐ *Creative Curriculum*, pp. 477–481

PREPARATION

Prior to the workshop, make arrangements for participants to have access to computers; perhaps there is a computer lab at the school or center that can be used. Have participants work at the computers in pairs, or have part of the group serve as observers, and then switch roles.

Arrange to use 15–20 software programs that require varying levels of child involvement (see the chart on page 477 and refer to page 479 for web sites that discuss appropriate software). Find out what software is already installed and use that if possible. If you will be bringing your own software to use for demonstration purposes, be aware that most software grants you a license to install it on only one computer. When you are finished with this activity, uninstall the software you have brought with you to avoid breaking the licensing agreement. Many software vendors offer demonstration versions that can be downloaded for free from the Internet. Also note that installing and removing software can take time; arrange to have this done with the help of the individual in charge of maintaining the lab or school computers.

Duplicate enough copies of handout 15A so pairs of participants can evaluate multiple software programs.

INTRODUCTION

Introduce the workshop with the following points:

• Most experts in early childhood education agree that the appropriate use of computers with young children can be beneficial.

• They feel that computers can provide effective learning opportunities for children when used appropriately.

• The purposes of this workshop are to examine the value of computers in the early childhood classroom and to look at how they can be used to support children's development and learning.

◀ ACTIVITY

Explain that participants will debate the pros and cons of including computers in the early childhood classroom.

Form two groups. Ask one group to defend the statement, "Computers have no place in the preschool classroom," and ask the other group to question or dispute the statement.

Allow about 10–15 minutes for each group to write a list of talking points on chart paper.

Post the charts on opposing walls.

Begin by having one group make a point and then let the opposing group respond. Then have the second group make a point and the first group respond. Continue as long as participants are engaged.

> **Possible responses:**
>
> **Against computers:**
>
> *Costs—initial costs and maintenance*
>
> *Security issues*
>
> *Requires skills that are too advanced for young children*
>
> *Isolates children, discourage social skill development*
>
> *Stunts children's imagination and creativity*
>
> *Contributes to health problems (stress injuries, visual strain, obesity due to sedentary nature of activity)*
>
> **In favor of computers:**
>
> *Promotes oral language and social development when children work in pairs*
>
> *Promotes cognitive development and problem solving*
>
> *Promotes fine motor control and eye-hand coordination through the use of the keyboard and mouse*
>
> *Reinforces and supports other learning in literacy, math, science, social studies, arts, and technology*
>
> *Helps children make the bridge between the concrete and abstract*
>
> *Provides equal access to technology (adaptive devices for special needs children)*
>
> *Is intrinsically motivating for many children*

After completing the debate, summarize the discussion of the pros and cons of using computers in the early childhood classroom. Present the following statement (page 489):

The question to ask isn't, "Should I be using computers in my preschool classroom?" but rather, "How can I make the best use of computers in my preschool classroom to help children achieve higher levels?" (Fouts, 2000)

If participants are not seated at computers, have them do so.

Introduce key points about setting up and equipping the Computer Area as a means of further addressing any points listed as cons. A few examples include these:

- Health and safety concerns can be addressed by arranging the computers so that the cords are out of children's reach, the lighting is appropriate so there is no glare on the screen, the monitor is positioned so that children are no less than 18" from the screen, keyboards are at an appropriate height, etc.

- Social skills and language can be promoted when two children share one computer.

- Creativity can be encouraged by selecting open-ended software.

- Locating the Computer Area close to the Library, Toys and Games, or Discovery Areas encourages children to use the computer as a tool for communicating, problem-solving, and gathering information.

- All children can benefit from using computers, particularly children with special needs (refer to pages 480–481).

If necessary, review specifications for hardware or any terms the group might want clarified. Discuss computer-assisted devices with audiences who work with special needs children.

Review the items in the "Computer" section on page 11 of the *Implementation Checklist*. Then have participants complete self-assessments of the Computer Areas in their classrooms. Have them identify any areas that need strengthening.

Lead a brief discussion about selecting software and websites. Review the "Software: Level of Child Involvement" continuum, found at the bottom of page 477, and the "Checklist for Selecting Developmentally Appropriate Software" on page 478.

Provide time for participants to explore varied software. Give the following tasks:

- Evaluate each program using handout 15A.

- Determine where each program would fall on the "Software: Level of Child Involvement" continuum.

- Identify the programs most appropriate for preschool children.

Invite participants to share their findings.

Point out the resources for selecting appropriate software and websites recommended on page 479.

SUMMARY

Lead a closing discussion of the value of including computers in the preschool classroom.

Summarize with the following points:

- Successful experiences with computers depend on how the computer is integrated into the classroom.

- The setup of the Computer Area and the software and web sites available to children influence whether their experiences are successful or frustrating, and whether computers are used appropriately or inappropriately.

- The computer is a tool that can benefit all children, including those with special needs.

How Teachers Support Children's Learning in the Computer Area

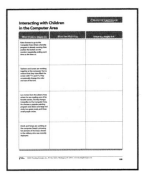

☐ Handout **15B**
☐ *Creative Curriculum*,
   pp. 485, 487–488

PREPARATION

Duplicate handout 15B.

INTRODUCTION

Introduce the workshop with the following points:

- The way teachers support children's use of computers will influence whether their experiences are successful or frustrating and whether computers are used appropriately or inappropriately.

- Teachers can help children learn to use computers as tools for problem solving, research, creativity, and fun.

- As in other interest areas, teachers rely on their observations of children to help them make decisions about how to respond to children.

Refer participants to page 485 and discuss the stages of computer use:

- investigation
- self-confidence
- involvement
- creativity and original thinking

Make the following points:

- As with all learning, children's use of computers follows a developmental progression as just described.

- Your interactions with children while they use the computer will help determine whether they use it constructively—as a tool for problem solving, exploring, and investigating—or not constructively—to dabble or do busywork. For example, sometimes children use programs randomly and with little purpose because they (and their teachers) don't know how the programs work.

- As you observe children's use of computers, think carefully about each child's developmental stage, and then determine how best to interact to address children's needs and enrich their experiences.

- Talking with children about their work on the computer is one of the most important ways of encouraging computer usage.

- Using open-ended questions encourages children to describe or explain their actions and extends their thinking.

Have participants read pages 487–488 or and then discuss these concepts:

- describing what children are doing

- asking questions to encourage children to put their actions into words

- asking open-ended questions that promote process skills

ACTIVITY

Have participants turn to handout 15B. Then give the following instructions:

- Pair up with someone at your table.

- Read the observation in the first box of each row. Determine what you might say to the child to affirm what he or she is doing. Record your statement in the second box.

- Next, think of two open-ended questions—one that encourages the child to describe or explain his actions, and one that promotes a process skill mentioned on page 488.

Invite participants to share examples of their responses with the entire group.

Discuss ways in which families might become involved in helping children learn more about technology. Invite participants to share strategies that have been successful in their programs.

SUMMARY

Summarize the workshop with the following points:

- The way in which teachers interact with children while they are working at the computer sets the stage for how children will use it—as a tool or as a toy.

- When teachers talk with children about their experiences with computers, they

    help children to reflect on what they are doing and why

    let children know that this work is valued

    build children's confidence in their ability to use computers

    promote thinking skills

The Creative Curriculum® Checklist
for Selecting Developmentally Appropriate Software

☐ Program has age-appropriate content and approach with realistic expectations for children's skill levels. Children experience success and feel competent using it.

☐ Child can use and adjust control features independently, without adult assistance.

☐ Program makes use of intrinsic motivation, not rewards, and is paced so children don't have to wait a long time for the program to load or for graphics or feedback to appear.

☐ Program offers choices that child can control.

☐ Content is meaningful and interesting and can be expanded. The software is open-ended and engages children in exploration and problem-solving activities.

☐ Child can set the pace for movement through the program and exit at any time.

☐ Child and/or teacher can set the level of difficulty.

☐ Feedback uses meaningful graphics/sound and can be individualized.

☐ Instructions are clear and simple and not dependent on the ability to read.

☐ Program appeals to a variety of learning styles and multiple intelligences.

☐ Teacher can track child's history using the program.

☐ Content and feedback are bias-free and violence-free.

☐ Program is accessible to all children, including those with special needs and those who are second language learners.

☐ Program offers good value for the cost.

From *The Creative Curriculum® for Preschool*, 4th Edition, p. 478.
©2004 Teaching Strategies, Inc., PO Box 42243, Washington, DC 20015, www.TeachingStrategies.com

Interacting With Children in the Computer Area

Observation	Reflection	Response
Kate chooses to go to the Computer Area where a favorite program is already running. Kate pushes the on/off button on the monitor repeatedly, smiling each time as she does so.	Kate is discovering that if you push the button, the screen turns on and off. She is exploring the physical properties of the computer *(Objective 25. Explores cause and effect; Objective 20. Coordinates eye-hand movement)*. What other ways can I help Kate explore the physical properties of the computer? How can I help her build language skills as she explores?	Say, "When you push the button, the screen turns on. When you push it again, the screen turns off." Ask, "I wonder what would happen if I push one of these letters?" While using a drawing program, say, "Watch what will happen when I move this mouse back and forth."
Tasheen and Juwan are working together at the computer. You've noticed that they have filled the screen with "T"s and "J"s. They occasionally change the color and size of the font.		
Leo moves from the Library Area where he was reading one of his favorite stories, *The Very Hungry Caterpillar*, to the Computer Area. He chooses a popular painting program and draws one large red circle, two green ovals, and three small purple circles.		
Derek and Sonya are working at the computer. Derek is showing her pictures of his Dad, a doctor in the military, who was recently deployed.		

Outdoors

WORKSHOPS

🔑 Key Points	⬡ Workshop	▤ Materials	Time (minutes)
The Outdoor Area is a total learning environment where children can grow in all areas of development—social/emotional, physical, cognitive, and language.	**How Outdoor Play Promotes Development** (p. 348)	☐ Materials, supplies, and equipment for learning stations ☐ Chart paper, markers ☐ Handout **16A:** Outdoor Learning Stations—Instructions ☐ Handout **16B:** Assessing the Value of the Outdoor Area—Learning Station Worksheet	90
An inviting outdoor environment offers children a variety of clear choices for very different kinds of experiences and challenges.	**Creating and Using the Outdoor Environment** (p. 350)	☐ Chart paper, markers, ☐ *Creative Curriculum* video ☐ Handout **16C:** Remembering the Outdoors ☐ Handout **16D:** My Outdoor Plan ☐ *Creative Curriculum,* pp. 497–510 ☐ *Implementation Checklist*	60–90
By observing what interests each child outdoors, teachers can respond in ways that extend learning.	**How Teachers Support Children's Learning in the Outdoor Area** (p. 354)	☐ Transparency **16E:** Four Types of Play ☐ Handout **16F:** What Observations Tell Us ☐ *Creative Curriculum,* pp. 514–516	60
Teachers who provide children uninterrupted time to explore the outdoors and demonstrate their own interest, excitement, and curiosity, nurture children's interest in nature.	**Nurturing Children's Appreciation of the Natural Environment** (p. 356)	☐ Paper, pencils, pens, or markers ☐ Handout **16G:** Nurturing Children's Appreciation of Nature	30–45

How Outdoor Play Promotes Development

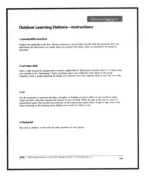

☐ Materials, supplies,
   and equipment for
   learning stations
☐ Chart paper, markers
☐ Handout **16A**
☐ Handout **16B**

PREPARATION

Locate sufficient outdoor space for this workshop as participants will be engaging in active outdoor experiences. Create four learning stations with the following materials at each station:

1. **Learning With Loose Parts**

    Materials: Select several from this list.
    chart paper, markers, tubes, tubing, lids, bottle caps, fabric, netting, ribbon, film canisters, nutcracker, carpet scraps, buckets, toilet paper rolls, measuring tape, ice cube trays, magnifying glass, measuring cups, clothespins, PVC pipe and connectors, paint brushes, assorted kitchen gadgets, wood pieces, pulleys, gears, rocks, leaves, twigs, paper, pencils, pine cones, and nuts

2. **Let's Take a Walk**

    Materials:
    paper bags, chart paper, markers, tape

3. **Art**

    Materials:
    water color paints, water, drawing or painting paper, modeling dough, crayons, marker, construction paper and tape or rubber cement for mounting completed artwork

4. **Playing Ball**

    Materials:
    variety of balls (e.g., playground or utility, foam, beach, bumpy, yarn, plastic baseballs, tumble/exercise, soccer, football, tennis, etc.)

Duplicate the handouts.

INTRODUCTION

Begin with a discussion about how participants feel about the outdoors. Ask them to think about and discuss at their tables what they enjoyed most and least about playing outdoors when they were children.

Next, have participants discuss what they enjoy most about being outdoors now as an adult. Invite a few participants to share their memories or the points from their discussions.

Make the following points:

- The ways in which you use the outdoor environment with young children are greatly influenced by how you feel about the outdoors.

- Children are sensitive to adult feelings and can be influenced by what you feel about the outdoors—the things that we enjoy about the outdoors are often the same things children enjoy.

- The purpose of this workshop is to consider the value of the outdoor area and ways it can be used to enrich the curriculum and support children's overall development and learning.

ACTIVITY

Form four equal groups. Explain the following:

- There are four outdoor learning stations, each equipped with materials and handout 16A with instructions explaining your task.

- You will have approximately 10–15 minutes to spend at each station. I'll give you a signal when it is time to change stations.

- After the end of the allotted time, you will return to the training room and complete handout 16B.

When participants have completed the handout, invite them to share their responses and any observations about their experiences.

Lead a discussion about the problems that prevent teachers from using the Outdoor Area effectively, listing the issues participants identify on chart paper.

Assign each table one barrier listed and have them brainstorm solutions to the problem. Reconvene the entire group and ask each table to report. Record their ideas in the appropriate column. Emphasize the importance of planning for outdoor time to overcome any barriers.

SUMMARY

Summarize with the following points:

- Outdoor play is essential for children's health and well-being.

- The time children spend outdoors every day is just as important to their learning and development as the time they spend in the classroom. In fact, children can be observed related to almost every *Creative Curriculum* objective during outdoor time.

- Teachers who truly want to take full advantage of the Outdoor Area as another learning environment thoughtfully plan and seek creative solutions to overcoming the barriers.

Creating and Using the Outdoor Environment

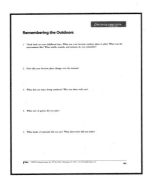

□ Chart paper, markers
□ *Creative Curriculum* video
□ Handout **16C**
□ Handout **16D**
□ *Creative Curriculum,* pp. 497–510
□ *Implementation Checklist*

PREPARATION

Prepare a chart listing the outdoor activity spaces discussed in *The Creative Curriculum*:

> sand and water play
>
> a track for wheeled toys
>
> a garden
>
> space to care for living things
>
> open space for playing games, building, and pretend play
>
> space for indoor materials that can be brought outdoors
>
> playground structures

Prior to the workshop, ask participants to sketch a map of their Outdoor Areas. Have them include a list of all equipment and materials available. Duplicate the handouts. Cue the video to the "Outdoors" segment.

INTRODUCTION

Introduce the workshop:

- No other aspect of an early childhood environment varies as much from one program to another as the Outdoor Area.

- Some programs have grassy areas, trees, plants, and playground equipment specifically designed for young children, while others have only asphalt and little or no equipment.

- The purpose of this workshop is to examine ways in which you can create an enjoyable outdoor setting for the children in your program, regardless of your circumstances.

ACTIVITY

Introduce the activity with the following points:

- The starting point for designing the outdoor environment is the children.

- To get started in thinking about how to make the outdoors a rich and inviting environment for your children, reflect on the outdoor experiences you had as a child.

Distribute handout 16C. Ask participants to read and answer the questions. Have them share their memories with others at their tables.

Refer to the chart of activity spaces (which you prepared earlier) discussed in the Curriculum.

Invite participants to share some of the outdoor activities they enjoyed during their childhood years and identify the category in which each one would fit. Ask if there are any other categories or spaces they might like to add.

Make the following points:

- Each of us is unique; we all enjoyed doing different things outdoors as children.

- When you create a well-planned outdoor environment that offers children a variety of clear choices, you are able to address their individual interests and needs and to promote learning and development.

- The key to making these different areas work is to define space, create easy-to-follow traffic patterns, and equip them well. By doing so, you will minimize injuries and maximize learning and fun.

Introduce the "Outdoors" segment of the *Creative Curriculum* video. Point out that many of the activity areas shown were either created by teachers or expanded with the addition of homemade materials (e.g., blowing bubbles outdoors, painting a building with water, and bringing cardboard boxes outside).

Invite comments about the video.

Lead a discussion about bringing the indoors outdoors. Invite participants to share ideas that they have used successfully. Have participants read pages 503–504 for additional ideas. You may want to have them brainstorm additional ideas for "Play Crates."

Next, have participants select a partner and share the drawings of their outdoor areas. Give these instructions:

- Identify where the activities listed on the chart paper take place.

- Identify the areas most frequently used by the children and tell why you think this is so.

Discuss the items in the "Outdoors" section found on page 12 of the the *Implementation Checklist*. Then have group members complete self-assessments of their Outdoor Areas.

Next, have participants develop a plan to create, expand, or improve upon the outdoor environment at their own school or center. Suggest that they choose from one of the following options:

- an activity area discussed in the Curriculum (e.g., gardening area)

- one or more aspects of the environment that needs improving as identified by their self-assessment with the *Implementation Checklist* (e.g., acquiring a variety of age-appropriate equipment for climbing)

- another aspect such as making sure the outdoor environment is accommodating to children with special needs

Give the following instructions:

- Read the relevant section(s) on pages 497–508. Also read the section, "Special Considerations" on pages 509–510.

- Develop a plan that includes

  the area or aspect of focus

  the tasks associated with the development, expansion, or improvement of this area including, for example,

  a list of equipment to be purchased, if any

  a list of equipment that could be acquired through donations from teachers, parents, or community members

  the names of individuals who will be responsible for accomplishing each task

  anticipated date of completion

Allow about 20 minutes for this activity. Have participants record their ideas on handout 16D.

Invite a few participants to share their respective plans.

◀ SUMMARY

Summarize the workshop with the following points:

- The outdoor environment, like the indoor, should offer children a variety of experiences and challenges including opportunities for active and quiet play, group and individual play, teacher-directed and child-initiated play.

- Safe, well-defined outdoor spaces equipped with interesting materials helps keep children engaged and promotes learning and development.

- In some settings, teachers have to be creative to make outdoor time enjoyable and interesting.

NOTES

How Teachers Support Children's Learning in the Outdoor Area

☐ Transparency **16E**
☐ Handout **16F**
☐ *Creative Curriculum*,
 pp. 514–516

PREPARATION

Prior to the workshop, ask participants to collect observations of one child during outdoor time on 3–5 different occasions.

INTRODUCTION

Introduce the workshop with the following points:

- The teacher's role in the Outdoor Area extends well beyond supervisory duties.

- Countless teachable moments occur during outdoor time and teachers should take full advantage of them.

- The purposes of this workshop are to

    discuss a framework for observing children outdoors that can help you to determine how to respond to children and extend their learning

    examine ways in which to interact with children to encourage them to take safe risks and nurture their appreciation for the natural environment

Show transparency 16E of the four different kinds of play.

Review each, giving examples of what children might do outdoors. Point out that these are discussed on pages 514–515.

Make the following points:

- Because so many activities are going on at once outdoors, it is easy to watch children without really seeing what is going on. Teachers must make a concerted effort to observe children purposefully.

- As you observe children, notice how they are using the Outdoor Area (refer back to the four kinds of play).

- All children are different; therefore, they will approach the outdoors in different ways. For example, there are some children who readily become involved in active play while others appear timid and a little anxious about the open and unpredictable outdoor environment.

Have participants turn to page 515 and read the bulleted list of things teachers can look for as children use the outdoors.

ACTIVITY

Distribute handout 16F. Explain that they will analyze their observations of one child outdoors. Give the following instructions:

- Take out the observations you collected prior to coming to the workshop.

- Use the handout and answer each question with the information from your observation notes.

- Next, find a partner and share what you learned about this child.

- Together, brainstorm ways you might enhance and extend this child's learning.

Allow about 20–30 minutes for this activity.

Invite a few participants to summarize their findings and plans for the child observed.

Remind participants that the observations collected during outdoor time can be used to assess each child's progress toward many of the goals and objectives of *The Creative Curriculum*. Review the chart on page 516 with the group.

SUMMARY

Summarize the activity:

- Observing children outdoors enables you to see how they use their skills in this unique environment. You discover parts of a child's personality you hadn't seen before and become aware of unexpected fears or surprising courage.

- *Creative Curriculum* teachers take full advantage of the Outdoor Area to help children progress in their achievement towards the goals and objectives of the Curriculum.

Nurturing Children's Appreciation of the Natural Environment

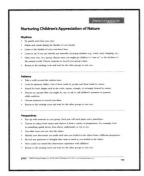

☐ Paper, pencils, pens, or markers
☐ Handout **16G**

PREPARATION

Prior to the workshop, locate a diverse outdoor area (e.g., one that has sunny and shady spots, trees, flowers, grassy area, birds, puddles, etc.) where activities can take place. Since participants will be spending time outdoors during this workshop, be sure to notify them ahead of time so that they can dress appropriately.

Participants will be divided into three equal groups. Duplicate handout 16G, making enough copies so that each group member will have a set of instructions. Cut them apart.

INTRODUCTION

Introduce the workshop:

- Teachers don't have to be naturalists to instill in children an awe of the natural world and a desire to discover and uncover what is around them.

- Children are intrigued by nature as it changes constantly and offers countless surprises.

- By providing children uninterrupted time to explore the outdoors and by demonstrating your own interest, excitement, and curiosity, you can nurture children's interest in nature.

Explain that in this workshop participants will have time to tune in to nature so they can then foster children's connections with nature.

ACTIVITY

Lead participants to the outdoor area. Form three groups. Give each group member a set of instructions and the necessary materials for one of the activities in the handout related to rhythms, patterns, or perspectives.

After completing the activities, invite the groups to share their experiences and ideas.

Discuss options for programs that may not have access to natural environments. Options may include taking children on outdoor field trips to parks, community gardens, bird sanctuaries, trails, etc.

SUMMARY

Summarize with the following points:

- Today, more than ever before, environmental education is vital.

- Children have fewer opportunities to be exposed to nature firsthand.

- If you want children to grow up to be people who care about preserving the environment, you have to start early to cultivate an appreciation for nature.

- You are models for children.

Outdoor Learning Stations—Instructions

1. Learning With Loose Parts

Explore the materials in the box. Choose someone to record what you did with the materials; how you used them; the discoveries you made; what you created with them; what you pretend to be using the materials.

2. Let's Take a Walk

Take a walk around the playground or nearby neighborhood. Each person should collect 3–5 objects that you consider to be "interesting." Upon returning, share your collection with others in the group. Together, create a graph depicting the things you collected. You may organize them in any way you wish.

3. Art

Use the materials to represent the ideas, thoughts, or feelings you have while you are outdoors today. Come up with a title that captures the essence of your artwork. Write the title at the top of a piece of construction paper then mount your artwork on the construction paper. Don't forget to sign your work. Upon returning to the training room, display your work for others to see.

4. Playing Ball

Play ball as children would with the other members of your group.

Assessing the Value of the Outdoor Area—Learning Station Worksheet

1. What did you enjoy most about these activities? Why?

2. What didn't you enjoy about these activities? Why?

Refer to the *Creative Curriculum* Goals and Objectives on page 530 for the next four questions.

3. Which objectives in the Social/ Emotional area of development could be addressed through activities such as these?

4. Which objectives in the Physical area of development could be addressed through activities such as these?

5. Which objectives in the Cognitive area of development could be addressed through activities such as these?

6. Which objectives in the Language area of development could be addressed through activities such as these?

7. How could you use these activities with children? What adaptations would you need to make?

Remembering the Outdoors

1. Think back on your childhood days. What was your favorite outdoor place to play? What was the environment like? What smells, sounds, and textures do you remember?

2. How did your favorite place change over the seasons?

3. What did you enjoy doing outdoors? Who was there with you?

4. What sort of games did you play?

5. What kinds of materials did you use? What discoveries did you make?

My Outdoor Plan

Area _____

Tasks	Person Responsible	Anticipated Date of Completion

Four Types of Play

- **Functional play**

- **Constructive play**

- **Dramatic or pretend play**

- **Games with rules**

What Observations Tell Us

1. Where did the child prefer to play?

2. What types of activities does the child prefer?

3. What equipment does the child prefer to use?

4. With whom does the child prefer to play?

5. How does the child approach a new piece of equipment or a new situation?

6. What kinds of things does the child appear to be curious about or interested in? Does he/she enjoy making discoveries?

7. What large muscle activities did the child participate in?

8. Did the child encounter any specific challenges? If so, what were they?

Nurturing Children's Appreciation of Nature

Rhythms

- Sit quietly and close your eyes.

- Inhale and exhale feeling the rhythm of your breath.

- Listen to the rhythm of your own heart beat.

- Listen to see if you can identify any naturally occurring rhythms (e.g., wind, water dripping, etc.)

- Open your eyes. As a group, discuss ways you might get children to "tune in" to the rhythms of the natural world. Choose someone to record your group's ideas.

- Return to the training room and wait for the other groups to join you.

Patterns

- Take a walk around the outdoor area.

- Look for patterns. Make a list of those made by people and those made by nature.

- Search for basic shapes such as the circle, square, triangle, or rectangle formed by nature.

- Discuss as a group what you might do, say, or ask to call children's attention to patterns while outdoors.

- Choose someone to record your ideas.

- Return to the training room and wait for the other groups to join you.

Perspectives

- Pair up with someone in your group. Each pair will need paper and a pencil/pen.

- Choose an object from nature and observe it from a variety of perspectives. For example, look at something upside down, from above, underneath, or eye to eye.

- List other ways you can view the object.

- Identify new discoveries you made each time you looked at the object from a different perspective.

- Record any questions or thoughts that came to mind as you looked at the object.

- How could you extend this observation experience with children?

- Return to the training room and wait for the other groups to join you.

Appendix

Using Your Continuum Cards

Prepare the continuum cards from the master set that follows. Copy the cards for each developmental area on a different color of paper (e.g., Social/Emotional—yellow; Physical—green; Cognitive—tan; Language—blue). Of course, you can choose whatever colors you wish. If you plan to use the cards more than once, copy them onto card stock paper for greater durability.